Praise for *Letters to the River*

"Sparrow Hart loves what is most wild in the natural world and in the deeper landscapes of the human heart. He is a keeper of myth, dream, and story, and in this collection of essays he shares reflections that open us to the interconnected myste wilderness.

"Gary Snyder writes that a shaman 'speaks spirits of plants, mountains, and watersheds… They a shaman is the healer who sings, then Sparrow Har Through these heart-opening essays we discover a profound listener to unspoken stories, a man of immense spirit, a singer with a wild and perceptive heart."

— *Stephan Beyer, author of* Singing to the Plants: A Guide to Mestizo Shamanism in the Upper Amazon

*   *   *

"In Letters to the River, Sparrow Hart addresses the challenges facing humanity in these perilous times. He describes the strategies and transformations needed to cope with whole-system change, using a provocative manner that employs word-play, poetry, and insights from shamanic wisdom, Jungian psychology, and a host of other creative sources.

"There are many fine books that confront the perils facing humankind in the 21st century, but none are as adroit in celebrating the "in-between spaces" where reason, emotion, and intuition produce a synthesis to help humanity continue its grand adventure."

– *Stanley Krippner, Ph.D; co-author of* Personal Mythology *and* Healing States: A Journey Into the World of Spiritual Healing and Shamanism

*   *   *

"Letters to the River is an open-minded exploration of the unknown, an inspiring and fascinating meditation upon nature's mysteries and magic. For a world struggling with the miseries of overpopulation and ecological destruction, the instructions are both practical and timely, and especially uplifting for those suffering the maladies of civilization -- depression, anxiety, and disconnection.

"I recommend this book both to fellow seekers and to those who have yet to learn to seek."

—Lewis Mehl-Madrona, MD, PhD, author of *Coyote Medicine* and *Healing the Mind through the Power of Story: the Promise of Narrative Psychiatry*

"Sparrow Hart is a gifted storyteller. Dancing between the visible and invisible worlds, this book expands our perceptions, tells the truth of who we are, and shows us the beauty of our inner and outer landscapes.

"Inspiring us to live in harmony with nature and all of life, reading Letters to the River is like being on a vision quest. This book is a gem!"

– Sandra Ingerman *author of Soul Retrieval and Medicine for the Earth*

*   *   *

"This is a generous book and from the heart. Artfully interfacing science and mythology, spirituality, shamanism, and earth wisdom, Sparrow Hart listens to and reveals the profound guidance from nature that true elders have been passing on for generations. In the easy-to-read fashion of a good story-teller, he reminds us that life is holy, that we all have purpose and work to do. The good news is we can do it successfully if we respond to the wisdom – the summons and the invitation – this book places before us."

—Tom Pinkson, *author of The Shamanic Wisdom of the Huichol: Medicine Teachings for Modern Times*

*   *   *

"From the wild terrains of Mother Nature to the realms of sacred transformation, Sparrow Hart guides us on the quest for a new story, a new dream where timeless voices of the sacred Earth whisper in one's heart, 'You belong.' The language is poetic, often exquisite. Like a sunrise that illuminates the dark and gifts us with a new day, its shadow and light reveal a landscape in which we recognize our own wholeness and intimate partnerships with life.

"Letters to the River is a fountain of wisdom, a gossamer thread of mystical content… a wellspring of natural beauty you can hold in your hands."

— ALisa Starkweather, *founder of the Red Tent Temple Movement, Women in Power, and Daughters of the Earth Gatherings*

*   *   *

"In Letters to the River, Sparrow Hart explores how to give birth to a personal and cultural story large enough to lead us into the arms of a healthier, more integrated world where human and nature share one voice. As a poet he listens to the muse of creation and the thrumming rhythms of the land, dipping into this fertile unified voice and transporting us to places of great beauty."

—Meredith Little, *co-founder (along with Steven Foster) of the School of Lost Borders, and co-author of The Book of the Vision Quest.*

Letters to the River
A Guide to a Dream Worth Living

by
Sparrow Hart

Cover design by Sandhill Design Group LLC. Photo by Gabriela
Schaufelberger, iStockphoto.

ISBN 978-1482370355

Dedication:

This book is dedicated to the Living Earth and all her children.

You've given me vision, purpose, and a path with heart. Guided by your voice and teachings, it's through your blessings my work and life has flowered and born fruit. May this book be a small gift in return for all you've given.

Acknowledgments and Thanks:

To my students and all those who've traversed the edge – of known and unknown; self and other; human and nature – who've entered the wilderness to face and find themselves. You've honored me with your courage, authenticity, and passion; trusted me with your vulnerability; taught me about soulful community; and, in the process, supported the living enactment my vision.

To my medicine teachers – Carlos Castaneda; Sun Bear; Wallace Black Elk and Grace Spotted Eagle; Steven Foster and Meredith Little... for sharing your knowledge and wisdom, your humor and human frailty. For sharing your considerable gifts while being simply yourselves.

To my family – Prairie Stuart-Wolff and Willie Allison... for loving and sharing your lives with me, and for putting up with my (occasional) quirks.

Dear friends and companions on the Journey –

To Blase Provitola, Garry Alesio; Ron Kearns; Larry Murphy; Phil Payson; Leo Horrigan; John Dore; Thomas Griffin; Bill Hesbach; Flynn Johnson; Dan Roden; Mark Knight; Steve Beyer; Richard Legault; Clearwater; RavenKind; Karen Swanson; Rita Millhench; Sebastien Michon; River Strong; and Tim Dalton... for sharing the path and "the Work."

To Alan Steinberg; Peter Thurrell; Mary Beath; Doug Campbell; Kate Wolff; Kit French; Rupa Cousins; Len Fleischer; Lauren Chamblis; Zana Burns; Kathryn Perrin, Erika Radich, Raven Seltzer; Rich Fain; Gary Stuart, Jensen Curtis, Gary Solomon, Sonya Bykofsky, and others too numerous to mention... for your friendship, support, and inspiration.

To my father – Leon Everett Stuart Jr. – for showing me that seeds of great love can eventually break through layers of pain.

And of course, to The Bears.

Table of Contents

Preface

"What's the problem with my writing?"

Sitting beside New Mexico's Mimbres River one spring day, I spoke these words out loud while jotting them down in my journal: I'd achieved some initial and easy success composing articles for magazines, but had grown increasingly dissatisfied with the limitations of the form and market. The box seemed too small, but my thinking about this – practical, rational, and what to do – had gotten me nowhere. Deciding to voice these frustrations to something outside my reasoning mind, I transferred the pen to my non-dominant hand, hoping an answer would emerge from an untapped and unfamiliar place.

My left hand responded immediately as the words "Your father" were scrawled in large letters across the page.

This was unexpected… and exceptionally interesting. I'd once used this non-dominant hand writing technique therapeutically in "inner child dialogues" for a year, the awkward scratchings of the left side providing access to a seemingly younger, more-innocent part of the brain. Leaning back against the trunk of a Ponderosa pine, I placed the pen back into my right hand, asked for more information, and let the left side respond.

Over the next hour I received surprising revelations about my inner world, including some disturbed soil that consistently undermined the foundations of the words I placed on paper. I saw how my father had tried to live his unlived dreams through me, pushing me to achieve his version of success so he would feel important. I resented this imposed pressure to succeed, and I rebelled against his values by quitting nearly every career I'd begun just when I'd become really good at it.

My father represented the critic. At various times he had humiliated me, blamed me for his heart attack, told me I was "a rotten son." To write the way I wanted required sharing my innermost thoughts and passions with the world, making myself vulnerable. Subconsciously my father – in the reincarnated form of editors and readers – waited "out there" to ridicule and tear me apart. The dialogue with the left side fascinated me. It provided fresh perspectives, a window open to emotional currents seething below the surface of the "problem." But it had yet to offer any solutions. Finally, I placed the pen back in my right hand and scratched out the words, "Great, but what do I do about it?"

The left hand answered directly and without hesitation: "Write to the river!"

From that point, I began. Often when leading vision quests, workshops, or wilderness programs, I would rise early and head to a nearby shore with pencil and pad of paper in hand. I sat by the Gila, Chama, Mimbres, or Pecos Rivers in New Mexico; Somerset Lake in Vermont, the Caribbean Sea in the Yucatan. There, at the edge of the water, I would face the blank page and, as if writing to a dear

2

friend, begin, "Dear River..."

Often these letters began with simple gratitude for the beautiful vistas before me, and for the senses through which I took in this magical and wondrous earth. Sometimes I'd start by just describing the landscape, and in so doing my eyes (and heart) would open to its miracles and myriads of interconnected mysteries. My perceptions began to expand, increasingly attuning themselves to those marvels of existence that continually support and feed us – most often below the threshold of our attention.

But simultaneously, something else was happening. As I spoke to nature as an admirer, apprentice, and lover, I developed, an "I-Thou" relationship with a far-different and more intimate rapport than any "I-it" relationship. This was an alliance of friendship, equality, and reciprocity. The Earth and those grand forces of Air, Fire, and Water became companions, guides, and mentors. They taught me – over and over – about interconnection, interdependence, and co-creation, and they ushered me into a story far larger than the one I knew. My human arrogance and self-importance began to shrink, and as they did, the mystery, majesty, and magnificence of what was all around me mushroomed. Thousands of cycles – momentous or miniscule – revealed themselves, overlapping and weaving into a thick-textured tapestry that made up each moment. Time filled with presence; "reality" becoming far deeper than it first appeared.

As I sat by the waters and my relationship with nature grew, more and more my identity slipped outside the small self I had always known. These meditations, or "letters," were often dreamlike, the sense of "I" roaming over territory somewhere in-

3

between my own reflections and the gaze of "someone else" looking back. Staring into the face of the natural world brought me to the border of inner and outer, self and other, human nature and Nature. The boundaries between "it" and "I" were blurring; I often had trouble telling who was speaking to whom. At times it seemed the letters were being written <u>from</u> the River rather than the other way around. The process of unlocking my heart opened pathways of perception where the landscape could find its voice through me. As I straddled this threshold at the doorway to the soul, I lost my bearings along with my sense of separation. I became enchanted and found myself at peace and back in the Garden again.

Physics has long known that observation strongly influences the results of any experiment. "Reality" – the reality we experience – is being shaped at every moment by whatever focus and attention we bring to the encounter. Perception is not passive: perceiver and perceived are polarities within a process, and each moment is a temporary snapshot of something more verb-like than noun. We are seeing our world <u>the way we are, as much as the way it is</u>.

Many selections in <u>Letters to the River</u> explore who we are and how we perceive. They question the nature of the line we draw between "self" and "world" and the assumptions that help construct the universe we experience. In so doing, they offer a glimpse into other possibilities. However, any inquiry that probes the nature of reality faces an obvious dilemma:

"Reality" is not a fact. The world is not something solid, separate, and outside us – we are inside and part of it. Therefore, the voice of these letters cannot be disconnected from the "realities" they inhabit, and they must speak not just <u>about</u>, but from <u>within</u> these worlds. They were written "at the shore." They dance between current and bank; their foundation shifting like gravel and sand between the seemingly solid ground and a far-more fluid reality. It's there and only there – in that place of "in-between" – that we can discover the true face of nature, and our own face and nature as well.

This book evokes and celebrates that place of "in-between," the experience of walking with our feet in two worlds. We mostly live in a left-brained reality of reason, logic, and unchangeable material realities. In this arena, we work, play, plan, and experience our "normal" life. Yet we also touch upon other modes of perception and being... a world referenced in myth, experienced in dream, and spoken of in spiritual texts and by saints and sages over the millennia. This realm – irrational, fluid, and hard to grasp – resists language and hard definitions, yet its emotionally rich landscapes – mostly ignored in ordinary life – are universally regarded as deeper, more profound, and more "real" than the marked and measured dimensions of our daily dramas.

These two realms have been referenced in pairs of opposites throughout the ages as physical vs. spiritual... sacred vs. profane... eternal vs. temporal... seen and unseen... concrete vs. formless... self and Self... known and unknown... left brain vs. right. Today these "separate" realms need to be united, woven together, and balanced to "connect heaven and earth" if we're to bring hope, inspiration, and a sense of grand adventure into the practical tasks of living well in challenging times.

In the pages that follow, the chapter introductions speak to and within the known world; the left-brain world of physical reality, logic, reason… ordinary life. They describe the lessons we must learn and the journey required to become whole. In this book's second half, these introductions are complemented by a selection of "Letters," which emerge from the unknown, singing within that irrational, fluid, and mysterious reality where possibilities are limitless and healing is ever-present and eternally available…

<u>Letters to the River</u> was written in natural landscapes, while sitting upon shores next to lakes, oceans, and "actual" rivers. In ordinary life, these rivers are facts. However, the River has always been a symbol pointing to The Source, that eternal spring from which life pours forth to create the forms of the world we inhabit. It also refers to the flow or stream of consciousness itself, the invisible foundation underlying and molding all we are capable of experiencing. It is the energy, the fluid, transcendent "stuff" that precedes and informs all the masks we wear and every face of god we can name.

The modern world is in crisis. Economic injustice, war, violence, ecological disaster – and their personal counterparts of greed, disconnection, depression, and loss of meaning – scream out from newspapers, talk shows, and therapists' offices. A sacred, fulfilling life seems far away. But our exile is of our own making. Close by, on the other side of the looking glass, the mythical lost paradise awaits. It's available if we want it.

We all can experience healing, find joy, and reclaim our wonder and innocence. To do so requires opening our minds, our senses and hearts, and letting go of some deep-rooted habits and routines. We have to reach beyond ourselves, be willing to dream again, step off the shore, and enter the water. If we do – washed of our "sins," cleansed and buoyed by the river of life – we can become ready to be touched by Grace again.

Amazing Grace. How sweet the song!

Everyone wants a home, a feeling of "rightness," a place they know they belong. Like most in modern life, I've been lost, hurt, miseducated, betrayed, and disillusioned. Yet we live on a magnificent planet: the beautiful, living Earth. We live within a miracle. Once blind, we still can see. Through these letters, these conversations, I hope to share with you a vision, a brief glimpse of what I found. I hope to point out a path – both new and ancient – that can guide us back to that Garden.

~ Sparrow Hart, May 2012

Letters to the River:
The Right Side

Introduction:
The Call to Adventure

Something's not working. Everybody knows it. The turmoil and breakdown of order, sustainability, and basic sanity in almost every natural and human system is overwhelming and disheartening. The list – war, economic injustice, environmental disaster, poverty, decline of democratic ideals and decency – goes on and on. When the system itself is at fault and every problem is interconnected, it can appear like there's nowhere to start and whatever we do won't make a difference.

The need to face "inconvenient truths" grows stronger every day. Wise voices announce we need a new paradigm. No doubt this is true, but how can we step outside and look at a reality we live within? When the ways we perceive and think about the world are a root cause of the problem itself, what can we do?

Through centuries of practice, hundreds of small, indigenous societies found ways to achieve peace within their communities and harmony with the natural world. Over millennia, sages, saints, and wise elders have shared methods and systems of knowledge for nurturing the best of human capacities, presenting pathways toward serenity, self-realization, and the amelioration of suffering. Though the modern era differs in many significant ways, the basic architecture of the human body and mind has not changed. The soul's journey remains the same, and the ancient myths of heroic adventure and initiatory rites of native cultures offer blueprints of where to go and what to do when faced with overwhelming odds and difficulties.

In traditional tales of this quest, the protagonist journeys beyond the well-known territory to a realm where he or she has never been before. There he/she encounters the unknown and extraordinary, faces challenges and obstacles that are difficult and frightening. The hero may meet monsters or magical beings; navigate dangerous descents through dark passages and labyrinths; struggle to lift an enchantment or overcome a curse. After this confrontation with the unexplored and unexpected, our hero must return to the world he put aside, carrying new powers, healing aids, gifts, or vision to the people and community.

This book is organized along the lines of that heroic journey. Today we face a task of creating a world worth living in, and doing so requires stepping outside the boundaries of what's known and familiar. We won't find the solutions we need by recycling the same old routines with better management, more efficiency, or greater effort, for it is the worldview or "dream" of the culture itself that leads to most of the dis-ease and dysfunction of modern life. Like the heroes and heroines of old, we must leave home and enter new territories of the mind, soul, and imagination if we are to find the answers we seek.

*　　*　　*　　*　　*　　*　　*

In ancient cultures, rites of passage and initiation were developed to precipitate a crisis – carefully orchestrated – that would dissolve an old identity and give birth to a new. The initiate was removed from the sphere of ordinary life; exposed to ordeals that tested his fabric, focus, and faith; and learned stories, secrets, and sources of strength before being reintroduced and reintegrated into the community with the new vision and power gained.

Today we are approaching a crossroads, a crisis or rite of passage that involves the entire planet. Outside the enclaves of the rich, the anguish and suffering of the world is immense, and the faith and fabric of millions is tested daily. The tide of torment continues to rise, and catastrophe – via economic injustice, global warming, political terror, or environmental disaster – now laps against the shores of whole populations who once seemed safe.

Joseph Campbell once remarked that yogis and schizophrenics live in the same ocean, one joyfully swimming while the other drowns. Our tide is rising. The surge builds, and the swells grow larger. Our choice is ultimately simple. We can engage the crisis, say "Yes," to this approaching passage, and enter the water. There we might discover our depths, chart new currents, or wash off an old way of being to reemerge refreshed and renewed. Or we can refuse the summons, steadfastly clinging to the shore until our resistance is broken, and the waves finally pull us under.

*　　*　　*　　*　　*　　*　　*

Our voyage is daunting, the current conditions severe. But the great and enduring myths provide maps and metaphors for navigating this passage. Included are three steps. The journey begins with a call to adventure in which the hero (or heroine) is compelled to move out of the familiar sphere of action, undertaking an odyssey that carries him beyond known horizons into a world completely unlike the one left behind.

The precipitating event can result from the protagonist pursuing something. A hunter tracks a deer or Alice follows the rabbit down the hole, and soon they find themselves in a reality radically different from any they've known before. Or the lead characters may be swept up by events beyond their control: Swirling winds pluck Dorothy out of a flat landscape and deposit her in the strange world of Oz. Swallowed by a whale, Jonah descends into the darkness of the abyss. Storms blow a ship far off course, and the crew is shipwrecked on dangerous and alien shores.

Often the quest begins because something is amiss at home, and the hero/heroine undertakes a mission to discover, resolve, or claim something. Civil war rages in the kingdom, and the protagonist searches for an oracle to sanction the rightful ruler. The king lies on his deathbed; his three sons seeking the Waters of Life to heal the ailing monarch. There are battles to be fought, fortunes to be found. Curses must be lifted, gods propitiated, dragons or monsters confronted or slain. The goal can be represented as a magic potion or treasure, a release from bondage, or a hundred other things, but – without fail – the summons requires the removal of the protagonist from ordinary life and precipitates an encounter with the extraordinary.

These myths do not just allude to antiquated fantasies. They cry out to us, their strange flights of imagination symbolic representations of the situations – inner and outer – we face today. Call them "make believe" if you will, but beliefs make reality, and our beliefs have formed the world – with all its problems – into the shapes we struggle with today.

Something **is** radically wrong in our kingdom. Monsters and dragons – greed, addiction, violence – wreak havoc in the realm. Curses and enchantments abound. The population is hypnotized by strange incantations (on hundreds of channels) while rainforests burn in the name of progress; politicians wage wars for peace; and truth suffocates under an avalanche of advertising and public relations. Who has the magic to lift these trances, confront this strange sorcery, and cast out the evil spells?

Over 150 years ago, Thoreau noted that "most men live lives of quiet desperation." Many myths have described a condition where "the springs have dried up; cattle don't give birth; famine and drought claim the earth." In one, the earth shriveled when Demeter, goddess of life and fertility, sunk into unending sorrow in response to her daughter, Persephone's, abduction into the underworld. Her grief – repackaged in a modern-day diagnosis of depression – continues on as a disease that runs rampant through the contemporary world. Today's life often seems meaningless and empty, and help is sorely needed, but our army of prescription drugs is rapidly losing ground in the battle with indifference and passivity. Climate change enters our inner world; the landscapes of the soul turn to desert. The pace quickens; the heat is turned up; modern man suffers burnout as the forests go up in smoke.

A tempest is battering the twenty-first century. Swept up and driven off course by its gale winds, much of the population finds itself shipwrecked and stranded in strange lands. The traditional moorings have eroded; the old signposts have crumbled. Mountains, forests, and neighborhoods are bulldozed for development; marriages, families, and pension funds collapse. War, crime, and sexually-transmitted disease pass as normal. Politicians lie; corporations plunder the national wealth; the moral compass spins in every direction till you can't tell the good guys from the bad. What are we to do? Fearful and adrift in a dangerous and disorienting landscape – like modern incarnations of Odysseus or Dorothy – how will we find our way home?

The crises of today are our summons to adventure. Like heroes and heroines of old, we must take leave of what's familiar, loosening the ropes that bind us to the dock of the known and ordinary if we're to search for a new vision and story. Our souls cry for a life more meaningful than buying stuff and accumulating the rewards of a materialistic society. We have yearnings, dreams, and desires that – to be fulfilled – will propel us into a psychic universe far beyond the stocked shelves and common clichés of today's mass-marketed culture.

People hunger for re-enchantment with nature and a connection with all life. They want communion with the sacred and communities where what they say and do makes a difference. But a great, heaving ocean stands between us and that new life on the far shore, and facing the depths means saying "goodbye" to the shallow end of the pool. Releasing one's grip on the old is never easy. The concerns for safety and security cry out piteously; the lure of comfort and convenience tempts us like empty calories of sugar.

But the longings of the soul are eternal, and birth is always attended by a little blood. Just as springtime follows winter, resurrection first requires a death. Our journey must begin by letting go. The ropes must be cast off, and the old dream must die to make way for the new song that waits to be sung.

The following three chapters begin with the known – the myths, assumptions, and models of knowledge and language we have inherited – and examine the implications and consequences of living within their codes and limitations. They describe modern life and its current consensus – the old kingdom with its decay and dysfunction – but their primary thrust lies beyond that familiar territory. They celebrate the lure and promise of a larger story, pointing the way to a grand dream outside the social agreement as we currently conceive it.

The journey calling us is personal, cultural, and political. It requires that we challenge our beliefs, allegiances, and definitions of who and what we (and the world) are. Ultimately this adventure is about our spirit and our souls.

In troubled times those of good heart have always sought the magic potion, the Golden Fleece, or the blessing of the gods. The great myths have survived through the ages to inspire, encourage, and guide us. The map is in our hands. Passion, adventure, and a heroic life beckon. A new vision of wholeness, healing, and a joyful re-enchantment of life – like hidden treasure –

awaits us. It's there if we but follow the call.

Sometimes a man stands up during supper
and walks outdoors, and keeps on walking,
because of a church that stands somewhere in the East.

And his children say blessings upon him as if he were dead.

And another man who remains inside his own house,
stays there, inside the dishes and in the glasses,
so that his children have to go far out into the world
toward that same church, which he forgot.

~ Rainer Maria Rilke [1]

Searching for a New Mythology

Myth and Reality

"This linkage with the infinite has of course been the intent of the great mythologies and religions; the healing creative and expressive arts; and the dreams we dream each night" [1]

Myths are more than charming stories told by people from long ago. Mythology continues as a living force that weaves through our lives, and – like fish living in water – it shapes our consciousness in ways so widespread and universal as to be overlooked or invisible. It creates the foundation and ground we stand on, but we often become aware of myth only when confronted with conflicting or competing mythologies. Then we then use the term *myth*, derisively, to describe *other people's* belief systems.

Beginning early in childhood, the fundamental task of culture is to integrate the individual into the larger frameworks – village, nation, cosmos – he or she will develop and function within over a lifetime. This weaving together of smaller and larger not only brings meaning, purpose, and a sense of belonging to the individual, but making these connections and identities (along with their attendant responsibilities) is necessary for any society to grow, adapt, and sustain itself over time. For millennia this task was accomplished by community rituals, the teaching of elders, and the transference of the creation stories and tales of adventure that made up a people's mythology.

These tools of integration have all atrophied or been shattered in modern culture. Today, the term "myth" is commonly used to describe something that's not "real," but in fact, it's <u>our myths</u> that <u>define what reality is or isn't</u>. All throughout human history, people have lived with diverse beliefs about the nature of the cosmos and the human role within it; have applied numerous criteria to judge "real" from "unreal;" and used different value systems to separate the important from unimportant. Within each of these systems, the world appeared authentic, palpable, even obvious, and people structured their lives and customs accordingly. To them, their world "made sense."

In the physical sciences, different facets of the universe emerge (and disappear) when we train different lenses – telescopes, microscopes, infrared sensors, radio antennas, x-rays – upon existence. Similarly, whatever the age or culture, people have examined the dynamic and evolving experience of life and living through a medium that results in their particular and unique perspective. One "instrument" through which we both view and create the world is our mythology, and it is neither neutral nor transparent. It determines which aspects of existence come into focus and which remain unseen or "unreal."

Myth is primary, foundational. There is no objective

universe and no human space – physical or psychic – outside of it. We see the world the way we are, not the way it is; and this fact is unavoidable. Myths create reality for they are the medium through which we "see." They shape our values, determine our truths and falsehoods, and define the direction of our greatest good and achievements. The belief that we are beyond or have transcended the world of myth is not fact, but rather, part of our modern mythology.

The glasses we wear inevitably conceal as much as they reveal. For every direction taken, innumerable alternatives must be ignored. For every treasure unearthed, a thousand possibilities remain buried. If we are unaware of our mythology and the power of myth, we can be deceived and led astray. Our cultural consensus – what's obvious to everyone – may be disoriented, dysfunctional, or downright pathological.

Adam and Newton: The Apple and the Fig

The current age desperately needs a new mythology. We've inherited ways of looking at the world that no longer work, that are unsustainable and have toxic consequences. We still live under the influence of paradigms that are centuries and millennia old, paradigms that are outmoded and unable to provide us with the insights and tools necessary to lead a life in balance, a life worth living.

Two primary myths dominate and structure Western consciousness in unhealthy ways. The first comes from our Middle-Eastern, Judeo-Christian heritage. Whether religious or not, Christian or Jewish or not, we have grown up still influenced by the worldview of tribal enmity adopted by warring desert peoples two thousand or more years in the past. Beyond the foolishness of original sin and the pervasive guilt (or outright child abuse) this doctrine has caused, much of Western culture continues to give allegiance to a mythology that 1) ignores the science of the day – evolution, global warming, systems theory, the insights of psychology, etc. 2) denies any central role of the feminine in creation 3) feels threatened by nature, and 4) is hostile or indifferent toward the living earth.

There may be historical reasons for this emphasis – a period of strife with older goddess and earth-based cultures with their totemic or animal deities – but two millennia steeped in this mythology has damaged our relationship to the feminine, the earth, and our bodies. And it has limited and suppressed the possibility of sacred communion with all the non-human aspects of creation.

The Judeo-Christian god is not here. "Our Father" lives somewhere else, neither on nor within the earth. He inhabits an abstract zone called heaven, and – unlike the great mother, Gaia – he's unreachable and unattainable within life. Our interaction and union with God (the source of everything sacred) happens in an after-life, only when we have left this sensuous world behind.

Over centuries, as this mythology rose to dominance in the Western world, the earth and all things earthly became unsanctified, foul, dis-*grace*-ful. Physical, sensual reality – instinct, sexuality, the body, and pleasure… everything that makes up our primal experience of life – was judged to be dangerous and evil. The Great Mother's qualities and beingness – soiled and dirty – were turned into epithets. Crusades were mounted; primal peoples slaughtered;

witches, druids, and homosexuals burned at the stake. The old gods of indigenous or matriarchal cultures that represent a fecund and fertile life and a connection to our animal powers were – like Snake – detested and turned into villains, while others – like Pan – became incorporated into images of Satan, the horned and cloven-hoofed demon.

The second guiding myth of modern times is scientific rationalism. Galileo, Copernicus, the Renaissance... The battles of the scientific revolution led to a dividing up of territory – the Church became ruler of spiritual life and matters of the soul, while science was given authority over the physical universe. Though quantum physics has left the intellectual revolution of the 1600's far behind, we still live in a psychic and linguistic world defined by the theories and discoveries of Isaac Newton, Francis Bacon, and Rene Descartes.

In this cosmology, the world is no longer dirty or evil, but it's dead, for the universe is ultimately a grand and complicated machine. It is a mechanism – like a clock – and mechanisms lack sentience, intelligence, and soul. These qualities are reserved for humans only, whose destiny and proper role is to mold and use creation for their (our) self-interest. The cosmos, defined as physical reality, lacks consciousness; therefore it cannot be sacred. The rest of existence – plants, animals, the biosphere (and oftentimes non-white, non-Christian peoples) – is comprised of lesser life forms, and their rights and welfare carry little weight in our calculations. Nature – no longer Source – becomes resource, and it has value only to the extent it serves and is useful to humans.

This mythology holds reason as the highest faculty, a faculty that can precede and define existence itself: "I think, therefore I am." Rational thought is what makes humans special. All other forms of knowing the world – sensing, feeling, empathy, imagination – are secondary or even suspect. Sensory life, possessed in common with the animals, is judged as base and primitive. The world of feeling –unmanageable and unsettling – gets in the way of rational discourse. And imagination is, of course, unreal and a waste of time. Stop dreaming and pay attention!

In this paradigm, the standard of knowledge and pre-eminent form of thought is scientific examination. This inquiry is based on objective, repeatable experiments. Experiments must be objective, for they concern objects, parts of the machine. The scientist must remain a neutral observer, uninvolved. He is separate, disconnected, and unrelated to the world he is learning about. Being neutral requires disengagement. He cannot participate, be involved, be part of the process. He is trained to live in his head, not within the world, and – like the detached and distant deity – he stands above and outside the interactions of all the dead or lesser parts of creation that he passes judgment upon. This "objective neutrality" has long been the prescription for teaching at most universities.

Eve... of Destruction or Renewal?

These two mythologies structure and underlie many of the daily dramas in modern life. They combine to create a sense of value that is abstract, above-it-all, and not present. Thought is abstract; heaven is abstract. Both are distant from and uneasy with physical life. God is not of the earth. He's unreachable, untouchable, beyond the sky, and without a body. The pleasures of sensual life are seductions, sins, obstacles blocking the way to joining the divine. That union does not happen here; it happens after life. Likewise, the scientist remains "above it all," his body or feelings a distraction, irrelevant and an impediment to scientific truth. He stays separate, observes, and does not participate.

These paradigms have created a value system and "reality" divorced from the feminine principle; from the emotions and senses; from the earth, our fellow creatures, and life itself. Concepts of "good" and "right" have come to be based on abstract criteria until what "makes sense" completely ignores the senses. Notions like "property rights" give humans permission to deny their relationships with and violate the lives and "rights" of the beings who live on the land, as well as destroy the land itself. Overvaluing abstractions at the expense of flesh, emotions, and the living has allowed thousands to be bombed, maimed, or butchered in the name of bringing them "freedom," "peace," "God," or "civilization."

These outmoded paradigms still underpin our lives. We act them out as we exploit and consume resources, destroy the habitat of other life forms, and assign value and a sacred dimension to only human affairs. They influence and define debates over schools, social services, forests, and wildlife. They lead us to consign children to twelve or sixteen years of intellectual training while ignoring their emotional intelligence, development, and maturity. They are at play when we deny people basic medical care based on economic criteria or use property rights or "development" to justify doing whatever we want with "our" land and resources.

In the realm of the psyche, these inherited stories are encompassing and invisible forces that structure our consciousness and shape our awareness. They make up the water we swim in and the air we breathe. But when the water and air are polluted, it affects our health and vitality. It limits our ability to experience wholeness, harmony, and joy. These myths disconnect us from our bodies, emotions, dreams, and the rest of life. They create a sense of isolation and alienation, keeping us stuck in our heads, numbed to our feelings, and emotionally illiterate. Their dark shadow hinders our search for meaning or a sense of belonging; and leaves us unwilling or unable to engage in those simple, basic processes that create a sense of community and relatedness.

The earthly values have been forced underground, and the fire in the sky has turned the earth barren. It is time for the hidden springs to bubble up, for the emotional, sensual, feminine principle to be resurrected from the shadows. A sustainable future needs a spirituality that puts us on equal footing with the plants, animals, waters, and biosphere. To live a vital and earthy life with any possibility of ecological balance requires myths that honor our place on earth and our relationship with this planet as a path and connection to the sacred. The divine principle – the Source of life, our Origin, our gods and goddesses – must become embodied and present, immanent as well as transcendent, and these entities or energies must be found, sensed, touched, and communed with through life rather than by leaving it.

The traditional values of primal peoples and today's discoveries in quantum physics both point to a universe that is mysterious, evolving, and interactive… a universe of engagement, participation, and co-creation. We will have to live in this psychic universe to become whole, or even to survive the crises we've already created on earth.

The letters of the New Mythology (p. 153 - 179) speak from that ancient and ever-renewing paradigm of a sacred and sustainable existence. To create or co-create a dream worth living, we will have to welcome back much of what we've lost, those powers and energies – those gods – spurned and driven into shadow by reason, religion, and righteousness.

The left side selections honor and celebrate all of the movements, directions, and powers on the Medicine Wheel of life. This includes Gaia, Mother Earth, the feminine… It includes Eve (and snake), whose curiosity, desire for knowledge, challenge of authority, and taste for what's sweet and succulent will serve us far better than the jealousy and judgment of a fearful father in heaven. When we've finally cast him from our garden, the springs will well up and the Tree of Life will bloom again.

It is a lie—any talk of God
that does not
comfort
you.

~ Meister Eckhart [2]

Sometimes we think what we are saying about God
is true when in fact
it is not...

I have come to learn that the truth never harms
or frightens.

I have come to learn that
God's compassion and light can never be limited;

thus any God who could condemn is
not a god at all

but some disturbing image in the
mind of a
child

we best ignore, until we
can cure the
dark.

~ St. Thomas Aquinas [3]

The Known and
the Unknown

The Great Mystery is not Meant to be Solved

Carlos Castaneda[1] applies a simple and elegant distinction
to reality: He divides the field of action and awareness (the world)
into two spheres – the known and the unknown, the right side and
left – and associates corresponding practices with each. These
practices are called *stalking*, the art of handling ordinary reality (the
known) in non-ordinary ways; and *dreaming*, the art of entering and
participating in the fluid and magical world of the unknown, the
non-ordinary reality.

We've been taught that learning comes from thinking,
study, analysis, and deliberation – the act of reasoning – and that
knowledge holds the keys to power and will open doors to success.
Our educational system promotes this primarily intellectual process,
where neutral, non-participatory observers study separate and
disconnected objects and events that make up the world. Applying
scientific analysis and method to the challenges of physical
existence has radically transformed the material, social, and psychic

reality we live in. But mesmerized by the considerable powers of thought, we often substitute and confuse this disconnected and disembodied intellectual process with the process of life itself – "I think, therefore I am."

Castaneda's system heads in another direction and leads to different conclusions than those taught in our schools and social institutions. In the magical and enchanted world of Castaneda and his cohorts, the depth, richness, and quality of your life has much more to do with the nature of your relationship to the unknown than how much you know in the world of ordinary, consensus reality. And a "man of knowledge," or seer, is one who molds his character and refines his personal mastery in order to explore those fluid and magical landscapes outside the borders of the known.

Thinking is just one possible way to engage with the world, and our obsession with it ignores other whole domains of experience. As Carl Jung noted, the capacities of sensing, feeling, and intuitive imagination – generally not nurtured in modern life – are equal, but alternative modes of knowing. Rarely given anything close to the 12-16 years invested in schooling the mind, these other abilities can be developed, and they can open windows onto alternative vistas with different, but vast potential for learning, action, and engagement.

In addition, we spend a full third of our life sleeping. This non-waking consciousness contains the realm of dreams, whose forms of perception and relationship have very different rules than those of daily experience, and where wildly-creative landscapes and possibilities for action beckon from outside the house of reason. To ignore or discard this consciousness, to label it inferior to rational modes of thought or irrelevant to waking life is absurd and irrational in itself. Yet we do, and by treating flesh, emotion, and imagination like undesirables, our potential to live with depth and passion atrophies, and the resulting emotional and imaginative illiteracy sends our national dialogues into swamps of the boorish and banal.

These negative side-effects of how we've been taught to think are major, but not the whole picture. The most significant problem with our inherited approach to knowledge is simply that the unknown is vast – far greater than the known. Like the iceberg whose mass – ninety percent – lies invisibly below the water, our perceivable and knowable universe comprises a small segment of reality. The known world – like a boat adrift on an immense ocean – is a minor fragment of existence, and to focus our attention and keep our energy tethered within the confines of this little sphere is to live in a prison of our own making.

Neuroscientists say we use less than ten percent of our brains to create, sustain, and act within what we know. And we know so little. For all our focus on knowledge, we have no idea about the relationship between thinking and matter; how particles emerge from nothingness; or how desire gets translated into movement and action. Meanwhile, our relentless internal dialogues remove us from our bodies, emotions, and imagination; keeping us stuck in our heads and unaware of even the most basic realities like the quality of our breathing moment to moment; whether we feel angry, scared, or hungry; or the deeper callings of our souls.

Since the unknown is so vast compared to the known, all

religions, philosophies, or forms of inquiry focused on or mired in the known will be limited at best, and foolish or dangerous at worst. We are taught and can try to be reasonable, but in fundamental ways we are not. Like a woman wanting to be a man or someone of color trying to be "white," pretending to be what we're not involves ignoring our roots, denying other, equally-rich heritages, and repressing large parts of who we are.

In the new worlds of quantum physics, the known is dissolving. Reality looks relative and relational. The quantum universe is probabilistic, a seething field of possibilities, and the old rock of reason has broken down into a shore of shifting sands. In this fluid landscape, there is no objective existence "out there." Inner and outer meet, interact, and dance together. In this rhythmic duet, the perceiver's intention, focus of attention, or lens looked through evokes and draws forth the emerging form of "reality" from the mysterious flux perceived to be outside in the world.

Primal cultures referred to the living presence of this "Unknown" as the Great Mystery. It was the source and origin of everything – all facts, shapes, forms, and expressions of existence – the wellspring out of which emerged all which could be experienced and known. The Great Mystery was a focus of reverence, the matrix and mother of our being-ness, the background and context within which we live, know, and perceive.

To experience the Great Mystery is to know God, the Source, our creator. To experience does not mean to think about or understand. To experience means to be intimate with. For millennia, developing a relationship of appreciation, gratitude, and respect with this Unknown was the primary task of life. Creating, nurturing, and sustaining this relationship led to a sense of belonging, finding one's place in the universe, and having a home. To do so resulted in deep feelings of peace, and a feeling of wonder, purpose, and connectedness with all parts of creation.

Shrinking Self-importance

Our modern culture of politics is based on self-interest, and the values of psychology are ego-oriented, emphasizing self-knowledge, increasing self-esteem, and getting what we want. Yet, at the core, it's these notions of self that make up a large part of our current problem.

An old Buddhist notion states that a primary cause of unhappiness is spending most of our attention and energy thinking about oneself, when that "self" simply doesn't exist. The self we have adopted – the separate self or ego – is a noun referring to the perceiver, the observer and judge at the center of the known. But this "self" is an abstract notion, a linguistic invention... an autonomous entity that requires and assumes a point of view outside and detached from the flow of existence... a point of view that has no actual reality.

Who am I? Am I a noun or am I really more like a verb? In the world of language, "I" am a noun, and nouns – as things – imply separate objects and assume disconnections. Language divides the unified field of experience. It can create polarities: up-down; left-right; good-bad. These distinctions may appear as opposites, but no part of a polarity can exist without the other. Left has no meaning without right; inner has relevance only in relation to outer; up makes sense only when associated with down. There is no meaning to left, east, or down in isolation.

This also holds true for the word "self." It too is part of a polarity, paired and related to whatever is defined as outer, or beyond the self. "Self" is meaningful only in its relationship to "world" or "other." Any attempt to know the self as autonomous or independent, as distinct from its myriad and changing relationship to that world is an impossibility. Yet, conditioned by our language structures, we pursue self-knowledge or self-esteem as if this self were a separate entity, an actual fact; and this tendency becomes a constant source of loneliness, disconnection, and disorientation.

To stretch toward the vast and magical Unknown, we have to move beyond this self. Castaneda's teacher, Don Juan, constantly exhorts him to "shrink his self-importance;" reminds him again and again that the "I" is not the center of the world. When this self shrinks and is removed from center, the world around it expands correspondingly, and feelings of wonder, magic, and magnificence develop and flower. Throughout history, the methods of all mystical and spiritual traditions have involved forms and techniques to break the obsession and constant self-referencing of the "I," and to open to the "Other," the vast and unknown realms beyond its confines.

The practices and avenues to move beyond the self can be many and varied. Some involve expressions of surrender, praise, gratitude, or prayer – an energetic offering in which we speak from the self (the known), but what we are intending and speaking to lies beyond that (the unknown). Others use the physical, sensory world (ordeals, fasting, breath, yoga, sound); evoke the emotions through fear, love, compassion, devotion, or ecstatic dance; address the mind, (usually in the form of quieting it, as in meditation); or nurture the imaginative/visionary realm through dreams, art, poetry, shamanic trance, or the use of plant allies.

These practices can range from austere to elaborate, easy to difficult; from vision quests and initiatory rites to the simple expression of gratitude. But at their core they share one thing in common: a shrinking or removal of attention and energy from the self in its ordinary and consensual reality, and/or a corresponding emphasis on all that lies beyond ... that changing, fluid, magical, and mysterious "world" of the unknown, and the profusion of possibilities to perceive and engage with it.

Beyond the Borders

The impulse and tug of the Unknown opposes the literal interpretations of sacred texts; chafes at the leash of our Cartesian-thinking world. It would undermine the foundations of the tower of reason and jump the fences round the well-managed and manicured lawns of logic to seek freedom on the other side.

This freedom does not mean license, chaos, or lack of responsibility. The power to throw off the shackles of consensual reality and effectively act in literal or psychological landscapes with different characters, energies, and rules takes courage, practice, and an inner sobriety. The discipline of meditation, the apprenticeship of a shaman, or the development of an artist includes a commitment to learning as great as that required for any university degree; a commitment that includes challenges to one's definition and sense of the self in addition to the effort required to become proficient in whatever skills and tasks are involved.

To respond to the lure of the Unknown is to celebrate the grand, heroic adventure: that archetypal journey in which the protagonist leaves home to seek something – a magic potion, healing gift, insight, or atonement – in those unexplored and unmapped territories beyond what we know. The landscapes and characters of these mysterious realms can be strange, wondrous, or frightening. Stories of these journeys can involve descents to the underworld, flights to heaven, battles with dragons, or times of fascination or fear in Oz or Wonderland.

But remember, myth is not just a collection of stories from the past. Myth determines what we consider real or important. In the world created by today's myths – abstract, ego-based, intellectual, and alienated from the earth – the vast landscape of the Unknown may include domains and territories labeled emotional, sensual, irrational, or spiritual. Entering this world might include forays into instinct, wildness, sensuality, the shadow… encounters with power animals, spirit guides, shamanic realities… explorations in dream synchronicities, conversations with ancestors, or interspecies communication… and much more. All these forms of engagement lie outside the current consensual circle of the known, and any (or all) could be labeled frightening, flaky, irrelevant, or simply unreal.

The Unknown is immense, stretching far beyond the boundaries – literal, conceptual, and perceptual – of the known. To evoke this Unknown, the letters to follow (pp. 181 - 206) affirm the presence of the Great Mystery through seeking out what is great and mysterious. Opting for fascination over fear, they aim to be entirely unreasonable. Profound or profane, they celebrate curiosity and choose clowning over catechism – hopping over the line and bouncing beyond the pale. They welcome you to let down your hair, take off that suit of seriousness or self-importance, and come along on this little romp.

When we get out of the glass bottles of our ego,
and when we escape like squirrels turning in the cages of our
personality
and get into the forest again,
we shall shiver with cold and fright
But things will happen to us
so that we don't know ourselves.

Cool, unlying life will rush in,
and passion will make our bodies taut with power,
we shall stamp our feet with new power
and old things will fall down,
we shall laugh, and institutions will curl up like burnt paper.

~ D.H. Lawrence [2]

The Role of Language

In the Beginning Was the Word

"Out beyond ideas of wrongdoing and rightdoing,
there is a field. I'll meet you there.

When the soul lies down in that grass,
the world is too full to talk about.
Ideas, language, even the phrase 'each other'
doesn't make any sense."

~ Rumi [1]

We don't live in the world. We live in our heads, and inside its corridors we perceive and shape the world to fit within the categories our language gives us. These categories determine how we organize the ever-changing sense impressions into a "reality." This means two things: First, the words we've learned enhance or limit our possibilities of perception. The Eskimo with his dozens of words for snow will distinguish far more in those fields of white than we do. Secondly, the structure of language – those rules of syntax that dictate the allowable associations between words – greatly influence the possibilities for relationship and interactions between the elements (words) of our world.

The noun, loosely defined as a "person, place, or thing," is the dominant and fundamental form within the English language. Our collection of verbs is then used to describe interactions among the various nouns, as in "John rows the boat." At first glance this seems natural and ordinary, no big deal. But, though we don't realize it, this arrangement programs us to see the world in a certain way. It tells us that *the world is composed of things* – separate things – and that change happens through those noun/things interacting with and upon each other.

But this does not have to be so. Many cultures have had more verb-oriented languages that do not predispose them toward a world made up of distinct objects. Their universe manifests differently, more fluidly, as a series of transient happenings, and they may observe and experience events and interactions outside the bounds of the linear causality required in a world of separate things.

Is the world made up of things? A stone, fork, or plate seems to be a thing, but what about a smile? What about a feeling, a mood, a dream, an idea, or week? We use these terms as if they were nouns and their meaning were simple. Do any of them have any 'reality' outside their relationship to a perceiver? Are any of them actually "things?"

Even a river....

The Gila River is one of my favorite places, and I have often sat upon its banks. When I mention its name, my memory takes me there, but where is "there?" I walk along its shores in spring, when the branches of trees are bare and the first bright green of new buds unfurl into the sun. In fall, those same buds, now fully developed as leaves, dry out and turn yellow-golden. I have crossed the river in summer and welcomed its refreshing coolness, while at other times of year my feet and shins are numbed to the bone. Its waters can be clear, emerald green, or black with soot and ash from fires upstream. Its current is sometimes quiet, gentle, and meandering; or it may froth with debris, ripping down cottonwoods and tearing away banks to make itself a new bed. So which river am I talking about?

Life, or "reality" changes constantly, but the words do not. The label "Gila River" has remained unvarying through decades of my visiting. As I speak of the "Gila River," I appear to be talking about the same "thing" each time I use the name, but those dancing waters won't hold still for a moment. The words evoke images in memory or imagination, and they seem stable when written on paper, but to what, really, do they refer? The river at this very moment – perhaps ravaged by winter floods – may be nothing like the images I remember. The river in my mind, the river in yours as you read these words, and the waters coursing through the Mogollon Mountains right now are different realities, different images or "dreams," all hiding within this one word: river.

The "river" as we think of it does not exist. Even sitting on its banks, it is less a "thing" than a collection of relationships – between hillside and valley, mountain and ocean, gravity and water; between boulders, banks, trees, ducks, and beaver – relationships that are innumerable and ever-changing. The unchanging word, "river," may be many things – a myth, a story, an assumption, a thought – but it is not the river.

Language and the World: Looking Through the Lens

As previously stated, we see the world the way we are, not the way it is. This is important to grasp. It implies that the world we perceive and act within has as much to do with our modes of perception and process as it does with any world we assume is "out there," real, and separate from us.

Whenever we observe the world, we are inevitably looking "through something." Imagine you are photographing a landscape. Using a telephoto lens, the cracks, faults, and fissures in a far-away cliff zoom into view, sharp and clear, but you're unable to see the wildflowers at your feet. To capture those flowers, you attach a different lens and crouch down close, but when you do, the mountain and its ramparts dissolve into a distant, blurry haze. Capturing any scene requires choosing a particular lens, and in so doing, different aspects of the vistas before you come into sharp detail, while others fade out and are lost.

All our interactions with the world have this quality. A telescope, infrared camera, microscope, or MRI will each give a very different picture of the "reality" they are looking at. Each focus is very limited, but useful, even critical, for the particular purpose chosen, while not relevant or even dangerous in other contexts. The magnified view seen through the microscope may save your life when battling an infection, but needs to be quickly left behind when navigating the freeway in your car.

Language is also a lens. It separates the stream of impressions into distinct groupings. Definitions and categories are necessary, unavoidable, and at the same time, arbitrary. They are not neutral. They cut, slice, and separate "reality" into parts, and they make associations which carry meaning or story, whether we are talking about different kinds of snow, what makes up "honesty," or whether someone is one of "us" or "them."

Constellations of Reality

Unraveling – even understanding – culture, language, and conditioning is difficult to do. For example, step outside tonight and look toward the northern sky, and you may see the constellation called the Big Dipper. It's one of the most recognizable constellations in the heavens, and many people learned its familiar shape in childhood.

But does the Big Dipper really exist? Is it "real?" Who decided to connect those seven stars in that way? Why not something else? It's quite arbitrary when you think about it. Of the thousands of stars visible in the night, we separate and group a few with 'lines' drawn between the dots to create images that we pay attention to. The Big Dipper, Leo the lion, Orion the hunter.......

Are those figures really there? In "physical reality," no lines connect the seven stars included in the Big Dipper, and the lines, obviously, could have been drawn in other ways. If my childhood had been different, I might gaze skyward and see a bridge, kangaroo, alligator, or anthill. One could look at the night sky and see virtually anything, and the heavens could be populated by completely dissimilar shapes and beings from the ones we know... as other peoples have done throughout history.

To create the Big Dipper, two important things have to happen. First, those seven stars have to be grouped together, seen in relationship to each other and not to the multitude of other stars in the sky. In doing this, thousands of relationships and possible arrangements have to be ignored or denied. Secondly, the relationship of those seven remaining stars has to be perceived in only one, particular way, lest we see a jack-in-the-box, deformed pear, knot of tangled yarn, or who-knows-what?

It is important to *real*-ize this process takes place with almost everything, every "thing" we perceive in the world. Our whole reality and known world is an interpretation as arbitrary as the Big Dipper, one that denies or simply ignores limitless other possibilities. But though my mind knows that familiar constellation isn't real in some sense, I cannot simply look at the sky and decide to not see it or see something else. The Big Dipper will be there for me whether I want it to or not. Once I grasp, accept, and constellate its image, it takes a great deal of determination and effort on my part to erase it.

Our culture's mythology – its creation myths, definitions of god, success, and what's important – is one lens through which we view the world. Our language, with its laws, syntax, and relationships allowed between phrases and words, is another; and it also constitutes one of the great factors that structure the reality we see. It "constellates" our world. It defines the dots with its collection of nouns and determines the relationships – connects them – in ways that are hard to undo.

The lens of English, with its emphasis on objects and their interactions, conditions us to see a world made up of "things" – separate entities that interact in a causal and linear fashion. It predisposes us to find or create nouns – consider the phrase "It's raining." – even when none exist. And like the microscope – useful, but not for driving the car – our language conceals, hides, and makes it difficult to perceive certain relationships that other cultures and languages may take for granted.

In the lens we have inherited, the possibilities for more fluid and interdependent realities fade from view. For example, the concept of the atom (the ultimate noun or separate "thing") dates back over two millennia, and scientists in "the age of reason" have practiced reductionism (seeking knowledge by reducing something to its smallest parts) for hundreds of years. Meanwhile, it's only recently they've noticed we live in "an environment." The disciplines that recognize relationships, self-regulation, and interacting wholes – ecology, mind-body medicine, and living systems theory, for example – are barely fifty years old.

This predilection to see a world of separate things obstructs our awareness of process and organism, those forms and fields of communication and coordination larger than the separate parts. As a result, ideas of synchronicities, the potential for worlds of relatedness among large groupings, and systems in constant communication and communion seem enigmatic, unfathomable, and difficult to talk about. Their existence feels somehow unnatural or unscientific, their reality consigned to the mysticism or hypothetical conjectures (like ESP) no matter what the data or evidence.

Language and the Self: Stasis and Ecstasy

Fundamental differences exist between language and reality, between categories and experience. All our experiences of ecstasy and joy – whether the arena is sex, sports, or religious trance – come from a breaking down of boundaries we put between ourselves and the "other"; from becoming one and in accord with the flow, with our partners, with the world.

The self is not a separate object. We are not nouns (or knowns). Like the river, we're collections of relationships, interconnections constantly shifting and too numerous to count. We're more like verbs, possibilities, potentials, as each moment we breathe, feel, perceive, change, and interact with other fields of energy. Our experience of the self and our relationship to the world are two sides of a single coin, and the quality of this involvement can range from ecstatic and inspiring to draining and threatening. To have an isolated and limited view of our "self" shrinks our possibilities of perception, engagement, and experience. It cuts us off from the potential of being a participant and a part of a much greater system and story. It can turn what's magical into the mundane, the sacred into the secular, and reduce what's profound to something petty or profane.

Language is mesmerizing. Like the proverbial fish in water, we grow and develop within it, spell-bound and unaware of its effects. A noun-dominated, prosaic language blinds and alienates us from the more fluid, interdependent, communal, and process-oriented aspects of creation, and its lens allows us to split mind from body, flesh from spirit, and individual from group, for they are... after all... different nouns. Everything has its pros and cons, and there's a power and prowess that results from this. Newtonian science with its bodiless, unemotional, disconnected observer has driven a tremendous explosion of technical knowledge within its narrowly-focused lens, a knowledge that has changed the "reality" we inhabit.

But today we skirt the edge. Poisons are released into the planet's life system by the ton. Weapons of mass destruction sit ready to wipe almost all life off the planet. People are massacred in the name of "freedom and democracy," their lands stolen in the name of "progress," "national interest," or "development." The inability to see the connections – between the systems and realms of living beings; between ourselves and others who share the planet; between the sacred and how we live daily – limit our choices and capacity to know more passionate, purposeful, and joyful experiences of living; more interconnected and soulful ways of being that perhaps can save us.

There are many alternatives to the reality we are living. Infinite potentialities, sacred journeys, and grand adventures of joyful communion await us. Realizing these possibilities will challenge us to move through the looking glass, to step outside the lens of consensual culture and language. Doing so involves changing who we are – changing the perceiver – and committing to knowing a different self, a self not separate, a self in relationship to the many other forms and faces of being.

"We need poets to rescue us from the awful contradictions we get into. Speech is literal and rational and cannot easily contain the depths of the mystery. For that we need symbols and symbolic language." (2)

Language is a great power, and wondrous. Whether this power is used well or not will depend on our awareness, intention, and perspective. Like spiders, we humans constantly weave our web of words. Our utterances spin into sentences attached to each other, and the threads – light, and barely visible – stretch across expanses of mostly empty space. Our stories, with their flimsiest sense of reality, create the world we inhabit and seem essential to our survival. They bind and capture bits of experience, making it palatable and possible to digest. If our desire is to be free and unencumbered and – like the fly – revel in the open expanses of air, the weaver at the center of this web may not feel friendly.

It's a common spiritual metaphor that people are asleep and living in prisons they are not even aware of. Language is hypnotic. We grow and develop within it, blind to its presence all about us. It makes up a virtual reality, and in an age of public relations, corporate-owned media, spin doctors, and opinion polls, one can doubt whether there's any reality to be found behind or underneath it. Fools rush in where angels fear to tread. Like the fly, it is easy to be forgetful, foolish, or careless, to become stuck in sticky syntax and captured in the net.

But there's no way around this. The dilemmas are unavoidable, and those who consciously spin stories are not immune from danger. The Hindu word "maya," loosely translated as "illusion," warns us that the hypnotic effect of our words and concepts may trap us and conceal the deeper reality beneath them. But *maya*, in its original sense, referred to a magical power within Brahma (the ultimate, formless, creative source) that could turn itself into the forms of the world. As such, these forms have the power to point to or reveal, just as well as conceal, a deeper reality beneath.

A hand moves, and the fire's whirling takes different shapes:
All things change when we do.
The first word, "Ah...," blossoms into all others.
Each of them is true.

~ Kukai [3]

In the first two lines, Kukai tells us of the interconnected-ness of all things... hand, fire, self, world. In the third line – *"The first word, 'Ah...,' blossoms into all others, each of them is true,"* – the phrase "first word" evokes and refers to primal experience. If our speech and words emerge out of that initial, core encounter, all that follows and blossoms forth from that point will be true. But if our words are inherited and not our own, or if they are disconnected and removed from primal experience, then everything – all speech resulting from that – will be false, illusion, bullshit.

Language need not entrap if it evokes or points to primal experience, what is ultimately ineffable. Among the Greeks, the arts – music, dance, sculpture, painting, poetry – were the province of the Muses, goddesses whose patronage and inspiration were recognized as sacred, a gift of the divine. Martin Prechtel, trained as a Mayan shaman in Guatemala, reports that among the Maya, their gods normally don't pay much attention to human beings. But these gods are like bears, and when people create beauty – through art, ceremony, and songs and prayers of great eloquence – the sweetness is irresistible, and, like bears drawn to honey, the Mayan gods... the sacred presence.... arrives.

The letters that follow (pp. 207 - 230) dance with language. Somewhere between swing, waltz, and a free-form rave, they spin around the hall; changing partners, bumping into walls, and seeking that space where movement and music merges into one. When that happens, there's no need to rest, for we're lying in the grass of that field, where a word like "everything" is magic, and "nothing" makes sense.

The Realm of Primal Forces

Entering the Primal Realm

What we choose to fight is so tiny!
What fights with us is so great!
If only we could let ourselves be dominated
as things do by some immense storm,
We would become strong too, and not need names.

~ Rilke [1]

The multiple crises of the world – each one challenging in itself – crowd upon each other like clouds piling up into a towering thunderhead. We all know a great storm is approaching; the necessity of major transformation weighs upon us. Change is never easy, and it's always disruptive, but to continue on as we are will be disastrous.

In humanity's great myths, the second stage of the heroic journey requires leaving home and entering a field of powerful and primal forces. The heroes and heroines have to bid farewell to all that's comfortable and familiar – the sphere of habit, routine, and cultural consensus – and immerse themselves in this novel and numinous realm.

Fantastic and frightening, the Realm of Primal Forces appears as a dark forest, the underworld, Oz, the labyrinth, the ominous and surging sea. It brims with magic and wonder, darkness and delights. It contains dangers and obstacles, tests and ordeals – dragons, wicked witches, enchantments, swamps, and storms. Odysseus, Orpheus, Jason, Alice, Dorothy... Our protagonists climb mountains, navigate through impenetrable fog, explore uncharted territories, set sail across dangerous seas, and journey to the underworld in search of some prize, for the answers they seek are never at home in the castle, town, or village. The stories depict a potpourri of purposes and expeditions to diverse and dramatic destinations, but this important and prototypical undertaking always requires a departure to somewhere else.

Metaphorically, leaving home tells us something: we will not find the answers we seek by doing what we always do. The profound distress – inner and outer – troubling our hearts and souls today will not be solved by performing our familiar routines faster or more efficiently, or healed through old clichés or common sense. Magic, truth, passion, purpose, or power – whatever we need to find our way out of the mess we've created – won't be discovered in Washington, London, Sedona, or Santa Fe. There is no easy way, no "secret" to be realized through affirmations, economic growth, the "law of attraction," the newest self-help book or diet – by playing the same old programs.

Superficial change is inadequate. Real transformation requires encounters in more authentic arenas and explorations of far-deeper domains. The archetypal adventures in the guiding myths take place in foreign territory, where everything seems strange. The alien landscapes require the protagonist to give up his roles and routines, his modus operandi; his beliefs, judgments, and opinions about the world and himself. This realm outside commonality, consensus, and culture holds the key to what we seek. The blessing of the gods, the wisdom of the ancestors, the lifting of a curse, a magic potion, the Golden Fleece, or – for Dorothy and Odysseus – simply finding the way home… all require a departure from the daily and immersion in the depths.

These stories are universal because they are symbolic maps that illustrate human growth and development. Psychically, the direction is clear. The journey requires an exploration of all that has been lost – unacknowledged, forgotten, ignored, repressed, or neglected – in becoming who we are. The heroic journey begins by leaving our normal, habitual, socially-constructed reality – the old story – behind.

Monsters

In these stories, leaving home appears dangerous and daunting. In a patriarchal culture obsessed with rational thought, the primal realm looks unpredictable and irrational. It's populated by gods and demons that are wild, natural, and instinctual. It's home to the dark emotions of fear, anger, grief, and confusion; it seems chaotic, outlandish, unfathomable… manifests as Hades, Wonderland, the disappearing Grail castle. Monsters lurk in the sea. Cerberus, a vicious, three-headed dog, guards the road to the underworld, and the treasures are hidden, hard to get to, or defended by dragons. Dorothy must kill the Wicked Witch, Perseus behead

Medusa, and Alice face the Queen of Hearts without losing her own. Dangers, dilemmas, and difficulties can appear at any turn.

The narrative expresses an inner truth. Releasing our grip on the old is stressful and frightening. The new landscapes are rife with magical powers and unprecedented possibilities, but they confront us with something alien and mysterious. Unusual, unexplored, and unfamiliar... the unknown seems threatening, and the potential for loss – our possessions and way of life; our companions, cherished routines, and desires for security and comfort – seems close and immediate. What – if anything – will we gain in exchange for all we might give up?

Internally, our habitual identifications and assumptions can start to unravel and lose their footings in the face of situations that are new, unexpected, and unusual. The familiar self clings to well-rehearsed stories and strategies to maintain its security and sense of importance at the center of the universe, but the shape of the universe has shifted. The rules of conduct or engagement have changed; now all our strategies prove useless. Our customary bag of tricks no longer brings any applause, and what we've formerly clung to like a rock now sinks us like a stone. The situation seems perilous; the "hero" becomes confused, anxious, and uncertain. We feel unprotected, sensitive, and afraid as – outwardly – "monsters" show themselves. Old defenses break down, and we feel exposed. Like a seed whose protective shell has split open, this vulnerable passage is necessary for the birthing of new life.

Allies

There is always danger in entering the uncharted waters

required for transformation to take place, but the stories contain a saving grace. The primal realm also contains the good witch, the princess, the fairy godmother… the sacred powers of the feminine. When the call is heard, the challenge accepted, and the commitment made, allies make themselves known. Guiding spirits, healing forces, and friends begin to come forth. Gods, oracles, winged steeds, fairies, guides… A stranger offers a song that can lull the dragon to sleep. The dwarf by the side of the road gives the youngest brother directions to the Water of Life. A message arrives in a dream or a bottle. A goddess appears and points the way. The dove darts down the channel that smashes ships and, as the rocks rebound and separate, the boat passes through.

Rich in magic, wonder, and innocence – gnomes, elves, the divine child, our natural selves – the Primal Realm represents a reclaiming of our imagination, creativity, and expression, a return to the Garden, a sense of joy and belonging on the earth.

Commitment

"A ship is safe in harbor, but that's not what ships are for…" [2]

Healing forces, guides, and helpers are there to aid us, but they only appear after the commitment to the adventure has been made. Standing on the dock before departure, like Jason, you sense, worry, think about the monsters in the sea. *"Suppose I fall flat on my face? If I leave this marriage… job… inauthentic life, will anyone else want me?"* Is your craft sturdy enough; is the crew trustworthy; are these maps any good? *"Will people think I'm crazy? Will living out my dream pay the bills?"* Fear is a constant companion as the hero steps across the line. He's heard rumors of what lurks in the forest, seen strange images and shadow shapes drawn beyond the borders on the charts of the known world. *"We need security, a retirement account, health benefits, more police, a strong defense. There are evil people out there."* Yet he must set sail into the storm and resist the urge to turn away.

Though this realm appears frightening and dangerous, ultimately, the greatest tragedy is to refuse the adventure. Trying to protect ourselves from what we're unwilling to face or experience comes at a tremendous cost. The seed is here to open; we are called to be whole. We can co-operate with those forces larger than the self by facing the aspects of life that seem dark or dangerous and, in so doing, cultivate and develop our courage, compassion, and our capacity to engage with them.

We cannot hide in the shell. Clasping to our comfort zones, security, and the known will kill the spirit. It requires suppressing our inner lives and trying to control the outer world in a vain attempt to avoid reality. Whether we choose to erode, soften, or break out of this shell, we must enter life, sinking our roots into the moist, dank soil; drinking of the earth and reaching to the sun to develop our full potential.

Ultimately everyone will be opened. Breakdown, disease, and death are unavoidable demons that await us all. We can come to them unwillingly, cowering, kicking, and screaming as the self's hard casing is smashed by their sword. But if we devote ourselves to our work by facing our fears and exploring the deeper currents beneath the still surface of our seas, we can develop the resources to meet those inevitable crises with serenity and an inner strength.

Allies await us, and help is at hand, but we will never know this if we do not take the journey. In times of crisis, the calls for security – political or personal – often represent a resistance to change, a denial of the new condition and the growth required to adapt and respond. In the stories of heroic adventure, we are both called and challenged to cast our lot, to face our monsters and the Unknown. Once we take that step, a beacon appears before us; companions and contributors arrive by our side. And, to quote Campbell, in every myth, <u>those of good heart invariably succeed</u>. Treasures are unearthed; the dragon is slain; the magic potion is found. We discover the miraculous spring that will support an abundant life.

Those who will not slip beneath
the still surface on the well of grief,

turning downward through its black water
to the place we cannot breathe,

will never know the source from which we drink,
the secret water, cold and clear,

nor find, in the darkness glimmering,
the small round coins,
thrown by those who wished for something else.

~ David Whyte [3]

David Whyte's poem – in this case about grief – speaks to the dangers and promise of the primal realm. Staring at the "still surface," all we'll see is reflections of our everyday images. If we want more than these shallow impressions, we must dive deep. Yet the prospect is terrifying – the water is cold, dark; our pulse pounds; and it feels like we will suffocate or drown. The descent, the journey to find creativity, the sweet elixir, the renewing vision at the wellspring of life, seems perilous. But it's only through facing this uncertainty and making ourselves vulnerable that we find The Source, the "secret water, cold and clear." And – surprise! – in this darkness we discover gold, treasures unavailable to those who approach the well unwilling to risk more than a pittance – a few coins and a wish – hoping their lives will change.

The Realm of Primal Forces is frightening. What's unknown and uncharted is vast, boundless, and powerful; and it's the hidden ground, the invisible foundation beneath all our self-serving focuses. But it lies outside the comfort zone. These new landscapes challenge the familiar assumptions, rules, and definitions we've built our lives around, and we must adapt, grow, respond, and change to meet them. Odysseus's adventures and ordeals transform him, and he returns to Ithaca a different man than the one who departed for Troy. The lion finds courage; the scarecrow acquires wisdom (a brain); the Tin Man obtains a heart. Parsifal is humbled, tested, and made worthy before he gains the Grail.

*   *   *   *   *   *   *

As today's crisis, breakdown, and unprecedented unraveling take place in human and natural systems, indications of a quickening of spiritual growth and awakening are emerging alongside as allies make ready to appear. Planetary consciousness, desire for a "New Age," and a sense of worldwide connection and concern grows stronger. This quest for a meaningful life – more and more – leads us outside the traditional avenues of God and country, church and nation-state. Shamanism, quantum physics, systems theory, and deep ecology all weave together, pointing toward a new paradigm of the possible human; while Buddhism and ancient teachings of the East adapt and take root in American soil. Words like "spaciousness" and "presence" – hardly nouns to describe a solid self – are used by greater and greater numbers of people to describe the essence of who they really are.

As the old order blunders forward creating chaos and calamity, many long for safe passage to the new dream that's to come. Like explorers of old, we face treacherous waters, buoyed by hope and the tales and intimations of worlds beyond our limited horizons. The outlines of tomorrow's shores may seem hazy, far away, and shrouded in fog, but they can only get clearer through saying goodbye to what's old and not working. When entering the realm of primal forces, we encounter our depths. We encounter our souls. And "for those of good heart," the journey is inevitably fulfilling.

Good heart. There lies the treasure. The values of daily life and the social world – strength, intelligence, riches, looks, power – are worthless here. The call is unmistakable; the summons inescapable. The grand adventure waits. Leaving home (and all that represents) is necessary, that first step to begin the journey.

The chapters to follow take leave of familiar territory and report from fields of potency outside the logical-rational mind. Moving from the mundane to the magical, they pursue passion and power through evoking possibilities of perception free from the old ideologies that gaze at the world through a lens of separation.

The River explores a fluid and changing reality that is – like water – real, but ungraspable. It celebrates the thrill in stepping away from shore, the pull and potential of the ecstatic through leaving what's static behind.

Dreaming and the Dream drifts and dances through a mutable and multidimensional universe where perceiver and perceived face off across the looking glass. Who leads and who follows when the "no-longer-solid self" waltzes with the world; and caterpillars ask "Who are you?" to men who dream they're butterflies?

Facing the Shadow reminds us that the archetypal adventure is not about sidestepping difficulties, that "the way out is through." Many of our cherished notions have a dark underbelly that keeps us stuck in patterns of arrogance, alienation, and fear. The heroic journey compels us to look deeply in the mirror; and to face those dragons (symbolic of all we'd rather deny or avoid) that stand between us and the treasure – the humility, kindness, and compassion; the larger sense of self – destined to be found by "the wicked who know they're wicked."

These chapters are an invitation to jump over the fence, plunge into the water... to release our rigid grasp on consensual reality and – like wise men or fools – enter those unknown realm of danger, delight, magic, and mystery. With no promises or assurances, they seek to inspire, spur, or seduce you into risking a real and radical engagement with life, for the hope and the chance you may one day marry her.

One night as I lay in bed
I asked my heart what it wanted
thumping so wildly

about to leap free from
inside my chest.

This is a fine day to die
it said, live as if
this were your last.

So I made a pact with her –
this bloody mother of my life

and every morning this prayer
pulls up the red-soaked dawn --

Strum your bloody strings
I said, pound the sturdy pulse of my life

and I will walk fearlessly
into the dark arms of death

having lived and loved so well
fed fully these moments
all you have given me.

~ Thomas Griffin [4]

The River

The Source

The history of civilization has been mostly written within great river valleys where the rich run-off from the mountains brought minerals and life-giving sustenance to the lowlands and waiting earth. The Nile… the Jordan, Tigris and Euphrates, Ganges, Yellow… Fertile fields created stable food supplies and surpluses that could support large populations. This abundance allowed cities – and a plethora of human passions and activities beyond survival – to arise and flourish. The freedom for large numbers of the population to pursue interests unrelated to food production led to specialization and the development of new forms of thinking and social organization – architecture, astronomy, writing, mathematics, art, philosophy, religion, government – that have created and seem essential to the world we live in today. Without those life-giving waters, people would likely have remained in those small, nomadic bands better suited to gathering, herding, and hunting.

For millennia people have treasured the healing powers of water. Explorers have ever-sought their magical elixirs and Fountains of Youth; spas and resorts have grown up around thermal pools. As a metaphor, The River represents the Source, that primal force, energy, or condition that creates and nourishes life. Moses was cast adrift on the Nile; Christ baptized in the Jordan. The springs where water emerges from the earth, and the rivers that flow from them, have been considered sacred, the bearers of grace, vehicles and expressions of the divine energy or Spirit that pours forth to sustain the world.

To be on the shore or in the River is to come close to the Source. In India, pilgrims hike high into the Himalayas to seek out the headwaters of the Ganges. In the lowlands, people flock to Benares, the holy city that straddles its shore. There, multitudes bathe, drink its waters, give offerings, are baptized, or cremated and cast adrift on its currents, for symbolically, to be close to the Ganges is to be nearer to god. It's a place of potential where the two worlds – the daily and the eternal – can mingle and meet.

A Fluid and Interdependent Reality

Row, row, row your boat,
gently down the stream....

It's no accident this nursery rhyme – simple yet profound – evokes water. Its lessons would be poorly represented by pictures of driving a car down the freeway or galloping on a horse around a racetrack. In those two images, the context – freeway, racetrack – is static. The path is laid out and unchangeable, and the human mind is primary and willful as it rides, accelerates, steers, and works to exercise control. But there's no control with a river. Rowing must take into account its motions, its meandering and mood, and we can choose to surrender, to synchronize ourselves with its movements –

and thereby be carried faster and easier than we would be otherwise – or we can ignore the flow and struggle, perhaps to capsize and drown.

In literature and philosophy, two primary metaphors have been used to describe awareness itself. In one, awareness is conceived as some form of space, inside which events and appearances arise, play out, and disappear. In the other, consciousness is represented as a stream, a flow of images, sensations, feelings, and phenomena. This River (whether referring to the flux of awareness or water running to the ocean) is a fluid reality. It is moving, changing, a process; not a solid entity. It sings; it trickles; it shimmers; it dances. It's a melody, a poem, a creative event… a symphony of relationships.

A river is also interdependent, part of a landscape whose threads weave together to dissolve the polarities of separate or one, cause or effect. Molded by and responding to forces all around it, the banks define and direct the current, but the River may build, destroy, or change those very same banks as it moves rocks, uproots trees, knocks over bushes, jumps its bed and deposits fresh mud and gravel. The banks define the river; yet the river creates the banks. They're interdependent, in relationship – they do not exist alone – and the river at this moment is a temporary snapshot in an ongoing and changing duet.

This co-creative dance plays out on grand scale as liquid meets solid throughout the glorious forms of the landscape. In one sense the mountains create the rivers. They force the atmosphere to rise up at it streams across the continent, cooling in the process. As it does, moisture condenses; clouds coalesce around the peaks;

droplets fall. The crags and contours gather and funnel the runoff, their shape and slope determining the rate of flow, the placement of streams, tributaries, rapids, and waterfalls.

But simultaneously, the water is sculpting the mountains. It carves canyons and gullies, erodes hillsides, smoothes boulders and rocks; breaking them down into gravel and ever-smaller pieces that turn into soil. Slowly – day by day and sometimes quickly – the waters wash or wear away those very ridges, moving them downstream while adding new features to the face of the mountains. This rich intermingling of rock, rain, and runoff causes seeds to germinate. It nourishes roots and paints the barren ramparts and stark outcroppings of stone with a palette of green, while seeding and sustaining the vibrant life – trees, grasses, fish, deer, herons – that begin to flourish on the slopes and in the valleys below.

The song of the River is attuned to rhythms that are connected to the great cycles of the earth and stars. It trickles, babbles, or roars, varying through the seasons in harmony with spring runoffs, summer rains, or drought. It may be liquid, harden to ice, or evaporate into vapor depending on temperature and season. It plunges down from high ground, runs through valleys and plains, and returns to the ocean. There its waters are lifted up by the sun once more and borne on the wind back to the mountains again.

The River is expressive, its countenance ever-changing as it journeys through and responds to varied and dissimilar landscapes. Moment by moment and mile by mile, its face reveals different moods.... roaring, frothing, meandering, or quiet. It is a verb, a process. It contains energy, a force, a fluid and mutable presence that takes many different forms. Its currents part around islands;

produce swirling eddies; splash and separate into individual droplets; then give up their boundaries to merge into larger entities once more. And like the River, there with the grace of god, go I.

Stepping Away from Shore:

Buddhist teachings emphasize impermanence and interdependence while exposing the illusion of the solid self. Like the relationship of the stream to the banks, "world" and "self" jointly mold and mirror each other. They are fluid, interdependent, mutually defining. Neither is objective, and neither can be known or exist by itself, except in relationship to the other.

As previously mentioned, in the old paradigm of knowledge, the world was stable, objective, "out there," and the scientist studied that world from a neutral and detached point of view. With the advent of quantum mechanics, that perspective on reality evaporated. The solid world exists no longer. Modern physics – like Dorothy peeking behind the curtain – has unmasked the separate observer and shown his neutral, uninvolved space to be illusion. Now there is only energy, and energy manifests in many different guises. Observation and attention are themselves energy, and this energy influences whatever is being observed. The world interacts and responds to this energy – our energy. Therefore, we are in relationship and "it" is no longer "out there." In the new world of physics, we no longer stand on the shore. We are in the water.

To be in the water is to be out of our element. We may think of ourselves as smart, sensible, the salt of the earth, but salt dissolves in liquid. To be surrounded by air is familiar and comfortable, but water tugs, pulls, touches us. It comes close, surrounds, and envelops as all distance vanishes. We are pushed, carried, directed... our usual sense of control washes away. As the seemingly-solid shore drifts out of reach, the river promises (or threatens) the dissolution of the self we've come to know.

Immersing ourselves in the current requires letting go of our familiar and separate identities – frightening – to fulfill the promise of a larger force and potential which propels us forward. Like snowflakes or drops of rain that fall in the mountains, something is pulling us toward a greater journey. We feel a longing to find our way home, to make our way back to the Garden... to find the Promised Land... to be reabsorbed in the great ocean of existence... but we can't get there by ourselves. The snowflake or droplet – small and separate like our own identities – must relinquish their boundaries to become trickle, brook, or stream and make that journey to the sea. They (and we) must surrender ourselves to something larger to realize our potential for a more boundless and far-reaching destiny.

My heart is torn open,
and I notice, surprised,
the pieces on the ground
waiting
to be put back together
into some new and unfamiliar shape.

Listening with the ache of all that is
and isn't
I hear the steady rain
falling into the earth
and imagine the shape of me
changing into a raindrop,
filtering down into a dark
loamy place where I would give

out my wet life (at last!)
against a tree root
and then, everything
would begin again
in a shape I would not recognize
as my own.
~ Lauren Chamblis [1]

Losing Interest in the Bank

To surrender to the current is to cross a boundary. Symbolically, through entering the river we become participants. We are immersed, inside, engaged with the world, no longer on the bank. We're connected, related, interdependent. In re-defining and re-imagining our identity, both world and self have become shape-shifting and fluid, and – though possibly frightening – this can be a source of both celebration and wonder. *"A schizophrenic and yogi are in the same ocean, one swimming while the other flails and drowns."* Why fight it? Resistance to the interdependent and streaming nature of self and world denies what is. This refusal is futile, fear-based, and a way of lying to ourselves, as it attempts to radically restrict our world and potential experience so as to not shatter our separate self-image and delusions of importance.

To step away from the water's edge is to release our hold on the chimera of that solid and separate self. It always seems safer to stay on shore, and if our goal is to play it safe, we should keep our little boats tied to the dock. But playing it safe is not the adventure we've come here for. The soul longs to experience life fully, to find wholeness, to become unfettered and free.

Our inner voice – shouting or quietly whispering – implores us to express, develop, and realize the potential within us, to complete ourselves. Our journey – personal and collective – has brought us to the shore, that transition zone where the solid bank meets the shape-shifting liquid. The land and its solidity represent our inherited notions – the old stories and consensual consciousness – while the river personifies a more fluid, merging, and streaming awareness. It is the place where boundaries dissolve, where everything changes and flows together, where nothing stands still. It exemplifies dream, emotion, alternate reality, primal awareness, the left side. The banks mostly attempt to control, contain (sometimes dam), and channel this energy, but the river – life – relentlessly, eternally courses. Sooner or later it will build up, overflow, and sweep those banks away.

Our first nine months were spent in the womb. This "memory" may underlie many stories and longings for a lost paradise, but that does not diminish its power. Our blood was formed in the ancient oceans, and the tug of the tide is relentless. It pulls, pulses, promises, and somewhere we know that in losing oneself – one world and identity dissolved in the endless streaming – we may discover ourselves anew in a different dimension, a more fluid and interdependent reality. Our souls long to participate, get wet, and enter the water… to "slip beneath the still surface…" to cast the lines aside and drift gently down the stream.

The letters in this section (pp. 231 - 249) invite you to trust the Source, to cast off caution… to enter the water, be buoyed by hope, to savor the cold splash of awakening. Common wisdom says be safe; stay at home; curb your dreams; don't make waves. But these are uncommon times, and the spirit sings for an uncommon life. A new dream is calling, encouraging us to release the ropes, let go the hold on consensus reality and the separate self. Often drowned out by the noise of traffic and television, it bides its time and whispers. If we grow silent, we'll hear it. "Enter the current, surrender and float… merrily, merrily, merrily, merrily…" There a greater myth and deeper dream is awaiting us.

If we're fortunate, or wise, we'll heed this call before the dam breaks.

This morning no sound but the loud
breathing of the sea. Suppose that under
all that salt water lived the god
that humans have spent ten thousand years
trawling the heavens for.
We caught the wrong metaphor.
Real space is wet and underneath,
the church of shark and whale and cod.
The noise of those vast lungs
exhaling: the plain chanting of monkfish choirs.
Heaven's not up but down, and hell
is to evaporate in air. Salvation,
to drown and breathe
forever with the sea.

~ Bill Holm [2]

Dreaming and the Dream

Reality

"Merrily, merrily, merrily, merrily... life is but a dream..."

"Life is but a dream." How curious! How profound! In our
current mythology, we consider dreams illusions, nonsensical,
chaotic. They are irrational, at best symbolic, and mostly irrelevant
to daily life. They do not satisfy the standards for "reality."

But most peoples throughout history believed we're
dreaming all the time, and the assumption of the modern world that
we are not makes us dismissive, and potentially damaging, to those
on another path. Unaware that perception may be active, that we
may be selecting and "assembling" the world we see, we call our
dream *"reality,"* and in so doing, we consign other states of
awareness – the enchanted landscapes of primal peoples; the ecstatic
journeys of shamans; the consciousness of the night – into the trash
heap of the "unreal." These rich cornucopias of association and
perceptual possibility are then seen as primitive, defined as

unimportant, and even labeled threatening; but the act of denying their value and validity leaves our own vision circumscribed and impoverished; and it can make us dangerous or destructive to all those whose consciousness roams outside our fenced-in yards of respectability.

I am a Verb

To entertain the idea that our assumptions about reality and life are just facets of a particular dream can feel sobering, frightening, or completely liberating. In our daily dream, the elements of the world (the nouns of existence) remain separate. I am myself; a tree is a tree; a stone is a stone. This separation remains relatively permanent – it will be there tomorrow, the next day, and the next – unless physical interactions intervene to change it. A stone can be broken, crushed into gravel, or ground into sand. The tree can be cut into lumber, chipped into mulch, burned to ash. I can die, be eaten by worms, decompose into soil.

But tonight I will lie down, close my eyes, and find myself in another world, one with a different set of rules and other options for engagement. The tree may tower above me, but this "me" might be taller, slim, or younger than the one I'm used to. I may observe this "me" from above, below, behind.... from a place outside those eyes housed in his swiveling head. Perhaps the tree will stretch, twist, and start to move; its branches becoming writhing snakes that turn their eyes upon that man called "me" below them. I become fascinated, frightened, begin to back away, run, grow wings and fly as the serpents slither across the ground in pursuit.

I have entered a different, but very real world. Call it fantasy if you will, but try telling that to the man running for his life! To him, it's you who are crazy and trapped in illusion. In the morning, this "I" may sit up, rub his eyes, and laugh about it. The ego and the assumptions of daylight reassert themselves, blind to the lie as they announce, "I had this strange dream last night." In doing so, conscious, ordinary awareness inflates itself at the expense of this other dimension, for in the reality of the night, <u>it was the dream that had the "I."</u>

But something happened, something unusual that makes no "sense" in the light of day. In the rules of our daytime awareness, objects make up the world. We are nouns. We are separate and remain so. But night casts its net and captures us in its spell, and in this new landscape, "self" and "world" are no longer so sharply divided. They move together, influence each other; they dance and respond. The tree is not static; it is not inert and unexpressive as it shelters, stalks, pursues, changes. And the self, the "I," changes alongside through mutual interactions within strange sequences of unpredictable calls and responses.

This dreaming awareness differs fundamentally from waking. In the dreamscape, we and the world around us change constantly. We transform shape and appearance; have many different points of view. Possibilities are unlimited. Perceptions can be local or non-local; awareness is not attached to or contained in "our body." And the world shifts with us, within and without mysteriously joined as objects and scenes mutate, move, and morph along with every other aspect of the dream.

Like a river, a dream is far more than a noun. It is not a fact, a discreet event with defined boundaries. It may have no beginning or end, for who's to say it's over when we awake? Morning comes;

75

the eyes open. But like a radio that tunes in a different channel when the eyelids rise, it's quite possible the dreamtime broadcasts continue on merrily, independent of the attention of the daytime-dreaming "I."

Dreaming is a verb, an activity, a process that continually changes the membrane along which inner meets outer and self emerges from world. In this non-separated, non-dual awareness accessed during sleep, we are the dreamer, the dream<u>ed</u>, and the dream. To primal peoples; to sages, shamans, and mystics; the fluid, mutually-defining and interacting relationship found in dreams – with its shape-shifting boundaries of "inner and outer," "you and me," "self and world," – mirrors the way the world actually works far more than the static and separate "dream" we label the *"reality"* of daily life. *Dreaming* reveals a different dimension – it demonstrates a different approach, another way to perceive and assemble the world.

The Common Nightmare

Across the world, fear, violence, distrust, and despair are spreading like an epidemic. The dream we currently live often resembles a nightmare. A crisis of spirit sits behind all the other crises – war, famine, exploitation, environmental degradation, and the breakdown of civility and community – that swirl around us. These dilemmas are not separate and isolated problems treatable by specific programs, legislation, rewards or punishments. They represent fundamental outgrowths of our core assumptions and cultural blind spots – the way we see ourselves and the world. They are products of our mythology, our beliefs… our Dream.

This Dream confines us in the smallest psychic space of any people in history. For all our abilities to manipulate matter, to create wealth, smash an atom, walk on the moon, or fool with the genetic code, we are shockingly unable to live well. We know how to fight, to make war on poverty, communism, drugs, or terrorism, but ignorance prevails when it comes to making peace with anything. We've lost any meaningful relationship and connection to the great cycles of the seasons, sun, moon, and stars; find ourselves unable to listen to or value the wisdom of our bodies, feelings, or imagination; pillage and pollute the land we live from; and have become strangers to or threatened by alternative reality states and other modes of perception sought by humans throughout the millennia.

A secular and social reality without a living connection to the natural, numinous, or non-ordinary to give it value quickly becomes shallow and meaningless. To identify with the separate self and be bereft of perceptual tools and processes that provide a sense of mutuality, reciprocity, and response-ability to a larger, living cosmos leaves us anxious, alienated, depressed, and out of touch with ourselves, the Earth, and each other. To be stuck in a lifeless, mechanical, materialistic universe deadens the soul, and it creates a standard of success that borders on the banal – getting more money to buy more stuff.

Dancing with the Other World

Modern life suffers in spiritual poverty from losing its living connection to the "Other World," variously described as the home of the ancestors, soul realm, sacred world, spiritual reality, or the Dreamtime. The universe is multi-dimensional, and the world is more than a collection or aggregation of lesser, inanimate "things." Our purpose must be far grander than amassing, using, or owning them.

Dreams are not opposed to reality though they've been defined as such in the paradigms we've inherited. Our myths, our stories, our dreams – and the possibilities and relationships allowed and excluded within them – determine what our "reality" is. We can cease wondering or arguing about whether our dreams are true, since the reality and truth we experience is a result of our "Dream." Instead, we must ask a far-more important question: Are our dreams worthy? Are they good, broad, or deep enough? Do our dreams locate us within the grand dramas and cycles of life? Do they create a sense of gratitude and wonder; connect us with the past, future, ancestors, and children to come? Is this dream inspiring, enlivening, guiding, and sustaining... or is it draining? Does it deserve our allegiance? Is it a dream worth living?

When your eyes are tired
the world is tired also.

When your vision has gone
no part of the world can find you.

Time to go into the dark
where the night has eyes
to recognize its own.

There you can be sure
you are not beyond love.

The dark will be your womb
tonight.

The night will give you a horizon
further than you can see.

You must learn one thing,
The world was made to be free in.

Give up all the other worlds
except the one to which you belong.

Sometimes it takes darkness and the sweet
confinement of your aloneness
to learn

anything or anyone
that does not bring you alive

is too small for you.

~ David Whyte [1]

"Anything or anyone that does not bring you alive is too small for you." This statement may be personal, about a relationship, dead-end job, or some situation you feel you can't get out of. But it may also refer to something larger, a whole way of looking at the world. Is this daily dream, the mass-produced culture of competition and consumerism, enough to satisfy us? Does it touch our souls; connect us with the earth, ourselves, each other? Is it a rich and sustaining soil in which those souls can grow, develop, and flower? Does this dream we're living bring us alive?

Imagination Running Wild

Imagine no possessions
I wonder if you can
No need for greed or hunger

A brotherhood of man
Imagine all the people
Sharing all the world...

~ John Lennon [2]

In sharp contrast to older communities where shamanism, primal awareness, mystical, and non-ordinary states were highly valued and sought for the wisdom, healing, and inspiration available there, current culture gives little or no attention to dreaming. In those more soul and depth-oriented societies, methods for nurturing and inducing *dreaming* – through plant medicines, fasting, ordeals, religious trance, etc. – were highly developed.

In the modern era, even when an individual takes an interest in dreams – with or without the aid of a therapist – the focus remains largely tied to the mundane. Dreams are examined for their symbols or meaning, which is to say, we approach them with our heads. We dream of a mountain lion and wonder if it's a symbol of power, or if it has something to do with cats or the constellation Leo. Our concerns remain wedded to the ordinary as we ask, "What does this lion have to teach me? What message does it have that will improve my life?" And it is this life – this ordinary life – that has our attention and allegiance.

But the history of humanity has been filled with other options. Imagine daily life as a room we live in, filled with all the familiar faces, activities, and things we give attention to. This room has a wall we can't pass through, a wall that keeps us from the room next door where magical things are known to happen. Each night we lie down in our ordinary room and close our eyes. Sometimes, we magically find ourselves on the other side of that wall, and there we cavort with angels, dragons, and mountain lions… only to awaken in the morning back where we started.

The common approach asks, "How can the lion help me? What is the message?" We examine our dreams hoping to enrich daily life. But in doing so, we bypass other, more intriguing possibilities. We might ask – as many have before – "What does the lion want and require of me? …How can I make this life (ordinary life) serve the greater dream, rather than vice-versa? …Could I enter the Dreamtime? …Could I live in the other room?"

The answer is "Yes, you can." Over the millennia, practices and processes have been developed to do just that. This fact challenges us to look at our lives through a different lens, to search our psyches for answers to questions too long ignored. Humans have the potential to remake themselves and ordinary life in service of the Great Mystery, to refuse to subjugate their capacity for *dreaming* to serve the social values of economics, status, or self-importance. We can start by withdrawing our attention and energy from those ordinary consensus and social values that are so dreary and soulless. We can pledge allegiance to something else, to the pursuit of the extraordinary, and in so doing, knock down the wall so that this world can be washed, cleansed, and – like the Nile in the spring – renewed in the flood of the numinous.

To paraphrase Jung, humans have four modes of perception, four ways to engage the universe, to know the world. He called these avenues Sensing, Feeling, Thinking, and Imagination. Our system of education trains us in one capacity – thinking, thinking, thinking – only, and, as stated, this capacity has become the foundation and standard for knowledge. This narrowing of focus is like buying a stool with one leg. You can commit your weight to it if you want, but all your postures and positions are condemned to be way out of balance.

In the current mythology, imaginary means unreal. But it is imagination, the language of symbols, which binds seemingly-discreet elements into wholes. It is imagination that creates the Big Dipper. It is imagination – coupled with people's agreement – that creates the United States, Indonesia, or the Middle East. Today's facts – from airplanes, to electricity, to hip replacements – first took form in someone's imagination. The elegant equation, $E=mc^2$, that ushered in the nuclear age, arose from a dream in which Einstein imagined himself riding a beam of light as if it were a motorcycle.

One hundred-fifty years ago, an "iron bird" or a "flying machine" was only a dream. In current "reality" that dream has become very real. But today, peace, economic justice, and a sacred relationship to the earth seem like far-away dreams. If we're to realize and manifest a more sacred and soulful life, we must step outside the one-dimensional dream of modern life in which dreaming and imagination are themselves categorized as unreal.

We spend over six years of our lives dreaming. When we enter the dreaming universe, the windows of the imagination are flung open. Impressions, associations, and possibilities proliferate, run wild, and overlap; refusing to stay in line. With borders and horizons vast and infinite, and landscapes more than three-dimensional, The Dreamtime possesses an ecology much deeper and richer than the circumscribed expanses of the day, and those dreamtime panoramas are potentially as real – and in many ways more so – than the unchanging and soulless flatland of physical reality in which modern "industrial man" has become imprisoned.

All aspects of a dream are relative – they exist in relationship to each other. I am a field of possibilities and potentials, and many of these remain undiscovered and unexplored. I will not "find myself" in isolation, for it is the world outside which changes, catalyzes, or evokes in me that which has yet come forth. Inner and outer shift and interpenetrate; they define and mutually create each other. In this world where everything is related, the many appearances and forms of being are all relative... relatives. We are in community. We are no longer alone.

Dreaming encompasses a far larger – not a lesser – universe than the one we are used to. Its spaces can be immense, microscopic, familiar, outside of time, or inside what's impenetrable; its territories without landmarks, colorful, blank, or nowhere at all. Science studies water in a beaker, but in the dream you can be the ocean itself. There one can learn how to joyfully... *merrily, merrily, merrily...* stream, flow, dissolve, reform, swim, or surrender. If we reclaim and embrace our capacity for *dreaming* and the multi-dimensional reality implied within, learning never stops, the horizons are endless, and we can belong and be part of the family of life again.

The letters I share here (pp. 251 - 272) honor the multidimensional, mutual, and creative interactions between perceiver and perceived. They celebrate *dreaming* and venture to evoke, enter, and expand our access to landscapes of magic and mystery. Symbolic, allegorical, personal, illogical… If we're to find, to realize, to bring a sacred dream into this world, we must be willing – joyfully willing – to reclaim our visionary capacities; to re-weave, knit together, and re-member all that has atrophied or been dismembered in our dark nights of detachment and separation. When imagination is finally welcomed back into the house of reality, poetry will replace politics, and creativity will once again bloom in the garden. The worlds of shamanism and quantum physics will crack open their gates of enchantment, and Spirit take wing over shimmering fields and circle a universe whose center is everywhere.

> *I live my life in growing orbits which move out*
> *over the things of the world.*
> *Perhaps I can never achieve the last, but that will be my attempt.*
> *I am circling around God, around the ancient tower,*
> *And I have been circling for a thousand years,*
> *And I still don't know if I am a falcon,*
> *or a storm, or a great song.* (3)

Facing the Shadow

Light and Darkness

Anything that has form, anything not completely transparent, casts a shadow. Psychologically, the shadow refers to all the areas of darkness we don't see when we turn our attention in only one direction – toward the light. Whatever this light represents – our values, beliefs, commitments, definitions of goodness… be they moral, patriotic, economic, etc. – the shadow refers to the hidden costs and the negative consequences that are invisible, ignored, or denied, yet inevitably accompany whatever good (or god) we are dedicated to pursue.

No one wants to face the shadow. The shadow – by definition – represents the parts of ourselves we take pains to neither acknowledge nor admit. It consists of all those traits we fear, are ashamed of, or simply don't recognize… that don't fit within the framework of the picture or image we want to show to the world. It is the cold, dark presence that follows us everywhere, and its effects can be felt by all those who are overlooked as our gaze remains oriented toward the light.

But life itself is whole, round, complete. Nature moves,

ebbs, and flows through repeating and renewing successions of death, decay, and rebirth. The seasons pass through springtime's birth, summer's expansion, autumn's constriction, and the dying back of winter with neither beginning nor end. Creation includes sunshine and shadow. It is yin and yang, up and down, night and day... embodying both sides of whatever the mind divides into opposites. Everything that is bathed in light also blocks the light and keeps it from reaching something else. All action – no matter how well intended – has effects and outcomes that can be harmful to someone or something else.

"God loves the wicked who know they're wicked, far more than he loves the righteous who know they're righteous." [1]

It's a dangerous illusion to think we can avoid the polarities inherent in the process of living, to assume that we can (or should) be "good" all the time. One can attempt to be against "evil" and seek "the light," but refusing to acknowledge the shadow side of the way we function ignores a great deal of life and who we are. This denial sets us against half of existence and demands we be blind to our own dysfunction. And when we turn our face away from the darkness within, it does not cease expressing itself; but it must leak or break out unconsciously, in ways we can neither see nor control.

If everyone in a crowd stands in a line and faces the same direction, whole expanses of darkness can disappear for the entire multitude. When people step out of line or – far better – stand in a circle, the shadows all become visible... visible to all those who have another perspective, who face another direction – their own – and whose source of light and frame of reference is not the same as yours. If one's commitment is to looking good, you will not embrace these other perspectives. They'll be dismissed, or labeled misguided, dishonest, or immoral. But if your intention includes knowing yourself fully, these contrary, uncomfortable perspectives can eventually be welcomed as allies.

"God loves the wicked who know they're wicked.... " Facing and coming to terms with our shadow is required to claim our wholeness. We must accept our repressed and unconscious impulses; our defects, dysfunctions, and unexpressed desires. One does not get to live in some shining city on the hill replete with just "good" situations and emotions. If we want to open our mind, senses, and hearts... if we want to feel and experience life fully, we must feel and experience it all. Love comes with grief and loss; immense wealth creates poverty for multitudes; your victory may be another's defeat. Creation and destruction work side by side; terror and wonder are holding hands. Consistently avoiding what is distressing or difficult requires that we disconnect, repress, and numb ourselves to feeling and experience all across the board. And many are committed to doing just that.

Let Us All Prey

Nature is rife with shadow. Life is predatory. Everything has to eat, and in that act something else is eaten. Lions, wolves, rabbits, fungus, bacteria.... one form dies so another may live. It's simply how it is. The fox kills the chicken, the lion the gazelle, the spider the fly. Cancer kills the host. Even sheep tear up the grass.

Nature is magnificent, intense, beautiful, sublime... but it is neither "nice" nor good. Sunshine makes crops grow and vegetable life possible, but it can also turn fierce and relentless until everything shrivels and dies. Rain germinates dormant seeds and makes fertile the otherwise-barren soil, but if the clouds don't disperse, those fields and all within them will be ripped away and washed downstream. Tsunamis, avalanches, tornados, floods, conflagrations... the great powers of earth, air, fire, and water all have their dark sides.

The assumption there's a literal place of all goodness – like heaven – with a corresponding territory for evil is both absurd and a life-denying notion. Of course these representations of perfect harmony or torment can't be found on earth, or even in life – hence the "after-life" – and they refer (if anything) to states of awareness, not locations in a physical universe. The real heavens and hells are found within the human psyche. They germinate and grow in the imagination and mind, fed by the way we think and perceive, and cultivated by our ability or inability to experience the numinous, to accept and love what is.

Accepting what is includes the darkness. Personal wholeness is not obtained through pursuing some abstract notion of perfection, for the whole of life contains death, betrayal, hunter and hunted, suffering, catastrophe, greed, selfishness, cruelty, and failure. Growth involves integration – not elimination – of the full range of human possibility and energy; and this integration requires recognition, confrontation, and acceptance of the shadow aspects of life. We live within a playground of creation and destruction. We must come to grips with the fact that "good" and "evil" are interwoven, and these labels vary by point of view. The fox's gain is the chicken's loss. We delude ourselves when we deny that we participate in this cycle too.

Every day, humans inflict suffering on a grand scale, damaging or destroying the earth and each other, with little concern or empathy for those who are different or labeled "the enemy." The notion that one's species (race, religion, country, etc.) is special and better than all the rest (the "righteous who know they're righteous") is a mythology with no ethical or scientific footing. To then use, hurt, exploit, or destroy those others without consideration because they're somehow beneath us is morally pathetic. Those who cling most fiercely to positions of moral righteousness mete out the greatest evil, for the denial of their own darkness leads them to attack others – the wrongdoing they see "out there" but a reflection of all they refuse to acknowledge in themselves.

Sympathy for the Devil

Healing ourselves, becoming whole and authentic, requires facing our shadow side, our wounds and dysfunctions, the "selves" or aspects we try to hide or deny. It requires becoming the wicked who know we're wicked. Relinquishing arrogance and self-importance and admitting our faults and failings is the first step on the road to participating in life with love, respect, and compassion. This ego shrinking, this "mea culpa," is not an easy task. To invite and welcome all our rejected attributes back to the banquet table requires an expanded vision of the self and a deepening of the soul, for our shadow elements normally lay outside the fence of the conscious self. They are uncomfortable, hard to admit, mostly unknown and unfamiliar. They do not look pretty. But they contain great emotion and power.

"Without Contraries there is no progression ....
Attraction and Repulsion, Reason and Energy, Love and Hate...
are necessary to Human Existence...

Good is the passive that obeys Reason
Evil is the active springing from Energy"

~ William Blake [2]

Blake turned the Christian cosmology of his day on its head. In reason, religion, and morality, in all the rigid rules that negated and repressed, he saw impulses that perverted humanity's capacities. In the flames of hell – which he identified with desire, body, and Eros – he found creativity, energy, and the fire of visionary and transforming imagination.

Joseph Campbell remarked that every *"devil is a god who has not been recognized... It is a power in you to which you have not given expression... Then, like all repressed energy, it builds up and becomes completely dangerous."* [3] Our labels of good and evil do not refer to facts in any objective world. Rather, it's the act of rejection and judgment itself – the refusal to shine the light on elements we want to hide – that keeps them in the dark. Then – ignored, unacknowledged, and unintegrated – they must either burst out unconsciously or be projected onto others, the resulting damage unable to be addressed while their existence remains discounted and denied.

These devils are the elephants in the living room, the monsters beneath the calm surface of the sea. They're tiptoed around, and no one likes to speak of them – violence, alcoholism, bitterness, greed, resentment... But these energies must be grappled with and befriended or they will remain demonic, emerging unexpectedly and in ways that are invisible to us. Desire unexpressed turns dark. What we resist, persists. We become whole only by welcoming back and integrating what's been excommunicated. Then the power of what was formerly in shadow becomes part of our gift, its expression no longer outside awareness or control. When we commit to finally enter the cave and face the dragon, we may be surprised and find our treasure too.

Making Apology to Snake

"The gods have become diseases." [4]

Historically, Snake is one of the oldest gods on earth, among the most revered of deities. He embodies primal awareness. He is physical-sensual existence, life force, earthly energy… lives with his belly on the ground. In Hindu cosmology, Snake's energy (kundalini) lies sleeping at the base of the spine, and all "higher" spiritual states depend on its movement and awakening. In Central America he appeared and was worshipped in the form of Quetzacoatl, the feathered serpent, his combination with eagle representing the union of earth and sky. Sacred to Athena and revered in most matriarchal, goddess cultures, he carries powerful medicine. The caduceus, the medical profession's symbol of healing, consists of twin serpents twined round a staff with wings at the top. But somewhere along the way, Snake became a pariah.

* * * * * * *

The Old Testament is an amalgam of stories from

wandering tribes in the ancient Middle East. Warlike and fiercely patriarchal, their cosmology denied, rejected, and erased all traces of the feminine principle central to the older goddess cultures they supplanted. Snake held an honored place in those societies, and this mostly accounts for his quick fall from favor.

According to this testament, the first humans once lived in the Garden, a holy place where they walked and talked with "God" when he visited in the evening. This Garden contained two trees – the Tree of Knowledge and the Tree of Eternal life – laden with fruit that was forbidden to be sampled. According to the story, Eve – at the urging of Snake – tasted and tempted Adam with an apple from the Tree of Knowledge. Jehovah, furious at their disobedience, and fearful they would taste the second fruit and become equal to him, banished them from the Garden, cursing them to wander the world in pain and suffering. From then on, the new sky god looked down on and repudiated the earth.

In the origin myths of these desert tribes, Eve, woman, and mother (in Latin, *mater,* the root of the word matter)… snake… the earth itself… instinct, sex, pleasure….the animal powers and all things feminine, sensual, or earthy… were demonized, and for millennia all things physical and related to the body have been denied their divinity and labeled the domain of the devil.

But every "devil is a god who has not been recognized." And every god can be a demon too. Snake still lives within us. He inhabits our "reptilian brain." To be whole (as well as honest), we must acknowledge and honor our other brains, our "lower" functions, our primal energy… our first three chakras. It was not Snake, Eve, or these core human faculties that caused the banishment from Eden; they were not responsible for "the fall." Jehovah, the angry, judgmental god, is the obvious villain in the Garden; his fear-fueling attitude (and the loss of our natural inheritance represented by Snake) resulting in dis-ease, discontent, and disconnection – our exile. Realizing our innate wholeness will require accepting and embracing Snake, our DNA, our sensual, earthy, and non-rational self. And it will require unmasking all those wrathful, righteous, and critical gods, who perhaps themselves need to be banished if we really want to know and return to paradise.

The Virus in the Program

Musicians with "soul" are generally those who've struggled with poverty, addiction, abuse… men and women who've paid the dues of pain and suffering, thereby developing a depth of character and experience that's reflected in their temperament or expression. Soul does not come from having to choose between Lexus and Mercedes.

Confronting the shadow is required in personal work. This involves being willing to look at who we are and how we think and act – accepting all those impulses and characteristics that run counter to the good boy or good girl image – if we're to deepen our sense of self… if we're to become adults. But facing the shadow is cultural work as well, and endless wars and massive military spending; growing prison populations; the epidemic of antidepressant drugs; pornography; child abuse; and an array of other social ills all point to the seamy underbellies of our religious and political dogmas.

Pointing this shadow out is a thankless task. As a nation,

America scrupulously avoids its darkness. Politicians endlessly proclaim the United States to be "the greatest nation on earth," while hiding the hideous behind curtains of catch-phrases and veils of euphemisms. We unilaterally attack or invade other nations to "protect freedom," name our war-making machine the "defense" department, and call assaults on the earth "development." Pride in one's country feels good, but the pursuit of feeling good does not encourage us to face the truth and look deeply within ourselves, to become those "wicked who know they're wicked."

In his 1984 inaugural address, Ronald Reagan spoke of the first president, George Washington, as being "less than a day's journey from raw, untamed, wilderness. There were four million Americans then." What's missing here? Let's start with the truth. Before the European settlers arrived, North America was home to well-over fifteen million Native Americans. By 1890, only two-hundred thousand were left, little more than one percent. The indigenous inhabitants of this land were free peoples – as free as any recorded in history – but those few who survived the slaughter were rounded up into stockades or put on reservations, and in many cases, denied the right to practice their religion or educate their children.

Praising freedom and the pioneers who tamed an "uninhabited wilderness" makes good politics, and it allows "us" to feel good and righteous. But these good feelings are built on outright lies. Telling the truth is harder. It would chronicle centuries of genocide. It would acknowledge deceit, greed, racism, rape, torture, and lying on the highest and lowest levels. It would report gatherings of frenzied crowds, chanting "Exterminate them!" and soldiers shooting native children for sport.

Revealing the truth would involve confessing centuries of the slave trade... kidnapping, rape of women, abuse, whippings, and hangings. It would shine the light on this sordid activity, recount the tales of men and women chained and packed like sardines in the dark bowels of ships, seasick and unable to escape their own excrement, fifty million dying and tossed overboard in the passage.

Truth would require we speak about the land: Massive herds of buffalo slaughtered in thirty short years, a hundred million magnificent beasts reduced to a few dozen individuals; the gray wolf and carrier pigeon driven to extinction; the grizzly bear eliminated from most of the west; underground aquifers polluted for two hundred thousand years; the destruction of coral reefs; the decimation of the salmon; seas fished out; the whales' fight for survival.

Truth would speak about an economy based on weaponry and an addiction to war; a military budget greater than all the rest of the world combined; bases for armies and armaments in over two hundred foreign countries. But our tongues are strangely silent on these matters as the patriotic band plays on. Instead, America continues to label itself special, blameless, the envy of a jealous world; innocent victims of terrorist attacks, righteously waging wars that claim hundreds of thousands of lives to avenge 3800 dead. Truth, integrity, and honesty are also casualties, acceptable collateral damage in the campaign to conceal the shadow.

"It is tragic to see how blatantly a man bungles his own life and the lives of others, yet remains totally incapable of seeing how much the whole tragedy originates in himself..." [5]

A virus inhabits the program. The operating system is unstable and heading for a crash. Behind all the banners of freedom and progress marches a crusading army – fearful, ill-at-ease, and dangerous – and the current epidemics of anxiety and depression signal deep-rooted disease. Ultimately we are all – human and non-human alike – connected, woven together within the fabric of life. But our inherited software – religious, patriotic, and commercial – denies this connection, and it keeps us from seeing that the wars we wage on the planet and each other is a form of killing ourselves. Like smoking, drinking, or any other addiction, it provides a short-lived rush, but somewhere below all the denial we sense the truth and feel angry, frightened, or cynical. Modern man is anxious. He's alone and alienated. He's not at peace. But he gets another prescription, installs a satellite dish, changes the channel, and goes shopping to fill the hole.

Land of the Free; Home of the Brave

"It is not because the mechanism is working wrongly that I am ill. I am ill because of wounds to the soul, to the deep emotional self, and the wounds to the soul take a long, long time... and patience, and a... long, difficult repentance, realization of life's mistake, and the freeing oneself from the endless repetition of the mistake which mankind at large has chosen to sanctify." (6)

Decades of avoidance, hypocrisy, and TV-watching have dumbed us down, removed us from Nature (the world's and our own), and left us passive and purposeless. We've become dogs in Pavlov's kennels, off to the next war, ever-ready to kill, cower, or consume when someone pushes the right button. Like any addict,

America is long overdue for a cold, hard look in the mirror, and what we see will not be pretty. But losing face is a small price to pay for finding one's heart again. And every day it becomes clearer that it's a necessary price if we're to avoid losing everything.

"Land of the free..." They say the truth will set you free, but breaking through denial and telling, feeling, and dealing with it is not an easy task. And – at least initially – it will not make us feel good. Good medicine often tastes bitter. Jung wrote: "One does not become enlightened by imagining figures of light, but by making the darkness conscious." [7] Making the darkness conscious takes time and *a long, difficult repentance...*"

"Home of the brave..." It takes courage to tell it like it is. Political soul-searching is just as difficult, (and in some ways more so) than personal – there are vast forces arrayed against it. But ultimately they must go together. Individually and collectively we have to be willing to take responsibility for ourselves and our acts – to grieve, make apologies and amends – to have any hope of healing those wounds to the soul and becoming the real and whole human beings we're capable of being... to give up the "good boy" or "good girl" and become adults.

Pain cannot be avoided. Attempting to sidestep it is futile and always results in even greater suffering. Facing our pain is the beginning of healing. Kahil Gibran wrote that "Your pain is the breaking of the shell that encloses your understanding."[8] Breaking the shell may be frightening, but it is the first stage in a growth process. It's an opening; a letting go of attachment; a young seed's time of vulnerability; an entry and extension toward the world that promises new life.

Every saint has had his dark nights of the soul, and these encounters with darkness are not aberrations or deviations from the path. They are experiences of deepening, vital stages in the work of integrating the shadow and truly seeing all that is. They are part of the maturation process, allowing the necessary suffering that develops compassion. They both test and temper the soul, for our souls must be strong enough to accept and endure the ebbs, flows, joys, and sorrows of life, and tender enough to treat the earth and each other as sacred and holy.

Death precedes resurrection; springtime follows winter; darkness leads to dawn. The way beyond is to go through. The essays that follow (pp. 273 - 300) are songs that invite, name, and summon forth the shadow. They acknowledge the predator-prey play of existence and honor the dark gods necessary to a passionate, sensual, and embodied life. They accept the promise and the pain that comes with loving fiercely: the hurt and hope of birth, and the gratitude and grief in dying. And they welcome all our tears – heartfelt and too-long held back – that shall support and sustain those new seeds just waiting to open.

The Return

Completion

"We can only begin to green the current wasteland by personally engaging in more levels of reality, by investigating the range and depth of the ecology of inner and outer space, and by bringing back rich traveler's tales of our discoveries." [1]

The third and final stage of a heroic journey is called the Return. The protagonist has heard the summons and set off into a realm of great and primal forces, the sphere of the Unknown. S/he vanquishes demons, unearths treasure, slays or subdues enemies, rescues lost souls, and overcomes obstacles in pursuit of magic, a treasure, gift, or relief from some difficulty. After all this, the completion of the adventure entails coming back from that magical realm and re-integrating with the life that was left behind.

But things have shifted. Our lead character does not merely return to the same house and look for a job as a waiter or secretary. S/he has acquired new perceptions, capabilities, and insights. The inner condition must manifest in the outer. The final task involves becoming an agent of change and making a difference; manifesting a transformation of self or surroundings that brings benefit, which alters the community one set out from.

The stories often show the central figure returning with a gift. This gift or "medicine" can be abstract or concrete, simple or complicated. It could be wisdom, the blessing of the gods, or a new tale that needs to be told. It's been portrayed as chests of gold, healing herbs, love potions, magical wands, or cloaks of invisibility. As metaphor, this gift can represent truth, a new vision or commitment, a relationship to the Other World. One could call it power, truth, authenticity, higher synthesis, or connection to soul... but the cycle is complete only when this fresh energy is brought to bear in healing and renewing the unhealthy or dysfunctional situation one began from.

Dangers in the Return

After a profound encounter with something extraordinary – a sacred dream, with "God," spirit, truth, purpose, or direction – the task of establishing this in daily life is daunting. In some tales, this return home can be the most dangerous part of the adventure. Odysseus requires ten years to make his way back to Ithaca, to his beloved Penelope and son, Telemachus. He and his crew are battered by storms, tempted by sirens, captured by Cyclops, bewitched and turned into swine by an enchantress. By the time he spies his homeland, all his men and ships have been lost – and even then, he is not safe. His court is overrun by scoundrels. Dukes and lords scheme to bed his wife, dispatch his son, and steal his kingdom. Forces are in play that would be threatened by his reappearance. Many do not want him back.

In Grimm's fairy tale "The Water of Life," it is the youngest son who finds the gift, the life-giving liquid that will heal his dying father. But his older brothers deceive and betray him, stealing the magical fluid in the hopes of winning favor with the king and, ultimately, gaining his throne and possessions. In doing so, they would take what is wondrous, precious, and sacred, and use it in service of values that are social and profane – wealth and power.

This conflict between the old order and the new, between the sacred and the profane, shows itself as danger in tales of the return. Whether personal – habits, routines, the attachments of the ego – or political, the old order does not give up easily. Individuals, ingrained tendencies, and institutions are protective of their power and position. They have a stake in things remaining as they are, and if the new energy cannot be co-opted, it can face outright assault. Wealth, privilege, and social position do not easily hand over the keys to the vault.

There is no guarantee that change – personal or political – will be welcome, no matter how brilliant the idea or needed the message. Forces of inertia or injustice will need to be confronted. Politically, justice, peace, equality, ecological balance, available health care, access to goods and services – all fine goals and noble aims – will be seen as a loss of power and profit to some. Change is nearly always inconvenient, and it will appear threatening to all who want to avoid their own call to adventure. Safety and "security" become catchwords representing an unwillingness to face and confront one's fears, while resulting in a life forever ruled by them. The castle may be full of scoundrels, and like Odysseus, you may have to find allies and fight to claim your throne.

Danger in all its various disguises – resistance, co-opting, betrayal – can play out in an individual's psyche, as well as in family systems, work environments, or on the great stage of history, as the values of the old order seek to dominate the thrust of the new energy. The utopian vision of Marx is crushed by the iron fist of Stalin; gurus and spiritual teachers cash in on their popularity and fame. The great new hope of JFK, Obama, health-care reform, etc. is soon mired in the morass of moneyed interests; the teachings of Christ are overwhelmed by the Church's obsession with opulence and authority.

The challenges portrayed in The Return alert us to the difficulties inherent in bringing a new vision or dream into being. As the hero arrives home and attempts to integrate into his or her community, a balance, an understanding and accord must be struck between the sacred and profane, the magical and the mundane. A successful return requires having a foot in both worlds. One must not forget one's journey, one's time in the realm of primal forces. The connection to living fully, to the depths of soul and the numinous world of spirit, to an order of values outside social rewards, needs to remain strong. If we become distracted and let our attention be captured by the common concerns of social reality, the gift will be co-opted. The new wine will be repackaged in the same old bottles. Encounters with the soul will become stories for the ego's enhancement; and the creative vision reduced to a slogan in the next advertising campaign.

There's a corresponding danger if our allegiance remains wholly with the sacred at the expense of the conventional and practical. Our ideas and intentions will go nowhere, our hazy hodgepodge of poorly-articulated visions and airy-fairy dreams lacking the incentive or grounds to galvanize or motivate anyone. The world is a play of light and shadow, terror and wonder. Cooperation and symbiotic relationships characterize every natural system, but so do predator and prey. Child-like innocence can be charming. Vulnerability, openness, and surrender may be required to discover and embrace a larger dream. But naiveté and an other-worldly aura are sorry strategies for engaging the world. Monsters, obstacles, and challenges of a different sort lie in the return to daily life as well.

If we do not address the important issues here, something crucial can easily be lost. A negotiation, a reconciliation and agreement – between doing and being, between new vision and current definitions of reality – is vital if the return is to be meaningful. Forgetting either our sacred responsibilities (our connection to something greater) or the demands of daily life makes us one-dimensional and devoid of depth. Abandoning our footing and ground in either world is like losing a leg. Vision will become crippled; all meaningful movement cease; and we will become incapable of walking our talk.

Finding Fertile Soil

The Return is the final stage of a death-rebirth cycle. The hero leaves the old story behind. He traverses territory outside the lines and limitations of his worldview and cultural consensus. The encounter and engagement with what's perennial or extraordinary lifts the veil, and it leaves the protagonist with fresh perceptions, values, powers, and allegiances. These new seeds must be brought home and planted in the soil of community, relationships, and daily life.

In the natural world, every seed is protected by some kind of shell. Inside the shell is the germ, the source of new growth and new life, but initially this germ is tender and vulnerable. If conditions are hostile – bitter cold, lack of sunshine or water, barren ground – the outer coat must perform its protective function, waiting until the seed is in a situation where those conditions can support the blossoming of the emerging life.

Growing a garden can be a delicate matter. The creative impulse or the inspiring vision (the kernels to be germinated) need fertile soil – allies and situations that welcome the new way of being. It requires sure and steady work – weeding, watering, fertilizing, and pruning – to insure conditions remain favorable to foster a fresh idea into reality. Whether we plant roses or apples, marigolds or marijuana; whether we intend to bear beauty, justice, peace, or spiritual nourishment to the world, husbanding these seeds through to harvest requires effort and consistency for there is no lack of forces – weeds, scab, scale, and beetles in the natural world; hostility, indifference, laziness, or attachment to comfort in the human – that can reduce our dreams to rubble.

Dealing with inertia, resistance, and the voices of the old order requires perseverance. The challenges are not finished when the central characters in the stories have arrived home. The work of the Return requires help, support, and allies – fertile soil; it is rarely done alone. Like those heroes and heroines of old, we must return to our people, our tribe and community, and face all those voices – in the world and in ourselves – that drain our energy, deplete our resources, and hinder us from bringing the new dream to fruition.

A particular example of the Return in modern life is the road to recovery as practiced by the members of Alcoholics Anonymous (AA) and other recovery communities. In this specific variation on a more far-reaching and recurrent theme, the journey consists of Twelve Steps. The call is heard and the journey begins when the central character first breaks through denial and admits that something is wrong in the kingdom. (Step 1: *"We admitted we were powerless... that our lives had become unmanageable."*) "He" then explores the realm of primal forces by facing the monsters and dragons. He does this by conducting a "searching and fearless moral inventory," an encounter with darkness in which painful feelings are confronted and responsibility taken for his dysfunctional behavior and perceptions. As in the perennial myths, the descent into this unfamiliar and uncomfortable emotional landscape is not without guidance. The steps form a map and include a series of practices and principles to live by. Allies are found through acquiring the help of a sponsor, surrendering to a Higher Power (Step 3), and discovering s/he is not alone through the fellowship found in the meetings and in the program itself.

Having had a spiritual awakening, our protagonist begins The Return, a journey back to the world (recovery) through admitting and making amends for his wrongs, serving this greater power in daily life, and – via sharing these teachings and principles – bringing the message (gift) to others. Twelve-step "recovery" contains many elements of a death and rebirth experience, and it has been literally life-saving to tens of thousands. In this particular path to a transformation of consciousness, one's shadow is faced; old patterns of isolation, self-absorption, and willfulness are let go of; and the hero begins a process of atonement (at-one-ment) through surrender to a set of principles in service of a larger force or story. Recovery (regaining what was lost) is a re-membering, a renewal of the spirit and soul in which the hero returns – free from shame and with a sense of belonging – to the human community. And there s/he rebuilds a life with new depth of character... with serenity, humility, compassion, and a gift to give.

*　　*　　*　　*　　*　　*　　*

The materialistic and superficial culture of the twenty-first century seems a far cry from an earlier age of adventure, but the psyche and physiology of the human has changed little in the last ten thousand years. Campbell called the heroic quest a "mono-myth" because it describes a process of transformation and growth that's archetypal and universal. With the whole globe surveyed by satellites and linked by the web, the opportunities for outer discoveries appear far fewer. The bold undertakings of our age will more likely be emotional, spiritual, intellectual, artistic, or visionary. The cross-pollination of technical sophistication, ancient wisdom, brain research, psychological awareness, and the implications of quantum and systems theory offer us a glimpse into the potential flourishing of a new dream – new medicines for the heart and soul emerging from a creative synthesis of sacred traditions, ecological awareness, and more life-sustaining possibilities of perception.

The chapters that follow speak to issues and concerns of the Return – to the actions, allegiances, and attitudes required to bring fresh energy and new vision to the world.

Christ was born in a manger to teach that God must come to earth. Spirit and Soul addresses this need to join heaven and earth, the sacred and the profane; to bring our inner and outer worlds into alignment. It explores the integration and symbiotic relationship of vision and task, recognizing that authenticity and integrity will only be found when we walk our talk, when our values and actions match. The ancient teaching, *"As above, so below"* is illustrated through the image of the World Tree, whose beautiful canopy reaches for the light through depending on an equally well-developed system of roots that descend into darkness.

Nature celebrates what is natural, untamed, and wild; what existed before – and still shimmers beneath and beyond – the cages and constraints of culture and convention. The selections point the way back to the Garden, invite us to worship Snake, celebrate sex, and invoke that immanent and sensuous spirituality that fed our souls before shame separated man from beast, god from man, and heaven from earth.

Einstein once remarked that great and intractable problems of life are never solved at the same level of consciousness at which they are conceived and created. Living in a Larger Story explores the importance and necessity of finding a more expansive framework for our lives.

All spiritual traditions recognize the ego – the separate self and its willful action – as a root cause of our problems, the continued feeding of which can only get in the way of possible solutions. These paths of knowledge emphasize shrinking self-importance, the removal of attention and energy from the ego and its self-reflecting dialogues so other "conversations" can be heard.

The way we feel about ourselves and the world is shaped by the stories we tell, and many current accounts make us feel aimless, isolated, and angry, creating enemies in an "us-against-them," dog-eat-dog existence. Other stories can touch our heart, open our eyes, and connect us with the myriad miracles – great and small – that make life and each moment possible.

Our myths will, and do, govern our values; establish what's important or not; and determine the universe and reality we live in. Living in a Larger Story affirms the potential for a journey... a path... a life that brims with wonder and joy through identifying with forces and energies far-larger than our separate selves. It celebrates the grand adventure, along with the sense of gratefulness that comes from focusing on what's truly great.

> *What we call the beginning is often the end*
> *And to make an end is to make a beginning...*
>
> *And the end of all our exploring*
> *Will be to arrive where we started*
> *And know the place for the first time.*
>
> ~ T.S. Eliot [2]

Spirit and Soul:
As Above, So Below

Spiritual Reality: Forms and the Formless

Spirit is not some "thing" that can be seen, tasted, smelled, heard, or touched in any common sensory way. Neither will it be captured and categorized by logic, reason, or any set of rules thrown up by the new brain. Our inherited predilection toward nouns, separate objects, and literalism hamstrings our thinking when we attempt to speak about spiritual "reality."

We can consider spirit as analogous to energy. Though recognized as the fundamental "stuff" of the universe, Einstein's equation, $E=mc^2$, implies that energy possesses relativity or fluidity, the shamanic quality of shape-shifting. Since energy has no fundamental form, we cannot apprehend "it" directly, but only as it manifests in gravity, movement, matter, heat, light, etc. Though appearing in many disguises – including matter – none of them fully reveals or embodies energy itself – there's no unchanging, perceivable essence hiding or waiting behind the various configurations it takes. Matter can be transformed into heat; heat can be turned into light and vice versa. Magnetism and movement can produce electricity. Mutable and mercurial, energy reveals itself within a vibrant field of potentialities, a pulsing network of possible relationships and expressions.

Like energy, Spirit is ultimately formless. We can sense it as movement, peace, vibrancy, love, presence, connection, or relationship, but this "not-thing" has to arise and manifest into form for us to experience it. We're touched by the beauty of nature. Drifting clouds stimulate our imaginations; a view of the mountains produces a sense of timelessness. The tenderness between lovers, the feelings toward a child, mystical visions, and inspiring stories of saints and gods impact, arrest, or inspire us. These expressions of spirit hint at – they evoke or reveal, but they do not define – that which is fundamentally indefinable.

In perceiving spiritual reality, the organs of perception are not limited to the usual five senses. But whether we experience chills up our spine, apparitions appearing out of thin air, tingling in our fingers, a sense of peace and serenity, an inner knowing, or the arresting power of a dream, the formless must first come into form. It must show up and somehow make its appearance in this world. It must become in-form-ation.

When communicating about spiritual life, we are referring to a realm outside our ordinary and daily individuality. In this relative and shape-shifting reality, one's self is not limited to its usual description as a solid, separate, clearly-defined entity. We too are fluid, more verb than noun. Capable of adapting and taking multiple forms, perspectives, and attitudes, our spiritual identity is coherent, but changing, like a stream, cloud, or river.

The more we lose contact with this spiritual reality, the greater likelihood we will believe in our separateness and be stuck in "the clothes we wear," the concrete casts of our habitual social descriptions – "I am a human; a man, Christian, or Muslim. I'm a Republican, patriot, pacifist, or seeker. I'm a nice guy, feminist, law-abiding citizen; a healthy person." Our egos and social personalities cling to these selves, yet we also (and always) have the capability to transcend them. When – in our deepest places – we know and experience the limitless and adaptable freedom of the spiritual realm, we can incorporate and express ways of being and relating that are outside all the old definitions we've held to so fiercely. The greater the disconnection from that boundless, infinite world, the more likely we'll cling to and aggressively defend that small, but comfortable prison we call home.

The World Tree

The World Tree is an ancient and widespread mythological image. Lofty, weathered, and broad-branching, this presence standing at the center of the world represents the axis of all that is. Its limbs spread out through space, reaching toward heaven, while its roots snake down through the soil to grasp the dark earth and seek those deep springs that contain the waters of life. The World Tree extends into the Upper and Lower realms, combining and manifesting them in the Middle World where we humans mostly live our lives.

"Spirit" and "soul" can be conceived of as movements, complementary directions life energy takes within this Tree. The spiritual urge is analogous to the rising of sap, whose impetus travels up and out toward the infinite sky. It seeks higher states, elevated consciousness; it longs to open and flower. It wants to transcend; break free of the bounds of space, time, and the forms we find ourselves in; to experience oneness, the source of all that manifests. Spirit spreads out, diffuses, radiates, finds rapture in the heights. Spirit moves beyond, breaks free of form and dissolves into light... enlightenment, illumination.

Soul stirs in the opposite direction. Soul brings the energy of the heavens down to earth. As the tree gathers sunshine, it harvests this sky-sourced radiance, fixing and concentrating it into saps and sugar compounds that are stored in the roots over winter. It turns light into carbon-based form. We develop our souls – become more soulful – when we carry the grand and universal vision (sky) into the nitty-gritty – the limitations, struggles, and darkness – of the lives we lead.

Soul is earthy; it seeks depth. It grounds, establishes a foundation, creates an underpinning. It generates reliability, steadfastness, and character. Soul embodies, concentrates, transforms radiance into reality. It creates structure, mechanism, conduits and channels through which the transcendent, compassionate, and non-dual perspective can manifest in the theatre of everyday life with all its difficulties, limitations, and conflicts.

Rare among animals, humans – like trees – stand erect, our spines aligned along the vertical dimension. The human vertebrae and the tree's wooden trunk symbolically represent the staff, whose vertical thrust joins earth and sky, matter and spirit, temporal and eternal life. By opening a conduit upwards and down, the trunk/staff/spine creates an axis, a pivot and center point around which the horizontal dimension, the temporal circle of our lives, revolves.

Heaven and earth, above and below… In the World Tree the poles are joined, balanced, although in different seasons of the year the movement in one direction or the other becomes more dominant. The sap rises in springtime, and the growth of summer moves upward and out, beyond what was there before. Budding, leafing, unfurling, and flowering; the barren earth of late winter explodes in a riot of new forms and color.

Come autumn, the trajectory reverses; the elevator descends. The direction is downward. The photosynthesis that peaked amidst warm weather's expansive greenery has created food that must be stored for winter in the root system beneath. The energy of life becomes concentrated and migrates underground. The blossoms of spring culminate in fall's fruiting; seeds drop to earth to await springtime's resurrection. Branches grow bare as leaves flutter to the ground. Outward existence contracts. The sap seeks out darkness and depth. The action moves inside, under the surface.

In a healthy ecosystem, these opposing impulses sustain and feed each other. All the expansion above the ground must be supported by what's below. If the purchase of a tree's roots is limited, it cannot grow tall without toppling. Similarly, the leaves will fashion little food into flesh, and root expansion will not take place when the canopy is constricted. The tree must develop in both dimensions, and to blossom and thrive, humans must do the same. Our branches and roots must be connected. Above and below, outward and in, spirit and flesh… earthly and spiritual life must be in balance. "God" and earth need not, must not, be opposed. The sacred and daily dreams were not meant to be separate.

Breakdowns on the Spiritual Highway

But the myth of separation – heaven and earth, mind and body, matter and spirit – is the foundation upon which modern life has been built, and this has resulted in an oppositional, polarized, either-or world. In one account – the common paradigm played out in most of contemporary society – we ignore the sacred and live a success-centered lifestyle, the focus on status, power, or possessions. Our awareness stays focused within shrunken horizons, and we forage in fenced-in feed lots mired in the mundane and material. Without tools to form a living relationship to the transcendent (or to the depths of the soul), we wade in shallow waters; our psychic universe an undersized container that quickly empties and needs refilling as each new acquisition or experience inevitably becomes old. Lacking any grander vision… thirsting for and always seeking "more"… life becomes a meaningless collection of acquisitions, roles, and routines with little purpose or direction to guide us.

Conversely, others may seek the divine by rejecting matter, flesh, and all those "messy" relationships. Seeking transcendence by turning one's gaze exclusively to the sacred and away from the commitments and struggles of everyday physical life can be a form of hiding. Searching for a sort of "spiritual bypass," the pursuit of higher consciousness and shamanic or non-ordinary experiences becomes an escape and avoidance of life's hard issues – our emotions; the shadow's expressions; our struggles with power, shame, sex, self-esteem, or freedom… the shit we need to face.

114

Altered states and expanded awareness do not provide reprieves or free passes that allow one to skip over pain and difficulties. A caterpillar turning into a butterfly may be a popular image of transformation, but we conveniently forget that the caterpillar spins a cocoon and disintegrates, and the butterfly's emergence involves a life-or-death struggle. "I" am not going to become a butterfly. The self I know will not just evolve to become lighter, freer, and more beautiful. The ego, the self, the "I," must die, be broken, or dissolve in order for real transformation to take place.

The teachings of Jesus and Buddha have been an inspiration to many, but it's not the tales of enlightenment or connection to the divine that arouse our reverence. Both are associated with miracles, states of rapture, and spiritual union, but their truly magnificent act – of choosing to embrace human suffering – is what gives rise to devotion. They did not use their illumination or "god-realization" as grounds to leave behind the hardships of human life in favor of a vacation in Blissville. In Latin, compassion means "to suffer with," and in saying "Yes" to the pain, limitation, and struggles of the world, Christ and Buddha showed their hearts and souls were equal to the breadth of their awareness.

> *"And so long as you have not experienced this -*
> *to die and so to grow -*
> *you are only a troubled guest on the dark earth."* [1]

The resurrection of Christ and emergence of a butterfly both involve death. The caterpillar – that grubby, consuming self – perishes to be reborn in another form. Christ, identified as biological man, surrenders his life to return as godly or spiritual man. The message here is quite clear: the times of contraction; the losses, deaths, and struggles are important, and they cannot be skipped over. For spiritual growth to occur, the self-protective shell of the circumscribed personality must be shattered or undone in order to serve the larger, transcendent purpose.

This shrinking or shattering is painful. Incorporating one's "Christ energy" is rarely simple or easy. The leisurely escalator ride to a luxury hotel of happiness must be foregone for a date with hammer and nails. Resurrection happens after death, redemption after the fall. The dawning spiritual realizations of saints and sages come after the dark nights of the soul. Without these difficult encounters, "higher consciousness" rings false – its airy and insubstantial fixation on the light impractical or hypocritical; its proponents unable or unwilling to walk their talk.

As two-legged creatures, walking the "good red road" on the path of heart involves having a foot solidly planted in each world – the sacred and the mundane, the daily and the dream. Spirit and Soul must evolve together to be healthy and whole. Left... right... left... right... To move forward and live in balance, each step must support, receive from, and give to the other. If we favor or do not develop one side – either one – we'll surely become stunted or topple.

Joining Hands: This World and the Other

Tension and paradox can play out between spirit and soul, between the affairs of this world and the other. On the one hand, the forms of the world – rules, roles, and routines; social groupings, language, and habits of thought – obscure the fluid nature of reality and can distract us from experiencing the fundamental unity underlying all. In this sense, the concrete world conceals the divine, and it represents a limitation or illusion to be transcended.

But the sacred is also revealed *through* creation. Sound emerges from silence, forms from fluidity, creation from the void, being from nothingness. Life cycles between these polarities like breath moving in and out, or waves rolling onto shore. As Blake said, "Eternity is in love with the productions of time."[2] These seemingly-opposites will define, disguise, or disclose each other as we expand and contract, assimilate and eliminate, venture forth and come home.

We are part of this world as well as the Other. Day to day, we grapple with physical existence, social structures, the material world and all its manifestations. We live in families and communities, sire children, and share the earth with other forms of life. Attaining spiritual realization is not the only thing of value in our time here – what we do and how we act is equally important! A baby may look like Buddha – open, vulnerable, alive with fascination, curious without constriction – but babies are completely helpless, unable to communicate or control their limbs or bowels. In India, some "god-realized" saints and sadhus sit immobile, uninterested or barely able to feed themselves, their outer manifestation hardly distinguishable from a homeless man in a diaper.

This imbalance – completely immersed in the sacred world and unavailable to the daily – is polar opposite (and would appeal to few) to what's common in the West. We are here, in Earth School. Escaping to or living in the other world, at the expense of this one, skips half the curriculum. We must be engaged in both to be whole. Sun Bear, a Native American teacher, said, *"If your vision doesn't grow corn, I don't want to hear about it."*[3] Becoming fully human involves leading functional and soulful lives that make a difference in our communities. As the lives of Buddha and Christ demonstrate, illumination isn't an end point. After we're "born again," we have to grow up and act like adults.

Enacting one's vision and creating a dream worth living requires moving between the known and unknown. Spirit represents the light side of the unknown. Transcendent and beyond... it dances behind and weaves through all forms of the world, yet it must also inform our lives. We know there's more to existence than the roles and routines of consensual reality. Something calls, and we're enticed to journey out beyond what we're familiar with. This journey may be frightening, but the far-greater tragedy is to refuse the summons, for – as Jung once noted – most neurosis comes from living a life that's too small for the soul.

Illumination, spiritual insights, and mystical visions are beyond our control. We can seek them – through ritual and practices of many kinds – but we cannot make them happen. Vision comes like the blossoming of a rose. While this flowering is the reason we plants roses, our powers are limited: We can't pull the petals out of the stem. Instead, we cultivate – we water, weed, and fertilize – that the bloom might come sooner, last longer, be fuller.

The tilling of the soil and feeding of the roots represents the work of the soul. It is something we <u>*can*</u> do. Addressing our shame, resentments, and hurts... confronting our shadow, loves, and longings prunes and thins the tangled vines that choke out the light. Dealing with the thorns and wounds; facing our past; weeding out our addictions and avarice – though hard work – are within our power and attainable. Soul work makes itself manifest in the known and daily world, but this expansion of depth and character brings power and presence – something magical and extraordinary – to the loves, limitations, and losses of ordinary life. The encounter with darkness develops authenticity and integrity, and it creates a foundation that can support and sustain the possibility of truly living out those greater and grander visions.

Meanwhile, spiritual explorations opens the door to the left side, increasing our capacity to engage creatively with the fluid and shape-shifting unknown, to improve our relationship with what is beyond the ego or conscious self. This expansion of awareness can usher in greater insight, power, and possibility, but vision does not necessarily make us happy. Experiences of great clarity or connection are often bittersweet. Episodes of profound oneness or peace can be followed by anger or sorrow as we realize the foolishness, suffering, and self-inflicted waste in the way we normally live. Seeing the grand picture or being swept away in the flood tides of love can make us feel like an outsider, unable to step back inside the box and take on the roles, relationships, and ways of thinking we were once comfortable in.

Spiritual realizations must be incorporated, brought from the imagination down into this world. Incorporation means embodiment. They must become real; they must grow corn. Black Elk, an Oglala Sioux holy man, said, *"A vision without a task is but a dream. And a task without a vision is drudgery. But a vision with a task can change the world.* "[4] It can be tempting to reject one side or the other – the daily or the dream… to swing the pendulum to the opposite of what we've been pressured or programmed to do – but the new story insists we bring them together. Rich encounters with the Other World will often – and should – thrust us into more profound confrontations and engagements with this one, demanding we become deeper, wiser, and far more human as we approach the divine.

Doing this requires expanding our sense of self, building a container in our hearts big enough for the paradoxes and polarities, and strong enough to welcome and accept it all: the deaths and rebirths, insights and disillusionments, the springtimes and falls. Heaven must be brought to earth and into the world; it must be found here, now, and enacted within life. And all the descents, our experiences of depth and encounters with soul, must be honored and resacralized.

The Letters herein (pp. 301 - 327) celebrate a life that embraces earth and sky, soul and spirit, inner and outer. The cultural myths that separate heaven from earth, spirit from flesh, make it hard to find balance or locate the center. Establishing this new center involves both finding and creating fertile soil – new myths, visions, attitudes, commitments, and communities – then breaking open our shells and planting our seeds, trusting in sky and earth, sunshine and rain. It will require determination, desire, and discernment. It will take courage and a commitment fed by the faith that somewhere between the sacred cows and all the bullshit, there'll be enough fertilizer for something good to grow.

Nature:
Coming Home

Human... Nature

"Oh what a catastrophe, what a maiming of love when it was made personal, merely personal feeling, taken away from the rising and setting of the sun, and cut off from the magic connection of the solstice and equinox. This is what is the matter with us: we are bleeding at the roots, because we are cut off from the earth and sun and stars, and love has become a grinning mockery because, poor blossom, we plucked it from its stem on the Tree of Life and expected it to keep on blooming in our civilized vase on the table."

~ D. H. Lawrence [1]

Human nature and human awareness, or psyche, arise within the field of Nature. Nature in its widest sense includes the energies of the cosmos – fireballs, supernovas; cold, black emptiness; distances, stars, galaxies beyond comprehension – as well as the elements and forces of the familiar planet we inhabit. Nature is grand; nature is magnificent. It encompasses earth, air, fire, and water... amoeba, bacteria, soil micro-organisms... oceans, volcanoes, viruses... plants, animals, humans. All the faces, forces, and forms – organic or inorganic – we can name are part of and happen <u>within</u> Nature. Nature is the context, the primordial condition, the ground of being within which all life emerges and passes away.

Creating and maintaining the bridge between daily life and the cosmos; between human nature and Nature has always been a primary task of culture. Doing this has required a rich toolkit of creation myths, rites of passage, stories of adventure, along with community rituals, and instruction from wise elders. Today these tools (along with elders and a sense of community) have been lost, and the core wound of our time – beneath all the other wounds we medicate or react to – is the breaking of this link between humans and nature, a severing of connection that leaves us without a sense of belonging, and without any relationship to something far greater than ourselves.

As a result, we suffer from spiritual dislocation, from soul loss. In fundamental ways, we do not know where we are, how we feel, or what we are related to. Unfit for heaven and afraid of hell, our myths claim god is not here, in Nature, and that Nature is… in one way or another… a threat, source of sin, or something to be ignored, used, or domesticated. These stories separate matter and spirit, pit heaven against earth and human against Nature. In so doing, they deny us contact with the great forces and cycles of life, and the deep, abiding structures of our souls.

Seeking an Unbroken Life

Inner and outer conditions reflect each other. Modern existence is fragmented and disconnected; the tapestry of life is frayed. Time and space have been chopped into pieces, the daily world broken into bits. The surface of the earth has been drawn and

122

quartered, sectioned and carved into nations, states, cities, streets, and blocks. The once-seamless landscape is cut by roads, divided by property lines, split into lots, and fenced-in with chain link and barbed wire. Forests are surveyed, sold off as grazing tracts, paved in asphalt, and divided over and over again as logos levels the land; the flat black expanses painted with parallel lines to make "parking space." And some actually come to blows over these temporary little pieces of "turf."

Utility lines crisscross the formerly-beautiful and spacious skies, its expanses blocked by skyscrapers and clouded by jet trails. Stars disappear behind street lights and smog. City "blocks" are broken into buildings, then further fractioned into offices or apartments; the spaces separated by walls and cut up into rooms, closets, and cubicles. In the labyrinths of steel and concrete making up most urban areas, the earth is barely visible… and this we call home.

Time has also been hacked to pieces and glued back together in artificial groupings. The natural cycle of a year is still acknowledged, but the revolutions of stars and phases of the moon – barely visible in the polluted skies – are mostly forgotten. Days are clustered into groups of seven, and appointment books divide those into fifteen minute segments, each one needing to be filled. People pay attention to calendars, watches, work-weeks, and vacations; obey clocks that have no relation to nature or the body. As we labor the day or night shift, take lunch or coffee breaks, the body's biological rhythms become more and more attuned to mechanics and economics. The bell rings in the classroom; History is over; English begins. The whistle blows; workers rush home from the "plant." Evenings are given over to fast-food servings of "prime time" television, its empty calories packaged into quick-paced scenes cut by changing camera angles and interrupted by thirty-second advertisements. It's a free country. Pavlov goes to bed smiling. We awaken with alarm.

Nature is organic, interdependent, and seamless, but our urban and suburban environments are artificial and almost entirely human-created. There is little that is natural within them, and people stay inside their flat-surfaced cubicles with bottled water and conditioned air. Americans spend over 95% of their time indoors, and most everything they see, hear, smell, and feel – TV, radios, computers, furniture, deodorant… their entire sensory reality – has been created by an industrial process.[2] The average teenager recognizes over two thousand corporate logos, but less than ten native plants. The "world" that most people live in is a virtual one. It's abstract, ideological, and in important and fundamental ways, unreal. We don't have technology. It has us, and we live inside it.

The word "human" comes from humus – to be of the earth. In this sense, actual human beings are disappearing like many other endangered species. Large, abstract entities – institutions and corporations – own and control the resources we use, seeds we plant, and food we eat. The technological drive also results in a general speeding up of life, as subliminal images cascade through commercials, information downloads in gigabytes, and we converse on cell phones while rushing through traffic.

In addition, civilized life and compulsory education train us to disassociate our senses, and this affects how we perceive and what we see. Years of schooling teach children to sit still, be quiet, and focus on the blackboard, computer screen, or page – to ignore all senses except the visual. Academic institutions limit physical, fleshy life to gym class or recess – good preparation for a sedentary life at the office or in front of the television. Other than sex, sports, or violence, where does modern man find a full-bodied experience? To have all your instincts and abilities alert and working together – common (and necessary) in nature – has become, for the civilized human, a rare, almost altered-state experience.

We have reversed figure and ground for, in truth, the sensory splitting characteristic of contemporary consciousness and "normal reality" is an altered state – a dissociated, numbed-out, and painful altered state. Socialization has resulted in a general narrowing of focus and an alienation from other modes of awareness accepted as common throughout the indigenous world. As Don Juan tells Carlos Castaneda, *"Our true mind, the product of all our life experiences... rarely speaks because it has been defeated and relegated to obscurity. The other, the mind we use daily for everything we do, is __a foreign installation__."* [3]

Gaia... Mother... Matter

All this (and more) makes it difficult to relate to natural cycles that are grand and cyclical, or appreciate a *presence* that may express itself in evolution, seasonal changes, or the slow turnings of eternity. The awareness and perception of this presence – woven all throughout the natural world – constitutes the primal human spiritual experience. It is the foundation, the core experience upon which the structures of most religious beliefs are built, and it should be palpable to us. And it might yet be, if we could only stop numbing ourselves into shock and letting our natural senses atrophy.

As technology and the vast, impersonal pressures of modern life remove us from our roots and interaction with this natural habitat, it becomes ever-more difficult to truly know who we are. As humans, we're born from and grow out of this living earth, but how will we "meet our maker" if we forever stay inside the environments that we have made? [4] To discover our human depths and claim our authenticity, we must step outside both the physical forms – apartments, cars, computers, and classrooms – and the abstract and disconnected ways of thinking that keep us separate and an observer instead of a participant. We must encounter, engage, and embrace that world – Nature – which has created us.

Nature is whole and unified, and within her embrace experience is not divided. In those places where she's still allowed to exist, we can rediscover an awareness where all faculties function in unison, where our perceptions and the strands of our lives can be woven back together. You watch the sunset while feeling the rock against your back, a breeze cooling your scalp. The rivers, wind, rattling leaves, crickets, birds... all blend their songs as you catch the fragrance of pine. The environment is seamless. Time and space join. Sensations merge in synesthesia.

The natural world is multidimensional and multisensory. Away from mechanical, impersonal life and the perceptual splitting required for reading, driving, or computer screens, every moment is visible, audible, tactile... pregnant. There we can once again experience at-one-ment as the head finds the body and the new brain touches base with the old.

Accepting the Reptile Brain

"The subconscious mind is a database of all our habitual learned perceptions (that) require no conscious processing.
We've overestimated the power of that conscious mind...The subconscious mind actually represents the operation of almost the entire brain... (and) is a million times more powerful than our conscious mind. Therefore... the programs in the subconscious mind will overpower, ultimately, the programs of the conscious mind. Consciousness is generally oblivious of what those programs are...it doesn't see them. Our conscious mind may have great intentions, (but) our subconscious mind is usually running the show." [5]

According to neuro-physiologists we have three brains. The oldest, called the reptile brain, sits atop the spinal column. It controls our instinctual selves and many important processes we never pay attention to (metabolism, temperature regulation, PH balance, digestion, etc.) Our second brain, labeled the limbic system or mammalian brain, surrounds the reptile brain. Associated with deep emotional states, it seeks communion or resonance – and senses disharmony – with the world. It is capable of rapid learning and functions mostly below the level of consciousness. The third, a later evolutionary development, wraps itself around the other two. Called the "new brain" or neo-cortex, we use this brain as we talk, think, and act. It is the rational brain, the locus of the ego, and we commonly identify its self-conscious activity as "me."

But we are far more than our conscious mind. The subconscious is "a million times more powerful" than our conscious selves. We have bodies, mouths, emotional reactions, dreams, penises, vaginas. We seek power in order to feel safe. We want to eat, have sex, be comfortable, and get our way. Even our seemingly "rational" minds spend large amounts of time in internal dialogues fueled by desire, fears, hurts, resentments, or anger.

What's irrational, instinctual, and animal defines much of who we are. We are part reptile. As a fetus developing in the womb, each of us grew fins, gills, and a tail, which were later reabsorbed. Our intestines and viscera undulate in peristaltic waves, mimicking the motions of a snake. A sea of hormones sloshes through the blood, capable of overwhelming the separate self, all distance and detachment swept away by the tide. The power of the subconscious is vast, evolving over millions of years to help us adapt, survive, and thrive in intimate contact with the dangerous, powerful, sensuous earth. Becoming honest with ourselves requires accepting and embracing our archaic and primitive roots – our nature – and admitting that we, with many an unconscious agenda and allegiance, may be dangerous too.

Gods of the Earth

The historical conflict of matriarchal and patriarchal cultures often involved a conflict of gods: earth vs. sky, solar vs. lunar. The sky gods – usually associated with patriarchy – transcend and look down on the earth. They represent things universal, eternal and unchanging, unaffected by time or place. If your god lives in the sky, you can travel for thousands of miles and he is still above you. His face remains the same; his expression is constant like the sun.

The gods in heaven are unreachable. They rarely speak, except through fire and thunder, and it's rare they get involved. The relationship mostly consists of worship and sacrifice, not touch, and qualities of faith and perseverance become important because of the virtual absence of actual contact with these gods.

The earth gods are more visceral. They express themselves as living forces and make themselves known through the senses. They capture our attention through beauty; they speak in omens, signs, and acts of power. They display themselves – here, and in the present – imbuing the living earth with magic and mystery. Pounding surf, glorious sunsets, the songs of whales, and the majesty of mountains... the migration of salmon or swallows... a woman's menses... the pollination of flowers – all speak of wondrous powers and intelligence. Establishing a relationship and communion with these powers and entities comprises a core spiritual impulse of many primal cultures.

The gods of the earth are here, now, immanent in body and landscape. They're present in the stones, wind, springs, groves, and caves. Their faces are many – fairies, gnomes, sprites – and they evolve, change, and participate in life's movements and dramas. They express the eternal through stories and cycles of growth, decay, death, and rebirth; like the phases of the moon, the turning of seasons, and the rivers which give themselves to the oceans and are replenished by the rain.

Earth and sky gods represent two complementary sides of a polarity. They are sacred twins, embodying the duality of life and expressing different paths within the paradox of spirit. On the one hand, spirit is transcendent and insubstantial, like air. We cannot grasp or lay eyes on it, but it surrounds and brings life to everything we perceive. We deduce its presence by its effect on what we do see... the swaying of branches, the ruffled surface of water... the movement of clouds, the swirl of flames, variations in sound. This face of spirit is distant, abstract, and formless – like the mind – both invisible and everywhere – not contained or limited by anything. Sky (and most male) religions evoke and celebrate this untouchable and invisible presence.

But humans have fleshy bodies. We have longings, desires, needs, and specific organs of perception. We cannot perceive apart from the forms – one does not touch, taste, or hear nothingness. Life is not lived in the void. But The Presence revealed and made manifest... the process and play of energy expressed within and through the forms of life – here and now, changing and impermanent, arising and fading away to be reabsorbed and arise again – can be perceived and participated in, for these powers play through us too.

The bubbling spring that quenches our thirst also brings life to the hillside. Seasons turn; the warm winds wane; shivers soon skim across the skin. The wet earth turns green, and then dries to golden. We approach the darkness hand-in-hand with Persephone as grain is cut, threshed, and ground into flour. The energy of Ceres becomes cereal, fueling and feeding human bodies who must themselves grow, give birth, and sustain more life. Aphrodite... Dionysius... Gaia... Pan... Bacchus... Krishna... Kali... These grand powers – creative, destructive, divine, and demonic – play through the ever-evolving panorama of life. And in all these mysteries, movements, and melodies the earth gods celebrate.

The Sacred Marriage

A full and healthy spirituality embraces both heaven and earth. The Western tradition has been well-versed in stories of ascent, mystical union, and rapture. But life encompasses birth and death, and the descents, falls, and confrontations with our flesh, wounds, and mortality can lead us to the soul. In these encounters we can discover our purpose, our commitment to this adventure, and how to bring our unique voice and gifts to it. Rather than transcendence, the earthy (and feminine) spiritual path seeks embodiment and expression, the bringing forth of our uniqueness, power, and radiance to give back; to feed, befriend, and fertilize the flowering of the world.

For millennia, the feminine gods of nature have been demonized or cast into exile, and our lives are disconnected and severely out of balance because of it. Some primal peoples, upon hearing our stories of original sin and banishment from Eden, feel sorry for us. They shake their heads sadly and wish us well, for they are still living in the Garden – or would be if we'd let them.

But the rituals and practices of older earth-goddess cultures could never be completely ignored. Christmas, celebrating the birth of Christ, was placed around the winter solstice, a far-more ancient observance that honors the cycle of returning light. Similarly, Easter follows the spring equinox, where rituals of fertility have forever marked the resurrection of life after the death of winter.

Gazing skyward, we miss what lies right at our feet. To place paradise and spirit somewhere else and later has left little to celebrate in the life we live here and now. Envisioned over centuries as a test, an ordeal, some form of limbo, or hell itself, humans have responded with their remarkable ability to transform this life into the very hells they've been taught to perceive.

But, as Christ is quoted in the Gospel of Thomas: "*My kingdom is expressed all throughout the earth, and you cannot see it.*"[6] Heaven is not a noun. It's not some other place or piece of real (or unreal) estate. Heaven describes an experience – an experience of union that arises out of creative and harmonious engagement; a feeling of living fully; a sense of belonging, oneness, and friendship. Its depth and power grows out of a rich field of relatedness that results from cultivating and creating a meaningful life and making a difference in the realms in which we live and act. Heaven becomes present and manifest when – like those honey-seeking Mayan gods – spirit comes down to earth and earthly life is re-sacralized.

Bringing spirit to earth and into our lives is neither arduous nor unattainable. It's our birthright, our most natural way of relating and being, for we have been created by and grown out of the living biosphere. In our deepest core – if we can get past all the conditioning – our nature and Nature are one. We belong here. We are already home, and we need not live out the nightmare of being in exile. Redemption is ever-present, possible, and close at hand, because ultimately, "heaven" signifies the return and rediscovery of what we have always known... Nature... our natural mind, as Don Juan says.

The return home requires remembering an older and deeper mode of being, and this will take effort, intent, and attention. The gods of Nature have to be invited back. They must be valued, welcomed, and worshipped anew. To re-member is to heal what has been dismembered, and this remembrance and reawakening includes making amends with our bodies and with the body of Earth. It involves embracing our animal nature, our feminine energy, our instinctual self. When this journey is taken and completed, we will enter a sacred marriage, the union of heaven and earth. And we'll find ourselves back in the Garden again.

Pledge of Allegiance

For too long, civilized man has attacked the natural world, exploiting its resources while denying its sacredness or sentience. We've separated ourselves from the rest of life, but the result of our dominance has been spiritual poverty: a sense of exile; a loss of belonging; unease in our bodies and an inability to integrate our human affairs into a larger and more meaningful context. Energy flows where attention goes, and the return to the Garden is possible. Reclaiming our true heritage and living joyfully on this planet requires honoring the sacred dimension of daily existence. Giving our attention and allegiance to the natural world – and our own nature existing within it – begins the process of recognizing the sacred abundance around us, and it shifts our focus from the lonely, isolated, exiled "me" to an identity woven throughout a far vaster entity.

Nature has shaped, fashioned, and given birth to human form and experience. Nature is, literally, our Maker. Nature is Father and Mother... still present, having never abandoned us. Nature is God and Goddess... the grand forces and the larger, perennial story within which our story unfolds.

"From thee I receive, to thee I give.
Together we share, and from this we live."

Nature is the matrix and the mother of all we are. As such, we are all related... relatives... part of the family, and in this family, life gives to life. The grass grows. The deer eats the grass. The

133

hunter kills and eats the deer. The hunter dies, is buried in the ground, and the grass grows by feeding off the hunter. And the deer eats the grass... This story – on the one hand, of death, loss, and limitation – also expresses "sweet medicine" and the sacrament of communion. Here, within our earthy, fleshy existence, the great cycle of oneness is played out as each death leads to a birth; each individual loss is a sacrifice and an offering, an act of relationship within the universal giving that makes up the many strands in the web of life.

"Our Father who art in heaven..."

Our father in heaven is the sun. This father can be felt and sensed. He provides warmth and comfort. He makes sight – shape, color, perspective and the whole, visible world – possible. Shining his radiance upon us daily, immolating and consuming himself to shower us with luminous energy, the Sun embodies the archetype of unconditional generosity. The plants gather this glittering gift, combine it with minerals from the sustaining soil, and in so doing provide food and sustenance to the whole animate kingdom. And from this we live.

We are children of the sun and the living earth. I know this as fact. Over and over I have sought out the land – the rivers, oceans, forests, and mountains – apprenticing myself to Nature, my mother and mentor. I've been instructed by her seasons, her stories, her powers and polarities; heard the call of the wild, stood out in storms, listened to loons and been guided by the wind. I have fasted, prayed, quested for vision, meditated, and participated in rituals to help me remember. She has challenged, humbled, and touched me; taught me more than any course or university.

She is fiery, dark, surging, and brilliant; her powers enduring, ephemeral, wanton, destructive or playful. In darkness and light I have been made in her image. Each time I have offered my heart and reached out to the earth, it has reached back toward me – helping, healing, touching, and teaching – opening doorways into enchanting and extraordinary experience.

Who is your God? And who will you serve?

I honor the animals, the plants, the mountains, and the rivers. I honor the woods, the rain, the rocks, and the slow turning of stars. Each year, the cold contractions of winter are followed by germination and growth throughout spring and summer. It's in this temple I bear witness to the presence of a dying and resurrected god. The Source of Life, her sacred mysteries are expressed all throughout this sensuous and animate landscape. Above, below, before, behind, beside, within… this is the Promised Land. We walk on holy ground. And to know God… to know ourselves, our place, our purpose… to her we must pledge allegiance, and to her we must be true.

The Nature letters (pp. 329 - 354) express gratitude and praise for the grand cycles, those forces older, deeper, and greater than ourselves. We live within a biosphere. We are inside the body of Gaia. We are a node of perception within a net, a cell within a much larger being. Life has produced millions of species – of which we are but one – and each has its unique medicine – states of awareness and powers of perception we can barely fathom. There are more miracles happening daily – around and within us – than in all the texts of sacred literature. Nature is calling; she is close by, powerful, present. This earth is alive, aware, magnificent, and holy... and far more mysterious than we could conceive or ever imagine it to be.

The wonder of it all... How wonderful!

When I was the stream, when I was the
forest, when I was still the field,
when I was every hoof, foot,
fin and wing, when I
was the sky
itself,

No one ever asked me did I have a purpose; no one ever
wondered was there anything I might need,
for there was nothing
I could not
love.

It was when I left all we once were that
the agony began, the fear and questions came;
and I wept; I wept. And tears
I had never known
before.

So I returned to the river, I returned to
the mountains. I asked for their hand in marriage again,
I begged – I begged to wed every object
and creature.
And when they accepted,
God was ever present in my arms.
And he did not say,
"Where have you
been?"

For then I knew my soul – every soul –
had always held
Him.

~ Meister Eckhart [7]

Living in a Larger Story

The Larger Story

*"The decisive question for man is: is he related to
something infinite or not? That is the telling question of his life.
Only if we know that the thing which truly matters is the infinite,
can we avoid fixing our interests upon futilities, and upon all kinds
of goals that are not of real importance."* [1]

The old paradigms of religion and science – our roadmaps
to the world and the soul – have left us fractured and fearful;
alienated from our bodies, emotions, and dreams; and disconnected
from the earth and those who inhabit it with us. The current
epidemic of anger, anxiety, and depression is not an accident, but a
direct consequence of the way we see the world and live. Our dream
is too small.

We were not designed and put upon the earth by someone
from somewhere else, whether we imagine a distant deity or a
spaceship from the Pleiades. Our origin and evolution is here. To be
precise, we do not even live <u>on</u> the earth. The biosphere surrounds
us, and we live within it and its ongoing development. This planet is

137

not merely a prop or stage for the human drama, a background to these beings – us – who are special. The earth is primary, the literal and metaphorical ground of being, and it will continue to be here long after we are gone.

The truly important story must begin with the earth and the universe. This saga, in which we have grown out of, and along with, a living planet, should point toward living harmoniously and symbiotically with the larger body we find ourselves in. Attuning our awareness to this larger chronicle holds the potential to inspire and renew our vision, reorder our priorities and return us to our proper place. Participating in this narrative requires us to reduce our self-importance, and to contest the fables of religion that our creator is somewhere else, and those of science that insist the world is mechanical, objective, or soulless. It will necessitate experiencing other modes of awareness – sensual, emotional, and imaginative – that challenge the linguistic assumptions of a reality of separate and unchanging objects.

"The goal of life is to make your heartbeat match the beat of the universe, to match your nature with Nature." (2)

We are not sinners or disobedient children. We are not nouns, static and separate individuals. Each moment we are dancing with the universe in infinite movements above and below the bandwidth of our consciousness. We breathe, feel, perceive, change, and interact with other fields of energy at levels ranging from the molecular to the magnificent. How we interact with what's "other" can vary; it can be ecstatic or alienating. The old myths limit the possibilities for perception, engagement, connection, and communion. They turn the sacred into the secular, reduce the profound into something petty or profane, and eliminate the magical for the sake of the mundane. And in so doing, they diminish our potential to participate in a larger community within a greater universe.

We are Storytellers

In many stories of the past, some god or myth has deemed a particular religion, culture, species, or belief system – Jews, Communists, capitalists, Christians, Nazis – most favored or special. These assertions –parochial and arrogant – inevitably lead to wars, aggression, and atrocities against those considered inferior, whether they be other species or our own. For thousands of years people have asserted "us-against-them" tales and theologies that justified what's unjustifiable with divine or enlightened inspiration.

As our gaze expands to see the whole planet floating in inky and infinite space, these claims appear ever-more foolish and dangerous. In a continually evolving universe, where galaxies, stars, and species wink out and die, what is our role or destiny? What is our "medicine," our gift; our contribution to this new narrative that's far longer and larger than us?

Most likely it will include our creative imagination, our ability to tell stories. Of all our capacities, it seems to be the one most particularly human. Many creatures run faster, see better, live longer, or have capabilities of sensing and perceiving that we can barely fathom. But we have a unique magic in the ability to make pictures and weave webs of words that explain the intricate workings of large and small or span infinite distances of time and space. Our tales, whether of myth or science, illustrate the breadth and depth of creation. They can describe the birth of galaxies, the forces inside an atom, or the evolution of species. They evoke the unconscious or unknowable; speak of past, present, and future; and bring the processes underlying mind and perception together for consideration in this very moment. We possess the power and the potential to conceive "the universe" itself, and to tell its story. (3)

This is strong magic and formidable medicine. This is the miracle that has been developed in us. Fifteen billion years of evolution has led to the beautiful, flowering earth, and in humans it has brought forth poetry, science, and art. Stonehenge, Machu Picchu, the Odyssey, Mona Lisa, Taj Mahal... Temples, shrines, and creativity flower in a landscape that once was devoid of life. The universe has created us – along with all the rest – and gifted us with the power of vision. We have inherited and been entrusted with a remarkable aptitude to discern, assemble, and weave all these strands of perception together. It is a sacred gift, and it's our responsibility to use it well. To do so we must create images that connect us to all life. We must tell stories that make us feel hopeful, at home; stories that open us to the wonder of it all.

Our guiding myths need to grow, to become large enough for our souls. If you were to wear size-six shoes on size-ten feet, you would hobble around in pain. If we have size-ten spirits, and our images of meaning or success offer us a petty life – competing to beat out the other guy and buy more stuff, going to war or destroying the last wilderness so we can consume more resources – we'll feel anxious, trapped, root-bound, and live as emotional-spiritual cripples. And mostly we do. Open any newspaper and read the reports.

We were made for more than the dreary dream of materialistic life. We are more than consumers, and larger than any of the self-centered ideologies that would make one proud to be an American, Christian, Californian, or college graduate. We are part of and surrounded by the miraculous, and we live within it. But the old descriptions and dogmas shrink our landscapes, and we need fresh perspectives and processes that can open our imaginations and perceptions to who we are and might become.

Visioning and storytelling are both creative and co-creative. We were born from this earth; we're a marvel of the universe's creation. In the new dream and paradigm to come, creation and creativity will express themselves in the cosmos, the earth, and in the very narrative itself. No longer separate, our inner life takes place within the greater saga. Self and psyche become a field where we play out the relationship of known and unknown, and the unknown in ourselves – just as in the world – is vast and magical.

As such, life can be experienced as a glorious adventure, a rich exploration – ever-challenging and mysterious – as we co-create a journey into the Unknown along with other "relatives" in the great family of life. To embrace this grand undertaking while rediscovering a sense of home and belonging within our family is a dream worth living. As storytellers within this story, we have an important part in this evolving drama. And if we're to play our part well, we must begin, and commit to telling it like it is.

Tragedy and Comedy:
Laughter in the Catastrophe

"(Comedies), in the ancient world, were regarded as of a higher rank than tragedy, of a deeper truth, of a more difficult realization, of a sounder structure, and of a revelation more complete. The happy ending of the fairy tale, the myth, and the divine comedy of the soul, is to be read, not as a contradiction, but as a transcendence of the universal tragedy of man.... Tragedy is the shattering of the forms and of our attachments to the forms; comedy, the wild and careless, inexhaustible joy of life invincible." (4)

Self and world; world and self: A feeling of serenity and a renewal of our sense of belonging results from expanding our notions about our personal identities as well as our vision of our place in the cosmos. The ancient Greeks recognized two primary forms of theater, tragedy and comedy. Tragedy expresses the truth that – as Buddha said – life is suffering. This core insight cannot be denied or avoided. We won't escape this drama without enduring pain. Everything we love will one day be taken away from us. Grief and loss are included in the price of admission, part of what we must accept in being here. Everyone and everything dies, and we must eventually say good-bye to all we care about.

Fame, wealth, status, comfort, and health are all fleeting and impermanent. The more we cling to anyone, anything, or any way of being, the more we will ache when it is threatened or eliminated. Suffering is unavoidable. The effort to hold onto what we love or fiercely defend some value we hold dear will often increase our own pain or inflict pain on others. Tragedy mourns the human tendency to identify with and become attached to life's impermanent roles, relationships, and modes of expression, and the unavoidable suffering as they change, fade away, or die.

Comedy – to the Greeks a higher art – takes a different point of view. It recognizes a true essence beneath or behind the roles we play, and though we must experience life through its many forms, it celebrates the ever-present potential of connection with something larger beyond them.

A light bulb (the form) burns out, but light – as energy – lasts forever. Identifying with something greater than our bodies and our attachments to the ways and means of the moment allows us to lighten. We begin to see the play of other forces in the ebb and flow of the shifting images of existence; see the beauty and humor in the arising and falling away of things.

Like the weather, seasons, and circumstances, we recognize we are not static – we can change and have done so many times before. We have been children, adolescents, adults; in love, divorced, sick, and healthy. We have grown, evolved, and developed through many selves and identities. Multitudes of other ways of perceiving or interacting with the world – each with their gifts, beauty, and lessons – offer themselves to us, and we don't need to take things so personally or cling to this moment so desperately.

Loss need not leave us empty; much is available to us. We are not just vacuum cleaners with our collection of attachments. Recognizing a presence – an essence beyond all the temporary identities we've assumed – leads to a sense of confidence and optimism, a sense of spiritual wealth and resourcefulness. We're greater than our own story, more than we are now. We can choose another path, change. Acknowledging our creativity opens many new possibilities. The social self, the ego circumscribed by its comfort zone and its assortment of habits, routines, and desires of the moment, ceases to be at the center of the world, and we can laugh – sometimes uncontrollably – as we gain detachment and distance from the story we tell about ourselves. There's no reason to complain or be permanently unhappy.

Making Ourselves in God's Image

The Greek concept of reality and... psyche is very close to... recent scientific understandings of the nature of physical reality. Psyche was not a thing, but a process, a dynamic continuum and relationship among humans, gods, and nature... one of radiating, but personalized fields that cross-fertilized all structures of reality, making archetypes available to men, and making intimate the universal patterns found in nature and story alike. [5]

Knowing and realizing a different, more unified self, one in relationship to the many other forms of being, brings a sense of renewal. It can be a delight to welcome the unknown and experience our essence as verb, process, possibility, potential. But embracing a more expansive self often necessitates choosing different, more expansive deities. A vision of salvation located in an afterlife and a deity who is harsh, punishing, and distant is an enchantment that needs to be lifted if we want to live in a more sacred and sensuous world. The god many have inherited – separate and judgmental, demanding obedience, seeing threats and sin everywhere – is not one worth keeping.

Incorporating a larger vision of the divine involves redefining ourselves, for our gods form not just an image of the universe's energy, but an archetype and pattern for our egos. In a monotheistic universe – like that of the warring desert tribes with their "one and only God" – there can be only one truth, one right

144

way of being, and any alternative opinions, truths, and approaches to living must be false and the work of the devil. *"As above, so below."* The pattern attributed to God and outer reality creates a mirror image in the structure of the self, and we think we should have one and only one voice in our psyche. To question or feel uncertain is to be somehow at fault, and we struggle to "get it together," not be in conflict, to be without doubt. And, having ingested the old patriarch, we judge ourselves, feel inadequate, suffer guilt and shame. We're uncomfortable with our complexity, duality, and uncertainty; we perceive them as moral faults.

There are many alternative images of god that can portray the energies of the spiritual realm. The Greeks, for example, populated Olympus with six male and six female deities, each embodying distinct capacities, energies, or concerns. Gods of war, reason... goddesses of home and hearth, eroticism... There's more potential for both compassion and creativity in a pan- or polytheistic universe. In these cosmologies, one's confusion, conflicting voices, or desires may be defined as the expressions of other forces – sacred in themselves – seeking expression and trying to be heard. Hera, Zeus, Ares, Athena, Apollo... Complexity ceases to be a problem, and attitudes of patience, tolerance, self-acceptance, and inclusiveness become virtues, important faculties to develop on the path of knowing ourselves.

The new guiding myth, with its grander and more-inclusive view of the sacred, will affirm that we have evolved out of an intricate, living cosmos, and as creations – children of the earth and universe – we possess their rich heritage and depths within us. Our task – the work of personal growth and self-realization – shall be to cultivate that inner richness, to coax out the wisdom that has been planted there. We must learn to till, water, and fertilize the soil in order that all the seeds in our psyches may open and flower. The psyche and self are verbs, processes, fields of relating, dreams. They are neither defined nor static; they are not facts. They brim with potential and possibility, and our sacred task – our path to the divine – is not to judge, repress, and eradicate, but to create conditions for their full and healthy emergence.

Gratefulness: A Natural Response to the Truly Great

Entering this larger story with its mysteries, potentials, and other forms of perceiving compels us to become respectful. It requires practicing and developing gratitude for what we have, opening our minds, hearts, and imagination to the magnificent living earth and those who share it with us. Rather than lesser forms of life, we must recognize them as companions in the grand journey, having arrived here with their own unique capacities, their special "medicine" evolved over the millennia that allows them to perceive and engage aspects of the world that remain inaccessible to us.

"Re-spect" literally means to look again. To respect is to honor, admire, and appreciate, and it sometimes means challenging our limiting judgments, accepting and exploring the possibility that things might be deeper and more complex than they first appear. Remember, *"We see the world the way we are, not the way it is."* Look again! Changing the world and its possibilities involves changing the perceiver and the lens he looks through. Opening our hearts and imaginations is necessary to open the doors. Something profound and precious is found when self-centeredness slips away and we lose ourselves within a deeper and broader narrative. When the eyes, mind, and heart all open together, waves of awe and astonishment can surround and suffuse the life appearing all about us.

> *Great Mystery, Source of Life...*
> *Thank you for this day... this life...*
> *for one more chance to wake up on this magnificent planet.*
>
> *Help me to open my eyes, my ears;*
> *my senses, heart, and imagination*
> *to the miracle and wonder taking place all about and within me.*
>
> *May I come to know you in the many forms of the living Earth;*
> *in the spirits of my fellow people;*
> *and in the tender recesses of my own heart.*
>
> *Help me to say "Yes" to this life exactly as it is,*
> *Without waiting for it to become just, fair, comfortable,*
> *or fit my ideas of how it should be.*
>
> *May I change what I can – myself –*
> *Learning how to water and nurture the seeds you've*
> *placed within me*
> *In the hope and faith they might take root.*
>
> *May they grow strong, flower, and bear fruit;*
> *Bringing forth beauty, and feeding a world*
> *Hungry for a dream worthy of the human soul.*

In addressing the "Great Mystery," we acknowledge something more boundless than our egos and personalities, something we will never fully know or understand, something that will always remain unknown. We give thanks because we did not make the world – it has made us. The enduring powers of earth, air, fire, and water have mixed and woven themselves together to create the many forms of being, ourselves included. Every day these energies feed, support and sustain us. Without them we would not, could not exist, and to forget that – to be disconnected from them – is to be shallow, uprooted... to live a spiritual death.

One can even be grateful for the ability to be grateful. Looking out on this beautiful world, our time here will be measured in decades. But the brain, eyes, ears, skin, and organs of perception that we look through took millennia upon millennia to develop. We are recipients of capacities and gifts we did not create, that were molded over eons as plants, animals, water, wind, and fire communicated, danced, experimented, and evolved in calls and responses across the vast tableau of earthly history.

"We are only a tiny fragment of history, but we carry the promise of it all. As travelers in an age which has lost its myth, our individuation task is a conspicuous note in a great song that has been sung from the beginning." (6)

What can we return for all we've been given? As the universe's storytellers, our ultimate and most authentic gift is to tell a magnificent story, one that honors the rest of existence and welcomes all the myriad forms of creation to sit at the table with us and celebrate. The letters that celebrate this larger story (pp. 355 – 381) affirm it's time to begin, to prepare and share this banquet of the soul. It's time to return, to finally come home. It's time to sing praises and join the song of creation, for our spirits have been starving and the voices of our relatives have been silent too long.

If not now
when? Who will sing
the praises of this place
if not you?
Can you make love
with limp excuses?
Just one word
in your own voice would cock the heads of robins,
but today they listen only to worms.
Every morning
a thousand birds
give the world a chorus of themselves
without hesitation or regret.
All through the day
the trees and sky
speak in the hushed voices of lovers,
and in the night
the grasses sigh in the warm hands
of the evening breeze
while fireflies flash their honest love
to the distant stars passing overhead.
When you are ready,
join the conversation --
it still needs the strong and delicate
sound of your voice.

~ Thomas Griffin [7]

Letters to the River
The Left Side:

Stepping Beyond the Shore

Searching for a New Mythology

Hard Labor: Giving Birth to Mystery

Mist rises from the surface of the river. My hands are numb. People will soon return from the wilderness and four days of fasting. Food, conversation, and companionship await them. What will we talk about? What is worth saying or speaking to each other? In the deep recesses of the soul, when the encounter with what's nameless draws near, can this meeting be reported, described, or spun into a myth or story that touches another?

We climb the mountain or walk to the desert. We enter the sacred river. Like Christ, Moses, or Buddha, we leave everything behind, seeking God, truth, the transcendent experience. The windows are flung open; the curtains part like the Red Sea; and something great and abiding floods in. How shall we carry this back to our people? Thoughts, language, and forms of convention seem flimsy. Our temperament and time, our body and being are so small, a mere vase that would contain the oceans. How can we return?

The problems before us are many. The old life seems banal;

society is petty and foolish. Commonplace culture appears an aberration – decades of buying stuff a squandering of potential, the whole assumption of our association a mistake. Do we come back as teacher, savior, or mechanic… or shall we stay aloof to avoid the toxic waste? In some middle ground between hermit and humanity we search for fertile soil. Can it be found?

What is our calling, our gift? What is our song, our story? What is our truth, our task that can carry the great into the small? We carry a seed that must be planted and protected, but the bulldozers, chainsaws, and steam-shovels assaulting the earth are blind to what's Sacred. Poisons and pesticides abound that would kill it. This seed must be pruned, watered, and weeded if it is to flower and bear fruit. It takes time and effort. It's hardly easy.

We will be alone, out of step, different… a lone voice facing excommunication. We will waver through doubt and dark nights, wonder what's wrong with us. The armies of Herod and the inquisitions of the church come in many guises. Indictments and interrogators mock our words as we stand like Galileo to proclaim the world does not revolve around us. Drink deep of this bitter cup that contains the blood of Christ, the hemlock of Socrates. Saviors get crucified; the great must face the petty. Gods must suffer to save their people.

Christ said love thine enemies. But they are still the enemy. It is not the humans we must battle; it's the nightmares they live within. What harvest can we expect from those who've never cultivated the fields of the soul? How can we tend this new dream that must be born from the dark blood of the old? Who can we call on to help?

The ancestors are still living within us. Our eyes and senses were refined over millennia in response to the challenges and calls of the earth. The reptiles and beasts designed our bones and brains. Gills and fins develop, dissolve, and are reabsorbed in each human fetus. Gaia and gods, eons of evolution, and the planet itself are on our side.

But how will they help us pay the bills? Yes, our mother and father are with us, but we must do our part. The saints have all lived simply, and to take more than we need violates our compact with life. Remember, we are already abundantly rich. Count your blessings and don't give Caesar more than his due.

The body is small. Life is short. The mind is word-bound, languaged, and limited. But a great mystery swirls around our tiny circle of the known. The sharp line between self and world must disappear. The spirit is infinite, and it's ever-ready to come alive within us. It calls out to the soul.

Yes, give Caesar his due, but do not pledge your allegiance. Be in that world, but not of it. Give your heart to the sacred, your soul to great Gaia. Embrace what's unknown and become your own great mystery. Reach toward the sun, and let its light fill your vessel. Don't hold it in. Give your attention and energy to what is eternal. That well is inexhaustible, though each body must eventually tire.

Live the life you were meant to live. Allies and guides innumerable are calling you to awaken out of the wasteland. The changing winds, the rising moon, the infinite heavens... clear running rivers, sacred trees, the teachings of Buddha... sunrise, seasons, the soaring circles of hawks.... We have been seeded by the

155

gods, prepared for an extraordinary life.

The tug of tides, the dust of stars, and the life-giving air is alive and embedded within us. You are the garden, so till and tend the soil. Cherish the humus of your humanity. Be fertile and let yourself be fertilized by the forces greater than yourself. You are pregnant with mystery.

And you are not alone.

The Muse in the Moon

The moon rises again over the Chama River, as words, images, and descriptions stream along a current through my mind. Something ungraspable courses on the tide – tugging and tempting – as my direction is drawn to mystical dreams on silver pathways across the water.

Artemis, Diana, Grandmother Moon... You are the feminine, the great and sometimes gentle Goddess, the light which grows, fades, and returns. Your movements mark the passage of seasons. Grand cycles are reflected in your waxing and disappearing from view. You are a shadowy force, the cryptic face, the rightful mother to a dying and resurrected god.

You hold sway over darkness and all that is mysterious and mortal. Your closeness offsets the solar force floating far above the earth, eternal, immovable, and unchanging. You are emotion and enigma, an antithesis or antidote to reason and abstract Apollo, values that rule the light of day.

One cannot approach the sun, but you reach into woman's womb and set her cycles. You illumine ancient altars of Astarte, observe the midnight dances, and draw wild and eerie wailings from the throats of wolf and coyote. You tug at the tides, trigger the ancient brain, and touch deep recesses of soul, where spirit and psyche move in unfathomable impulses of water.

For centuries the male gods have held sway, and their spires, temples, and towers all point to an unreachable heaven. Our attention and eyes turned away from you, your shrines have lost their luster. The festivals of fertility have been forgotten; your sanctuaries lie in ruins; your sacred groves are sacrificed for lumber. Your message is unheard; the quicksilver arrows of Artemis appear pointless. Invisible, but all about us, they lie scattered and broken, discarded and dusty, silent with nary a quiver.

Grandmother, what strange cycle is this that you have been waning for two thousand years? What secrets have you kept hidden throughout this long black night? Faded and disappeared, are you biding your time, awaiting some grand turning in which you'll rise and return to reign once again?

*   *   *

The river uncoils and undulates in a broad bend, then flows eastward into your ascending silver. Silhouettes of trees make a black ribbon along the bank. Within their dark arms the stream sparkles its way to the sea, the water effervescent and almost alive. I sit by your side with a candle, as others have done – by torch and campfire – for centuries. The atmosphere feels pregnant; invisible presences pass through the air like an approaching storm. Something moves softly through the grasses as a beaver slaps its tail, splashing downstream.

I sense and hope for a turn of the tide, a cleansing flood, the second coming of Innana, Isis, and Astarte. Tonight I will enter the dark water and swim into the moonlight, lured onward by ancient longings and an irresistible urge for that luminous disc in the sky. Like salmon splashing in silver and spent in their urge for spawning, I will hurl myself headlong, drawn to and drowning in your radiant light. I will follow your heavenly calling along its shining and gossamer pathway, and – like a dervish – whirl with blind devotion in a drunken dance for love of the night.

And I shall awaken in the waning moonlight, bearing witness to a new dawning of the dark.

Children of the Sun

Great Mystery,

The sound of water rushes by. The flood recedes, down a foot from yesterday, leaving debris and driftwood scattered all along the shore. Morning is a golden glow, and the flaming sun reigns in a cloudless sky, washing over the baking sand and stone. A bright ribbon of green lines each side of the river, but farther away, along gorges and rocky flats, the color quickly fades. The red-rock hillsides glisten with a sheen of sage, its light coating turning thicker in the presence of shade or a spring, the deepening hues highlighting the underlying architecture of the canyon.

Sunshine, rock, and the rare but explosive power of rain and runoff join together to paint an immense canvas of harsh and impossible beauty. The altitude is high; the light fierce. The earth turns sluggishly, but steadily, as Apollo's great chariot moves across the sky. At midday the landscape shimmers, panting like a dog in heat. A haze hangs in the air, blanketing everything. The colors are bleached, and a sense of over-exposure is palpable. The solar god glares down from the heavens, while mere mortals turn away and seek shade from his relentless radiance. Later, in the evening, slanting rays create shadow and contrast, and the red-rock walls reveal their fissures in glowing orange. As the fierce, flaming face damps his fires and slowly settles into his dusky bed, the desert cools. Insects call, and the thickets whisper with scurrying life.

We are all offspring of this blazing star. His hand is sometimes harsh, but we huddle and shiver in his absence. Among the mountains of Central Mexico, ancient peoples still sing and dance in honor of this first power – Tatewari, Grandfather Fire – and his prime manifestation, our Sun. The people of the earth are many, with their multitude of faces, cultures, classes, and customs, but deep in our hearts we are all children of the sun.

His is the flame that burns in each of us. The science is clear. Green chlorophyll in plants' leaves and limbs collects this cornucopia of energy, binding it with earth to produce stem, stalk, flower, fruit, sap, seed, and root. The animals – two-legged and four, swimmers, crawlers, and flyers – are, ultimately, all sustained by this vegetative vitality, ingested in flesh or fiber. Taken in, digested, and broken down, the power of sunlight is released and once again burns within us. It propels motion and thought; builds strength and sinew; makes possible all sense and sensibility.

Every day, medicine people offer a prayer of thanks. They cast their songs toward the eastern horizon in a gesture of gratitude given back to the source. *"We are one with the infinite sun, forever, and ever, and ever."* Father Sun is pleased, and his smiling face beams down upon us for another day. We cannot forget that, say the Old Ones. If we were to wander away and lose our sense of this sacred source, Grandfather Fire may no longer bless us with his shining countenance, and a great gloom would enter the world to mirror the bleakness of the human heart.

Some say it is happening already. Newspapers and television bellow out their fascination with shadow – "Stay tuned for a live update on darkness and death." – as slowly, steadily, we forget who we are and become what we fear.

Science and abstract thought add to our sorrows, striking

their blows against the Sacred. They turn the heavens' flaming furnaces into physics and something indifferent – a machine, not a miracle – that moves according to inertia and impersonal law. In so doing, we follow suit and become what we behold – masses and statistics, passive entities to be measured, molded, and manipulated – as the sanctity of the soul shrivels, retreats, and recedes in an objective, scientific, and secular world.

But the sun continues to shine, science and the news notwithstanding. Lift your eyes up to the skies and remember the source from which you come! Send out a song; speak your thanks to this shining sphere, for we are children of the light, born of grand and magnificent powers.

Feel the warmth beaming down and all around you! Know this force as your father, and be a light in the darkness. Remember his radiance. Remember your relationship and remember yourself! Feel yourself shining like the sun for, in the truest sense, you are. And in so doing, this world must surely become brighter.

The Burning Passion

And so long as you have not experienced this -
to die and so to grow -
you are only a troubled guest on the dark earth. **

The waters break over sandbar and shore along the Yucatan
Peninsula. The morning sun is born again, pushed out of the womb
of the sea, bloody and red. This ascending star blazes a trail across
the heavens, bringing light into the darkness and warmth to the
coldest heart. Forms emerge from nothingness; shadows retreat
before its radiance.

Praise be to creation, the savior has arisen! The shining one
smiles upon us and offers blessing in his beaming face. The earth
unfolds and flowers. Field, forest, leaf, and landscape open their
arms to receive his love.

Who could ask for more? Every day, the golden orb offers
his gracious gift, granting us life and rescuing us from darkness.
Unbidden, this marvelous offering, this precious present is placed
before us, yet many leave it – along with their eyes and hearts –
unopened. How can they turn away and ignore the obvious? There
is nothing more sacred. There are no more important things to
attend to.

Every morning he returns. For whom do the birds sing?
Who makes the grasses grow? I feel the warmth of his gaze on my
face. I need no catechisms, no stories of a resurrected god or
promises of a sometime salvation. This dawn I cast my sight to the
curve of the horizon. Rainbow hues streak the lightening sky, and I
sense the earth moving as his rising draws my vision beyond the rim
of the world and a glittering path is revealed across the water.

Alleluia.

The gods are great and generous. Remember to give thanks. Our father, the sun, the holy light... his love is received through skin and through sight. Separate and one, mixed with matter and bound in bodies of flesh and flame, we flutter like moths between his welcoming warmth and a sweet, burning annihilation.

*　　　*　　　*

Temples of stone slumber beneath twisted roots of the jungle. Pyramids and palaces lie earthbound and buried. The whispers of ancient peoples ride on the winds, their words of praise recalling warriors who offered their hearts to the sky. The old prayers of their priests struggle against the silence, their ecstatic and agonized voices choked by tangled vines that veil these stairways to heaven.

Those passionate days call across the distances, their songs of courage and carnage a counterpoint to our colorless concerns about the safe and secure. Comfort and convenience shackle our souls in well-furnished prisons, the drumbeat of our feeble pulses drowned beneath the blare of advertising and entertainment. We climb ladders of success leading nowhere as the gods of economics stare back with blank expressions.

Something in us still longs to climb those frightening steps, to leap with abandon into the arms of what's infinite and unknown, and to rise... reborn like the crimson sun; heart birthed beyond body and the bounds of human horizons; streaming its scarlet into the blue bowl of the sky.

It's a bloody and messy business, this earthly life, with its burning and bittersweet beauty. It's easy to wish it otherwise: to put the self at the center of a creation there to serve us; to insist on engaging existence only if covered by insurance; to demand compensation for hurts; to dream of dying in our sleep and awakening to angelic harps in an antiseptic afterlife. But it rarely goes that way, and we do great violence to the world and to the spirit in the service of such false gods.

The sun pours a pitcher of fire over the surface of the sea. The skin turns dark; the sands grow hot to the touch. The heart flutters like a moth, moving forward and back across the edge of contentment and crisis on the path toward its fate. The darkness of the cocoon appears appealing, memories of confining comfort and the simple satisfaction of endless consuming a relief from the relentless tug toward a far more dangerous destiny.

Some would stay there forever, but once the border is crossed, there is no turning back. The freedom of flight breaks old bonds, and new appetites send us dancing across sunlit meadows, our lust for beauty pollinating flowers until that final moment. Then, drunk with nectar and insane for ecstatic embrace with the light, we'll once again offer our hearts to the sun, flying toward the flaming doorway and burning from within.

** From Goethe's "The Holy Longing," translated by Robert Bly

Song for Gaia

The wind was relentless as it thrashed throughout the night. A boom box played in the darkness, the music mixing with the thunder of crashing surf. Words of a song floated like feathers through drifting dreams: *"What if God were one of us, just a slob like one of us....?"*

Oh yes, what if God was? But, which god do we speak of? God, the great Kahuna, the one, the only, the first and foremost...? That god was nearly always a goddess, a woman I believe: Nut, Inanna, Astarte, Lilith, Ixchel, Gaia... always and everywhere woman. She was Great Mother, the feminine face of the fruitful and fertile earth. Over the years we've developed, diverged, and differentiated, become distant and rational, but it's a wet and watery womb from which all life emerged. Today we live in our heads – self-centered and separate – but our genesis and ground originated in rhythmic and rocking waves of uterine union.

Our current god lives far away in a house called heaven. He sends his son for one short stay over the eons, leaves a book of contradictory and incomprehensible instructions for life, and assumes his petulance and absolutism passes for parenting. What kind of a god is this? Jealous Jehovah, the pathological patriarch. No wonder we feel angry, alienated, and alone! Petty and punishing, aloof, annoyed, abusive, or unavailable – he's the father of dysfunction, the archetype of abandonment. Thank god he's gone. Pray he never comes back!

Should we worship a distant deity, beg forgiveness from an abandoning father? Do we hope for a second coming, an encore for this kind of creation? What a foolish thought! Is it healthy to believe

– even for an instant – in a critical, judging God who has left us?

Gaia, the great mother, is with us always. She is, was, and shall be. Every day the garden blooms, and the thousand-petaled lotus unfurls... the ten-thousand things bursting forth into being. Buds, birds, and burrowing beasts; coconuts, cashews, and continents. Swans, slugs, sharks, and spiders.... dolphins, devas, disease and decay.... Mosquito and maggot; mountain and molehill; mother's milk, molten magma....

Silence and symphony, the sound and the Furies flow from her fingers. Seed and shellfish, amoeba and ant....

The joy and the hurt, sky and the dirt....
petals and pollen, the rising and fallen....
The egg and the semen, birthing gods or a demon....

Coyote and crow, and all that we know
Come tumbling out of her womb.
Giraffes and gazelles, the sights and the smells
of maggots and roses in bloom.

The fount of all wealth, the picture of health,
the cause of good fortune and Aids...
Cockroach and corn, and all that is born
must flourish, and then it just fades.

Pear and papaya, the fruits of desire
that rot or are turned into jelly...
Grasses and grains, all pleasures and pains
gestate in the globe of her belly.

Great art and slime, all creations of time,
her expressions and none could be finer....
The first word and last, the trifling and vast,
are spewed from her lips and vagina.

Chaos and confusion, her prolific profusion
Makes us smile, shake our heads, or just weep.

Vile or sublime, each disguise is divine
And nightmares can wake us from sleep.

The source of our rapture, we're seduced and we're captured
This passion can feel like a rape.
Often we're pleased, and at other times seized
By a love that can have no escape.

She is here, and we are home. She moves among us daily...
she crawls, flies, slithers, drips, or blows. We walk in her garden.
Look anywhere and you may find her! She lives in the heights,
hollows, and over the horizon. She's in emptiness and in everything,
in the longing and looking, in your eyes. She speaks to your ears,
your hunger, your heart; whispering, shouting, beckoning in
silence...

> A mystery or mess, our lives doth she bless;
> inner and outer, our lives are about her.
> She's matrix and mother, all one and no other.

Gaia.

Friendly or fearsome, hers is the first and final face. Froth
and ferment, fair, faithful, festive and fickle... she's former and
future, fact and fantasy, here and now, in nature and nurture.
Fashioned from clay, our soul and her soil are one. Fecund and
fertile, she's freedom, flow, fulfillment. She's fear, she's fun....
she's fundamental.

She has never left us. We are a part of God, not apart from
her. Always. And we are <u>still</u> in her garden. A gale, a garnish, a
galaxy... aflame and frolicking in fission and fusion, obvious and
hidden, she's everywhere apparent. We are so grace-full, so let us be
grateful.

Earth, air, fire, water;
mother, father, sun, or daughter.
She's divine; she's disordered,
and just what we ordered..

Yes, what if God were one of us? Just a slob like all of us?

How neat that could be.

Eternity in a Rest Area

Dear Spirits of this Land,

The stream of cars move steadily south, and my eyes are tired as I take time out in a rest area. Sleep calls to me, singing its sweetest song, but I have a plane to catch and must soon travel on.

I've stopped here to unwind and stretch, paused by this pavement to find you. My body is warmed by the sun and chilled by driving gusts as I take the time to pray and meditate, sitting on a small patch of grass next to the interstate. I try to tune out the highway and the chatter of parents and children who've stopped to rest or relieve themselves beside this black ribbon of asphalt. It's a struggle, and I wonder if I can find you here.

The sun is penetrating, the wind persistent. The landscape is vast and barren; the horizon lies far, far away. The sky is cloudless, the atmosphere hazy from blowing dust. There's not a drop of water in miles. Close-by, the earth seems subdued, confined and covered with blacktop and sidewalk; but it is vast all around us, the great expanse of desert stretching out past the edges of eyesight. It is immense, but not immediate; visual, an abstraction. Nearby, a postage stamp of grass and a few shrubs littered with cigarette butts, tissue, and cellophane wrappers struggle to hang on and assert their presence. I wish them well and appreciate the small comfort they bring.

This "rest" area is a caricature of ease, a reflection of our restlessness, a mirror held up to our myopic and anxious existence. It's neither refuge nor oasis. Living things struggle just to survive amidst the concrete and litter. Like passion and childlike innocence, there is so much that wants to live and grow within us, but it easily gets lost in the clutter of lists and limited possibilities. What's simple and natural is swamped by paperwork and possessions. What's spontaneous and sincere drowns in the tide of junk mail, entertainment, and distractions. Eros meets the Puritan ethic. The sensuous life is shamed as idle hands become the devil's playthings. Daily, dreams are crushed on the pavement as exuberance and enthusiasm encounter rules, regulations, and repression, the mind-sets of timidity, conformity, and materialism. And by the way, "Please keep your animal on a leash."

Can anything authentic thrive here, or has it become – as Chief Seattle said over a hundred years ago – the "end of living and the beginning of survival?" I pray we are better than that.

Out in the "empty" desert, rattlesnake and rabbit, raven, coyote, and vulture live out their lives. Having found nothing of value there, we have left it alone. In that harsh, but not hostile, habitation, they are far more at home on this earth than we are. They do not fill their days and nights with diversions. They're not prisoners of the highway, dashing off to be somewhere else. They neither posit nor hope for a better life far-off in the sky after they are gone. They survive, harmonizing and adapting their rhythms to sun and shade, to wind, cold, and water. They endure, breathe, and glide in air that is fresh, alive, and unconditioned; facing life and death daily, eyes unblinking, senses alert.

Comfort and happiness are elusive and empty goals. This great earth is round. Its movements and structures are cyclical; eventually we come back to where we started. We cannot run away from discomfort and pain (or anything) without, at the same time, rushing toward it. Going faster in our squirrel cage gets us nowhere. The microbes keep up with the latest wonder drugs, the insects with each new pesticide. Better weapons have not made us more secure or lessened our fear, for it is our fear itself that created them.

Our greatest dreams will not be realized by hurrying toward some fantasy-filled future over a distant horizon. It is time to stop running and enter the desert or the mountains – like Christ, Moses, or Buddha – and face our own wilderness in its diversity and desolation. Our salvation lies in encountering our emptiness and grieving our losses, not in larger homes and better security devices. Our promise will be found and fulfilled in freely giving away the best of ourselves, in facing all the deaths and dying so that in our final moments, there is nothing left to lose.

The path with heart stands outside the highway and all those well-marked lanes. It requires an enduring faith that can embrace the eternal and mysterious present as it journeys toward unknown destinations. An authentic and worthwhile future will be found within a living landscape whose invisible ways are wider, deeper, and richer. There we encounter life on its own terms – its harsh winds, stark and profuse beauty, its death and decay. There we can discover hope through developing the capacity to love it as it is, and in so doing, find and love ourselves also.

Heaven and Earth:
The Heart of the Matter

Turn your hearts to the sun. Say "Yes" to the new morning!

The rim of the world burns with crimson, and ancient chants play over and over across the hills: *"We are one with the infinite sun, forever and ever and ever...."*

My chest expands, arms rise up, face turns to the horizon. *"Great Spirit, I reach out my branches and leaves toward this heavenly father. Open me like a flower. Blind me with radiance. Fill me with light and warmth, and may your images of gold swirl within the dark depths of my vision."*

The mind of man is troubled. People are wounded, their attention distracted and captured by pettiness and pain. *Wash away our worries, bathe us in brightness! Draw our gaze toward what is truly important!*

I have wandered for so long, making my home in the mountains and canyons. I have sat by rivers, drunk from streams, and spoken with the sky and stars. I have sought shelter in caves and groves, sung to trees, been blessed by birds, beasts, and beauty. I've gazed into the faces of rattlesnake, bear, and elk, been taught by storm, fire, and wind. I've followed the tracks of the invisible 'til its presence has made itself known, my senses merging into streams that flow to the eternal oceans of awareness.

But I feel uncertain. Is there a home for me among my people? Can they be trusted? Is there love, a dream worth living, a simple and basic sanity? I see so much pain, anger, resentment, stupidity. It is inescapable – competition, separation, shame....

violence, cruelty, original sin.... money, materialism, self- interest....
Ugliness is everywhere!

Who are these people? Are they like barren soil, a once-
fertile landscape that's been ravaged and destroyed by bulldozers?
Can their ecology be tended, the scars softened with signs of new
growth? Are they evil, beyond hope, or merely children, frightened
and unable to escape the nightmare they're in?

Darkness, shadow, depression.... coldness eats at the hearts
of the people. Aimless and lost... caged, domesticated, and
dangerous... they pace like cornered and wounded animals. What is
my task, my role? Can I make a difference? Can I walk among my
brothers and sisters with the equanimity of Buddha, with the
compassion of Christ? Or should I just get out of town to avoid the
Crucifixion?

An answer takes root and grows in me, but slowly. Long
ago, Christ called upon his heavenly father, and Buddha faced down
armies by touching the earth. The earth is our mother; the sun and
sky our father. In the midst of all the greed, craving, and violence,
we cannot forget that, must not forget who we are. We stand upon
the living earth, and now we must make a stand for it.

Yes, I will speak out. I will speak to the earth, the living soil
we are born of, that has fashioned our bones and brewed our blood.
I will speak to the heavenly fire that sparkles in our eyes, the
shining light that brightens cold space, the burning passion that
scatters dark clouds and creates the warmth and possibility for love
to take root in our hearts.

I will speak to nature. I will speak to what's innocent, true, and longs to be free; shackled or confined by the cages of civilization. I will speak to the human whose allegiance is here and not in some angry or abstract afterlife. I will speak to the indigenous soul and all earth's children waiting within. I will speak of the chance to live in the Garden again.

I will not join the nightmare of normality. I will not bow to false gods: to fear, authority, consensus, and all their dreams of darkness. My vision will quicken with the glow of the sun, moon, and constellations, and I will have warmth in my heart and fire in my belly as I turn toward the light.

I am born of the living earth, the cycles of sun, stars, and seasons. By them I set my compass, and to them I must be true.

Dream of the Deer

Life is a great and holy mystery.

A deer wanders into camp, and – startled – bolts away, shocking me from sleep. *"Awaken, awaken!"* this herald cries. I look up; see her bound into a gully and out, slowing on the other side. She stops, sniffs, looks, listens... finally stalking off amidst the piñon and sage.

I arise, curl out of my sleeping bag, pull on my boots, and step away to heed nature's call, but it's nature's deeper call that continues to echo throughout my inner landscape.

It would be easy to ignore. This was likely a chance encounter, an interesting thing, no big deal. I could go about my business and make my coffee. I could write a letter, read a book, and look over my list of things to do. Everything I've learned steers me in that direction. Since a child, I was taught that God grants mankind dominion over the earth; that nature has no intelligence, purpose, or soul. This world is a place we find ourselves in and momentarily inhabit. Its flesh and body are just background to the human drama. The universe is random, circumstantial, physical. It's made for our use.

But I wonder what nature learns about us? The deer thought me dangerous, even though I was sleeping. But perhaps she sensed I was more than just sleeping – that I am unconscious, foolish, blind, and dumb. She surprised me, sounded the alarm, called to me – *"Awaken! Awaken!"* – startling me to a more alert and attentive awareness.

* * *

My people are lonely and lost. They wander through sterile landscapes of logic and language. They dream the dreams of Newton, Descartes, John Locke, and their science is a story of separation: "The universe is a machine – mechanical, savage, or stupid. We are different and special. Only human concerns have ultimate value. Our souls will find their home in the afterlife..."

Oh yes, something is dead, stupid, and mechanical. This dream itself is a nightmare. It pursues hard facts, cold reason, drab data and dissection. It is body without beauty, measure without music. It's a story without love, prose without purpose. It hungers for dead specimens, knowledge on a blackboard, life with a white lab coat.

The deer's soft brown eyes looked into my soul. The creatures observe us, and they sense our fear, our anxiety and disease. Our mad myth of mechanics severs thought from feeling, soul from body. We place origin and destiny in the supernatural, label life a fall from grace, then plunder the world for pleasure or profit. We are the Prodigal, profligate children. We spend our inheritance, cast the circle of creatures out of our story, forget our home and family. And the slop in the pig sty we've created will not fill our emptiness.

It's time to awaken from this dream, this nightmare. It's a curse, a foreign installation. It's poisonous to our humanity and toxic to those seeds that search out a deeper destiny. Love, beauty, compassion, and communion are wanting to take root in us. A magical universe is shimmering under the surface of self-righteous religion and all the hard and flattening facts. We must come home; remember what we've lost, what primal people always knew. A greater dream demands it.

The painted walls of mesas rise above me. Canyon wrens sing in descending scales. The desert drones a wavering melody through the throbbing cicadas. The earth moves; sun, soil, drought, and deer shift in dynamic balance. Great depth and beauty abound, and I must cultivate them in myself if I'm to meet what's already here.

I am not an object. I am not an observer, visitor, or steward. Fertilized by and reaching to sun and sky, I was born out of the womb of the living earth. She has touched, fed, fostered, and taught me, and I feel her arms wrapping all around me. But the deer's soft brown eyes remind me that my mind can go astray.

I belong here. Looking upon my mother's face, I've glimpsed her gentleness, beheld her bounty, and heard the deeper calling. Though daily I must dwell within the limits of logic, learning, and language, the soul lives beyond the borders of religion, rules, and reason. There – bound by love, desire, and longing – my words must tell another story, and I must sing another song.

Dawn and deer arrive together;
The morning magic, the moment strong.
She grants her gaze, her gift, her presence.
If she's the game, I'll play along.

The deer is dancing through my Dreamtime,
A bounding tale, a path with heart.
Its tracks are poems and prayer and promise,
Of becoming whole and not apart.

I will come back to the garden,
Eat its fruit and dance a jig.
For I am free, unshamed, unpardoned
Of Adam's apple, and Newton's fig.

The Known and
the Unknown

Truth and Beauty

One day, the eyes just open, and what was once unseen or far-removed comes flooding in. Flowers rise up brightly on the stream bank, bursting forth, laughing and optimistic. Thrusting themselves boldly and unashamedly into the world, like the child I once was, their germinating seeds feed upon spring's runoff as a flood of memories washes into the future.

My vision expands, attention lighting upon what is right before me. The first tight bunch of white-petalled joy I notice leads to another and another – the blossoms suddenly appearing everywhere, scattered among brown needles of pine and fresh tufts of grass. Spring returns, and new life erupts beside decaying logs and discarded piles of driftwood. The creek gurgles on joyously, its eternal song of resurrection and rightness carrying me beyond the banks of time. I stand on the shore of holy ground, in heaven, on earth, and in love.

"I think, therefore I am."

What foolishness! If we must be fools, let us be fools for love, for innocence, or any kind of sense at all. Deduction cannot make a duck. Thinking makes thoughts; it only rarely makes sense.

I did not make this world. It is older, wider, and deeper than I can fathom. It has secrets, undisclosed dimensions, and a silent presence unknowable by thinking. I sit on the bank and simply observe what is, trying to make sense of it all, but other forms of knowing break through the dams of discourse and carry me far downstream. I float in reverie, finding myself here and there, drifting, awash in feelings far richer than reason. I am awestruck, outside myself, both at one and a witness, as this man I call me sits on the shore and the river runs through him.

I wander happily through forests of feeling, wildflowered fields of possibility, and irrational regions in the land of the free. I bow down to no human governments and faithfully serve only the imagination. I shall dig in the soil, undermine the foundations of the tower of reason, for it is a fortress, a foreign installation, a garrison. I will prowl around its borders, cry out from the wilderness, assault it with poetry and song, confuse it with extraordinary and uncommon sense until – dizzy and flailing in its demonic detachment – it finally falls. And all the king's horses and all the king's men will find themselves lost, but unrestrained once again.

There is beauty in truth; there is truth in beauty. I gaze out with wonder, seeking the song or the silence beyond the surface of things... and I become what I behold. Vision is a verb, an act, a possibility of perception, a capacity to transform and reveal the world around us. It is a gift of attention, an offering of energy to fields of potential, to parallel worlds wishing to be born. It is the uncertainty principle, observer effect, the creative spark, first cause, original innocence. It is the wisdom of the fool in love with all that's unknowable.

*   *   *

Dusk settles into the valley. Flowers fade away into the soft hands of darkness. Stars will soon burn holes in the black paper of heaven. A chill passes through the air, and the sound of the stream grows stern.

Spirit, thank you for this day and night, for the infinite forms and faces you wear. Thank you for springtime, this foolish love, and the magnificent folly of my vision. Trees fall while new ones are birthing. Life is unreasonable. Life is suffering. Life is short, hard, and tragic. But the flowers keep reaching their hands to the sun.

I will be a bud, a blossom, a babe, but I will be yours. I stand before you like springtime's child, fresh from the source, a brook gone round the bend. I walk in the garden and see you everywhere. I am rising sap, gushing fountain, frothing water; but I am not alone. I am foolish and flaky, a madman and clown, guilty of innocence. I am deranged, devoted, out of my mind; haughty, humble, and crazy with wisdom. I am a wild man, a fool filled with love.

And in that, I'm certainly made in your image.

The Serpent and the Shadows

Dark shapes of mesas loom above as a crescent moon moves in and out of clouds. Shadows grow and dwindle in response to the passing billows; the sound of my footsteps echoes and sometimes scares me. The canyon is empty – save for ghosts and spirits. I stop, listen to the silence, and move on.

Its whispering continues. A breeze blows hard from the east, but the night is surprisingly warm, the clouds acting as blankets. Bursts of fire catch my attention, and I turn to face the wind as bolts of illumination flash behind ridgelines – gauzy flares, eerie and beautiful – highlighting the black silhouettes of the mountains. A storm is coming.

My boots kick up rocks as I weave through the sagebrush. The thickets glow silvery and fade to charcoal. The dark shapes of piñon and juniper seem foreboding. A sharp whirring pierces the night, startles me, stops me in my tracks, body frozen in the steamy blackness. Head turning, ears alert, something in my belly reaches out toward the darkness to my left, a few feet away.

I am not alone. Slowly pivoting, I turn to meet a rattlesnake, another soul who wanders in this lonely canyon. Two currents of caution and fear face off across the distance between us. Awash in mine, the surge slowly calming, I pick his shape out of the shadows – half lifted from the ground and ready – speckled against the speckled earth. A black tongue tastes the air and the flavor of my scent upon it. His nostrils sense my heat. His tail is a blur, appearing almost motionless. I hold my ground.

Danger and desire balance as equals. The gross calculations are quick and simple: He sees me perfectly, could cause me trouble.

He is hard to make out, and fast. I could probably kill him. I can easily turn away and move on; the encounter would be over. But we are both here, meeting in the night.

The moments are full; my attention is riveted. I am alert, but not alarmed. I still have options, choices. Fear sharpens my awareness; my body is alive. The Other, the unknown, LIFE itself – rich, dangerous, sharp, and primal – confronts me in that buzzing, coiling shape. It holds up a mirror: He too is life, a different life. Somewhere, somehow he may be just like me, and my merciful heart stretches out in kindness, compassion. We are one, brothers. But then again, he might be heartless, cold, alien, and utterly unknowable. Am I describing him or myself?

We are both present, at the edge of the unknown, meeting one another. I move to the side and crouch; my shields soften. The rattling sharpens, then subsides, the sound and his sinuous shape emerging and receding with the passing of clouds and moon.

Re-spect. Look again! Respect.

I could get up and walk away, his fear and troubles over. Or I could stay, waiting, stalking the edge of distance and defense, self and Other, until, slowly, they shrank and we touched. But this is not just my decision. I must "treat him as a powerful stranger. I must ask to know him and be known." *

… Respect.

"Friend, stranger, Great Serpent, little one... enemy, adversary, and teacher, what is your will?"

"Not tonight," he answers, "Another time, maybe."

I know he is right. He has other things calling him, and I am not ready. I push back, breathe in the fragrant air. The storm is closer, through still far off.

*   *   *

Twilight draws me onward into this panorama of black silhouettes, silver, and shadows; a landscape of shifting shapes, shrinking sight, and strange new sensings. Something grows within me... a peculiar preoccupation, a profound invocation, an inexplicable summons that pulls me past my fear.

Cautious and curious, I roam a rich and resonant expanse between fascination and foreboding. Awash in danger and desire – attentive, alert, and awake – I am immersed and adrift in an uneasy peace along the edges of darkness and dream. Frightened, but free, I slither through the shadows, stalking an unaccustomed clarity, an acute and intangible realization in this fly-by-night folly... in this calm before the storm.

* adapted from the poem "Lost," in <u>Traveling Light, Collected and New Poems,</u> by David Wagoner. University of Illinois Press, 1999, page 10.

Dancing with the Dark

Last night I dreamed of divorce and deceit, of love that flowers then fades, as the darkness gave way to the dawn. Morning approached, and night slipped off to a secret hiding place; its blackness absorbed in the fabric of space like ebb tides in the sand. The trail of dreams left faint tracks like footprints on the beach, soon to be forgotten, washed away in a stream of sunlight flowing out of the east.

Slate clouds are riding on a restless river of air. The great earth turns; the tides move in and out; waves continue to roll toward the shore of this tropical island. Friends are soon leaving, their vacations and time here over. Days pass by, and the path once before us now stretches out behind, the unknown becoming the known. Yet we stand once again and always in the present, facing out toward something we truly cannot see.

Always the darkness is there. We cling dearly to our candles, our lanterns, our flashlights. Reason, religions, and cultural traditions all shine their beams into the endless black. We pick a path through shifting shapes and shadows, and pretend we recognize the way.

Many follow well-worn maps drawn up by parents or priests. Some are led by longings, others just carried along by the current or their companions. Onward we go, in trust or terror, and far more innocent than we ever suspect. A few search for magical moments of inspiration or illumination, a flare to flood the fathomless twilight with flashes of brilliance. And for some, I hear, it happens.

Dawn breaks; the denizens of daylight awake. Becoming alert and aware, their agendas and actions gather might and momentum as the sun grows sated and climbs up the stairs of the sky. They turn toward the right, seek refuge in their house of reason, head out into the world committed to clarity, consistency, control. They plan, produce, "make progress"; search for strategies so things make sense; pretend to know what they're doing.

But the right side grows tired, and the light fades. Night arrives, and we return to what is left. There the guidebooks are useless. Our candles and campfires are comforting, but they illuminate but a small circle, a focus so finite and foolish in the face of what is. Shadows start shifting; our confidence and control seem less convincing. We drop plans and pretensions and fumble for words. The darkness is deep, but there we must go if we're to follow our dreams.

For now, the sun is ascending, and it is bright, sharp, searing to the skin. But on the far side of the planet, blackness blossoms as ebony enfolds the world in its velvet flowers. We are of this earth, and we must stretch between its polarities. We will not eventually find our way into the light, and the shadows will never disappear... for we are also fashioned by the dark and carry it within us. It has its rules, its riches; its deities and demons; and we must learn to live there.

Our dreams reveal doorways to the yet-undiscovered dimensions where fear and wonder walk hand in hand. The twilight is everywhere. The brilliant stars shine in an inky infinity; physicists marvel and theorize about a mysterious and ever-present dark matter. Shamans travel through death and beyond, bringing back gifts. Treasures are twinkling, and diamonds dance in caverns of carbon. We cling to solid ground, but are pulled toward the underworld, the oceans, the depths. Pluto is the god of abundance. Persephone, beautiful and pure, gives her promise and takes residence in the house of Hades.

The psyche moves in cycles of collapse and reforming, death and rebirth. A synapse sparks, an arc is closed, and a boundary separates inner from outer, known from unknown, self from other. We stand on shifting sands and waver between fear and fascination. The sun shines in the sky and scatters over the surface of the sea, but we sense the surge and deeper swells beyond the shore. We stay on our side; retreat to high ground; attempt to keep the darkness at bay.

Our resistance is fearful, but futile. The tug of the tide is relentless. The depths threaten drowning and dusky indistinctness. There, vision is veiled; identity is confused and chaotic. We are scared, surrounded by much that seems strange or secret. Peace is promised, but separation, sanity, and solidity must be surrendered.

But there's an expansive awareness in the anonymous abyss, an aliveness in what's alien. Clandestine passageways of pitch worm down through the false floor of the ocean bottom. A chasm and a choice yawn before us. The pupil opens, and the eye fully dilates as the darkness takes us. A line is crossed, boundaries become blurred, direction and defenses dissolving. We lift off on the wings of a raven and melt into the night.

Stirring up Trouble

Spirit of the Canyons,

A grove of oaks cluster in the sage flats, their bright green canopy a strange, leafy aberration among rabbit brush and dark-needled cedar. A bird sings a captivating lament from a barren-boned piñon. The first spatterings of rain tap on the ground, while ants scour the sand with relentless intensity, their fiery red bodies at home in the desert heat.

Thunder rumbles off in the distance, and somewhere the air comes alive with ozone and electrical charge. Great forces of creation crash over mesa and canyon, and the arroyo soon fills with red mud and a frothing roar. Clay, stones, and sticks are swept down from the hillsides as the river below swells and turns crimson like blood.

We are one with the body of earth, but who today lives in their body? Bound by the chains of convenience, comfort, and insurance, who dares to get up and dance with Shiva? The world is not a fact! The universe is emerging anew each moment and every day! This spring, cicadas are birthing themselves after years of dormant dreaming. The outpouring of brittle shells from their cast-away cocoons litters the ground. Canyon wrens catch flies, build nests, and hatch their young, while somewhere in the Galapagos, iguanas give up food consumed for millennia and begin to eat algae.

Wake up! There is more to life than consuming! Creation is not an event of the past. It is a principle, a force within the fabric of space-time surging through the seams of form, fate, and eternity. It is here, now, in the sing-song play of children, this storm bursting forth in flood, and in those words you're too frightened to speak. It is here – powerful, pulsing, pummeling the mesa, exploding in lightning and thunder. Nothing is determined.

When did you stop singing? When did you cease dancing? What chains have hobbled your wildness and left you so tethered and timid? Whose hands wrap round your throat and choke out the chance of truth and turn your strong gaze into something frigid, furtive, and false?

Wake up! You are not a statistic. Your life matters! Creation seethes in the cauldron on your forgotten back burner. Yes you! You are an artist, a poet, a teacher, something undiscovered.... a healer. You are a lover, a hero, the renegade. Pull yourself away from the TV and all its mindless drivel. Cease being the captured whore of corporate pimps and become a citizen of another, richer world.

You are a creator, not a consumer! You are a witch, a sorcerer, a shaman, a priest... something about to happen. Light the fire under your magical pot. Pick up that spoon and stir up trouble!

The World at My Doorstep

Throngs of insects search the water's edge, exploring invisible worlds around my feet. They move, stop, face off in strange dances; driven by mysterious impulses I can only imagine. Do they wonder about the dam upstream, converse about the causes of rising or falling water? Do they see me writing on the shore, or care about the human world we deem so important with its odd beings holding sheets of paper with strange markings that seem to speak?

Probably not. But there they are, striding across the mud and silt along the border of liquid and land. They are engaged, purposeful, peculiar. They are interesting, fun to watch, and embedded in something greater that we both share. Feelings of fondness and friendship weave through the fabric of my observations.

Curiosity is inexhaustible, and it pours forth as a force and sustaining passion. I cannot praise life enough. I want to know it through eyes of wonder, as a child at play in the garden. Abstract categories do not interest me... they seem dead, hostile, life-denying. I am no objective observer; the world is no object. The bugs and I share a sunlit morning; we're held in the arms of some grander being, fellow-travelers on a journey to whatever we might become.

I am the sum of all I see, touch, taste, think, and feel. Perception as much as person, I am sunlight on water, a billowing soundscape streaming in the ear. I am the pencil, page, those markings on paper; a mystery revealed in each emerging and unknown sentence. I am motion, membrane, a boundary between inside and out – hard, permeable, frightened, or friendly. I am the open circuit, the reaching hand that's completed and known only in touching an Other.

This Other knows me intimately in ways beyond myself. The river senses me on the shore. It speaks in kinetic conversations as it flows around my ankles. Swarms of insects detect my heat, smell rich or fetid stews in swirling exhalations, agitations, and imbalances blind to me. Do they feel my heartbeat? Is my pulse conducted through the earth I sit on, the atoms of clay and molecules of mud dancing differently when I am here? Infinite arrays of emanations fly out past the horizons of my awareness to be translated by unfamiliar receptors into pictures I cannot see. The unknown knows me, and I do not. I must find this Stranger to find myself.

*   *   *

There are no perfect maps to the mysterious. Charts and graphs are useless, reason irrelevant. What rules should I follow when there may be everything, or nothing, to fear? A good heart shall be my unerring guide, for friendship yields friends and allies. Bliss then, will be my compass, for it gives clear direction – the road of wonder appearing wonderful, the road of terror terrible.

The dangers are obvious. The sea may smash me on the rocks; the shaman faces dismemberment... but I must go. I hear the sirens' calling, a song so sweet it could lure me to my death. There are always monsters on the hero's journey. Sailors are wrecked upon the reef; the savior is crucified, the shaman torn apart. But the sea and stones remain fathomless, and the shaman shape-shifts into other forms. Death and resurrection, the miracle of spring, and the drama of Christ or Dionysus are playing out in universe, stage, and psyche. I shall become wolf, ocean, dolphin, or cloud… for the Self is larger than the ego and finds release in its dissolution.

Old boundaries blur. The shell is split; the egg is cracked; the world is stopped; while passageways to new universes open in the tearing seams. The dream body streams into the Other and becomes itself. The man of knowledge is no longer a man, the world no longer "out there." Paradox abounds. Waves break over polarities in the mind; the self becomes no longer separate or solid. Creation is inexplicable, but not unexplorable, and the great adventure takes us and not vice-versa.

The sun rises higher; the river continues to sing. My little friends explore the sand and debris in this ordinary world, but they are messengers of the extraordinary, guides who whisper of grand possibilities, deeper and radical knowing, the longings of the soul.

Praise to life and childlike wonder! There is wisdom in the child, and though it may be the wisdom of fools, it is friendly. In a world that is relative and related, what could serve you better? Children and clowns are sacred; fools see beyond the rules of the ordinary. The mind rebels at such simplicity, but the spirit smiles and knows the truth.

The world is made of infinite relations. There are no absolute certainties chiseled in stone. Why not wish upon a star? Why bow down to science, reason, religion or any emperor that is totally naked? The sages and Buddhas have an open, smiling face. They gaze upon the world with a different "I." A hardened stare will get us nowhere. Solemnity is unbecoming in the cosmic joke.

Children, clowns, fools… those whimsical, Buddha eyes twinkle with humor.

The river sings and sunlight sparkles like laughter. Something is dancing upon the water. It may be Christ, illusion, or me, but who doesn't love a dance? I will rush in, immerse myself, join it – a foolish thought – but there is so much to be found where angels fear to tread.

Drought, Delight, and Delirium

Dear Mountains,

The western ranges are bathed in light, and early morning blues, cocoa browns, and purples float in the bathwater. The canyons appear to be carved from chocolate, dark shadows marking the furrowed flanks of eroded slopes and steppes where clay, calcite, and salt deposits mix with remnants of ancient seas. Alkaline flats, borax hills, volcanic debris, and acres of ash lie together like strange bed fellows in the dream of a demented geologist, the outlandish made manifest in this twisted terrain called Death Valley.

As the sun strides across the desert floor, the hues wash out and fade into distance. Colors run off into gullies and evaporate in the baking heat. The sand dunes turn golden, their storm-swept, sculpted ridges of dust deposited over centuries by the incessant swirling winds.

I am cool, still in shadow, and enjoying my coffee in the shade of the Last Chance Range. But I can see the front lines of the solar army advancing up ahead, and in a few more minutes the soldiers of light will swarm over this camp. My clothes will be stripped off as I sweat and suffer in the heat of battle, rest and reinforcements not due till dusk. I will try to retreat, to melt into the landscape – my skin turning brown like the umber hills – and blend into a background of silence, sun, and eternity.

The quiet speaks like a relentless whisper. There is a constant humming, a buzz in the ears; I can hear my own blood pumping. Something grand inhabits this emptiness, the vast expanses of space and time filled with an invisible presence. An unknown guest stalks around the edges of awareness, and strange sensations tug at spirit, soul, and psyche. Ordinary life seems far away and useless.

Fire and air... fire and air. The landscape is stark, still, impassive; the composition of the senses unbalanced. All movement is missing, save for the steady shriveling of shadows. Light builds in increasing intensity.

Fire and air...

The air is invisible, conspicuous only in wind and the rise and fall of breath. It's intangible, fluid, everywhere ungraspable.

Fire... Light is formless, the foundation of vision, the unseen shaper of sight. Reflected, mirrored, mutable, particle, wave, energy, process.... it offers nothing solid to hold onto.

All definitions are breaking down. Time and space stretch out and approach the infinite. Everything merely is. A few creosote bushes stand in the rocky flats, ancient and wise, wordlessly whispering of survival and stillness. All else is barren, lacking water, flora, or any fertile soil for nouns or verbs to take root in. Only the indiscernible and inconceivable grows.

Unspoken questions rumble like an avalanche. Who am I? With nothing to do, see, or accomplish – a noun without a verb – I too am inconceivable, a stranger to myself, an unknown guest. In the background of outer silence, internal dialogue rushes to the fore – non-stop, relentless, and stupid – but soon it too runs down, a speaking with nothing to say. Outer mirrors inner and inner outer, but what do those words mean if I can't see who "I" am?

All these questions yearn for an answer, though none are forthcoming. They are merely movements of longing, the parts in search of the whole, a sense of the separate seeking oneness and completion. They are rivers moving downstream pulled toward a source; a child growing upward toward the womb; a human, made in God's image, imagining God. They are the ravings of a man standing before a mirror, asking of his reflections, "Who started all this?"

The sun climbs higher in the sky; the temperature rises. The atmosphere thickens with heat. My throat is parched, and I long for water, that cooling liquid, that primal power conspicuous in its absence.

"In the beginning, God's breath moved upon the water."

Wind and air... breath and water. I yearn to drink, to relax in its refreshing comfort – cool, womblike, silky, and soft – but today I am hardened, tempered by fire... my well has run dry.

All or nothing, nothing or all.... Who am I?

I continue to ask. I seek a response, a resolution, but all I hear is silence. Confusion and contradiction are bridesmaids of the unexplored and unfamiliar, and though I search for answers, it's a quest for source I seek. My examinations are but expressions of a longing, a hunger for the unknown by the known, a breaking down of boundaries, a baby step across borders that mark that small circle called self.

Great Mystery, you who are in all things and in nothing, thank you for this morning. Day defines night, and night defines day. Thank you for this time in this timeless place, this life within the lifeless horizon. My life, your life... this life made in your image.

The grand epic is still unfolding; the great story has yet to end. I am here, and I shall study this landscape like a book. Eternity stretches out to a far-off horizon; the infinite hovers like the heat. I will offer myself to the invisible presence all about me and celebrate the great folly of this task. Being, becoming.... alone, orphaned, born again and dying.... a universal loneliness is made everywhere apparent.

The enigma dances amidst the silence. My wonderings will continue, but any good mystery foregoes answers for wonder. I am both puzzled and peaceful. Though nothing is resolved, everything seems possible. And I am thoughtful, empty, in the desert and in love.

Standing at the Gate

The engines roar like a primal beast raging through the friendly skies, passengers crowded together like cattle packed off to market. Spaciousness has been sacrificed to order, economy, and efficiency, this cargo of commuters stuffed into an aluminum shell. The freedoms of flight are few, the choices reduced to peanuts or pretzels, window or aisle.

Travel brochures show palm-lined beaches and sun-washed decks of cruise ships. Known commodities are marketable, the experience a product that's planned and predictable, the vacations packaged and promoted as "including everything." More is better. Quantity replaces quality. Billions of burgers are served; the shallow sells.

Charter planes taxi down the runway. The destinations have multiplied, but destiny itself has become a forgotten word. Meaning remains immeasurable; it can't be exchanged for currency and never appears on NASDAQ.

*   *   *

Who will speak for the unknown? What would you offer for a life filled with mystery, unbound by common beliefs and beyond control or command? Who is prowling – passionate, hungry, and feral – below the surface of your saccharin world? Are you willing to encounter that hideous beast and find beauty there? What voice cries in the wilderness, unrecognized as your own?

Good citizens stand in line, conforming and compliant, moved more by authority, custom, and habit than by any hunger of the soul. They climb the rungs up the ladder of success, but their vision remains limited since they're always facing the wall. Society turns in on itself like Narcissus – self-satisfied, preening, and pompous – as progress offers up the promise of the next empty achievement. Reducing life's grand adventure to ever-increasing consumption, it struts out statistics about standards of living, boasting of greed and gross national products, while the heart is left to languish in loneliness and longing.

The populace is fearful. Dark shadows stalk all those sunny dispositions; a blackness lies behind the endless vacant expressions. Words remain unspoken while secrets eat away at their hearts, leaving them anxious and ashamed, so sterile and so nice.

Someone has been shackled and forgotten, and he wastes away in the dungeon. What has become of the wild self, our original nature, our sacred twin? We rush around frenetically, endlessly avoiding ourselves and this… "other." We lower our gaze, look no one in the eye – even ourselves – lest our soul mate or better half materialize in the mirror. We sense something moving behind the looking glass as we avert our face… and we're left to wonder if it's dread or loveliness that takes our breath away.

As what's frightening draws near, the houses of the known wobble on shaky foundations. The fabric of social reality begins to unravel in the face of a fearsome freedom. The earth moves; old forms fall flat, unable to wrest consensus from chaos or meaning from mirage. The confident facade cracks. Eyes stare anxiously into the mask of the mystery. The unknown appears and fades, its fluid form ungraspable to the solid self. Its smile is twisted, its whispered greeting enigmatic: "Do tell, how aren't you?"

Dogs bay at the edge of the clearing, some vicious from being beaten or too long on a leash. The collars rub the wrong way; the chains confine and start to chafe. Strange noises emanate from the forest, maddening and melodic, frightening, but somehow familiar.

Animals howl in horrible exuberance. Crowded images of death or dancing tug at the twin poles of an unacknowledged axis. Heaven and hell share the same entrance and price of admission. The trees sway though no wind is evident. Shapes shift in hazy indistinctness; the lush canopy blots out the sun. The air is musty and acrid with decay. The breath of god smells bad.

Old ties are loosening; the dam cannot hold back the tide. Walls weaken; expanding horizons leave us dizzy and disoriented. Routine and habit come unhinged; rules collapse in piles of rattling bones. Strange forces flood the shores of our psyche as docks of certainty collapse from rotten footings. There is nothing to hold on to, and nothing is everywhere near. The die is cast; the colors all run together; conviction washes away in the torrent. The mind reels as danger and desire join trembling hands. We grasp at straws before being swept away.

The Holy Ghost

Grand monoliths of rock look out from ancient cliffs on the mesas watching over this valley. Washed by rain, exposed to sun and storm, and scoured by wind-driven dust, sedimentary layers have been molded over millennia and formed into figures and faces. Silhouettes shaped of stone stare out across space-time – mountain lion, owl, snake... a grandfather and son. Archetypes, ancestors, and elders, these presences age over eons, and through them the eyes of eternity pour into the present.

Someone looks back, meets their gaze for a moment, and moves on. But another stops, enticed and captivated by fleeting impressions. Unfamiliar powers mesh, attention is arrested, and separation slowly dissolves as strange energies engulf us in a force field of something grand. Earth and stone stream into psyche, and the rhythm of the heart sings back. Inner crosses bounds with outer, present with past, ego with other. Time stops, and common sense is shattered by exploding reverie. Imagination bursts into flame; possibilities pour through doors of perception as though flung open. Synapses spark, and new neural nets snap into place, capturing schools of spawning images. Associations multiply in an undivided instant.

But the old self reasserts. We shake our heads and move on, lost in thought. Descriptions are inadequate. The words of a simpleton – "Wow... far out" – are the best we can do. Footsteps proceed automatically. We barely notice the ground.

*　　　*　　　*

Something wondrous has happened. Mystery has penetrated the ordinary self. A seed has been planted, the egg fertilized. Like Zeus appearing to mortals or God to Mary, the Divine enters us. But the joy of this potential and possibility is balanced by a great responsibility: Can we bring this fetus to fruition?

The burden is great; the labors are heavy. Habits, routines, comforts, and convenience call out to us, but yesterday's life is not meant to be saved. An acorn holds the promise of the emerging tree of life, but old, dead stalks can't carry the sap of a new stem. The old shell must crack, burst open, or dissolve. The snake must shed its skin; the caterpillar spin a cocoon and die.

New life must be welcomed, the garden tended. Fragile shoots must be watered, cultivated, and protected. They will not flourish on Main Street, rush hour, or ordinary life. It takes patience, awareness, attention. We'll become ill-equipped to run races or climb ladders of success. Can we shoulder this burden, bear this great response-ability? Should we keep this child or abort?

The virgin is safe for the moment – it may be weeks or months before anything shows. But growth continues unabated, and transformation is difficult. The old clothes don't fit anymore. Fashion falls by the wayside; what's eternal won't be contained in the fad of the day. Birth will make a mess of sheets that are whiter than white.

A rich stew simmers in the cauldron of creation. Its surface bubbles, ripples, and trembles as movement brews in the depths of the womb. Sooner or later, it stirs up trouble.

Change is threatening. Forces array against it. Herod's armies scour the highways, on the lookout for danger. The old king is frightened. The unknown scares the known, and letting go is hard. Security and shallow self-interest take precedence over potential and possibility. The miser hoards his misery; what's static shudders at the thought of ecstasy.

The ego schemes and strategizes how god can serve him, for the divine gift presents possibilities for power, wealth, and prestige. King Minos keeps the prize bull for himself and tries to trick Poseidon. The Promised Land is appraised for real estate; we calculate the lumber and firewood in felling the Tree of Life. Steamshovels billow clouds of smoke as the Sacred Mountains are mined for gold.

Which god will we serve?

Mary takes to the back roads and trails, for the new god avoids the cities. He will be birthed in a stable, among the straw, grasses, and animals. His surroundings are humble, his fingernails and hands dirty. Humility requires the presence of humus – this savior will be found on the common ground.

The citadels must be razed, the towers tumble. Spires and steeples, like leaves, must fall down to earth. Mesas and mountains loom over the valley as we sit by the river. Primal powers stir like deep currents. Ancient memories well up within us. We are moved, awed, awash in wonder. The certain and solid shore recedes as we are borne into fathomless possibilities. The mind reels. All matters of meaning stay on the surface – infinite, shimmering, and unanswerable – for words won't capture Beauty, nor tame the Beast.

I must face this one great question. Can I be faithful? Can I bear this great love and allow the Mystery to be born in me?

Great Spirit, gods and goddesses, help me to be true. I have walked to the mountains, fasted in the forest, prayed in the desert, and you are always there. I am grateful for your many blessings. But the devil always comes, like shadow and light, confusing my good fortune with his possessions. The collective unconscious can't be collected, yet the ordinary impersonates the extraordinary, and multitudes of false gods hide treasures in their trappings. The traps are set, the pitfalls are plenty. Many a predator hides behind an abundance of praying.

Help me, and this prayer, to be true.

The Role of Language

Words Upon the Water

Light and shadow dance among grays and golds as the sun rises behind blue slate clouds. An orange ribbon spreads along the horizon, weaving itself through the gunmetal billows and alighting on silver water. Waves roll onto shore. The surf is gentle, but relentless, as it scours the rocks. Solid stone slowly turns to sand, hard shapes swallowed by the shoreline and digested by the sea. A cool wind combs the beach grass and caresses the face.

Far away, planes rolls down runways and lift off the tarmac. Taxis weave through traffic and honk like agitated geese. People dash for elevators, grab pieces of toast and overcoats while rushing out the door.

Our utterances have such great power. *"Yes... No! ... Stop... Shame on you!"*

Experience is captured in their net and molded by their invisible fingers. *"Sin... Not now! ... Get lost! ... Shame on you..."*

These words echo down long corridors in a convoluted

maze of memories. The sounds take shape and become real as painful scenes are created and endlessly repeated. Truth becomes lost in the twisted, black passageways, and monsters spawn somewhere in the labyrinth. The mind spins in constant chatter; the soul becomes fractured and confused. Vision is restricted; we grow afraid in the darkness.

"Good... bad... whining... useless... "

The undeveloped psyche reels in shock. The foundation is untrue and the blueprints faulty, but language arrives on the scene like a busy carpenter. The tools are unpacked; walls are quickly thrown up and windows installed; vision becomes focused inside a frame. Functions are divided and space separated into specified sections: empty, opulent, or dreary. Roofs and gutters are added, nature and the changing seasons shut out. Wires are strung; power is funneled into specific outlets. Doors are fitted with deadbolts. Everything is done according to code.

The results can be devastating. Inside the buildings strange incantations may be spoken – *"Go away," "bastard," "punishment," "prick."* – as black magic and sorcery are practiced by evil wizards. The innocent are sacrificed, their hearts ripped out. Existence is judged, turned into essence, and twisted into terrible shapes. Truth is distorted; curses are cast which capture the spirit. Souls slip into trance.

The rituals are repeated relentlessly. Love, truth, and what's real are reduced to advertising slogans, the feeling of freedom forgotten. Priests, politicians, and peddlers of pornography compete for the now-mindless masses. Real fulfillment and satisfaction are put aside in favor of short-term solutions, temporary relief from the pain and emptiness. Trinkets are waved before the apathetic millions, promises and fantasy offered like scraps to Pavlov's dogs.

Language is hypnotic. It builds houses and hovels, palaces and prisons. Fine lines and structures of sentences stud the walls, and fascination with its expansive or restricted vistas can veil its forgotten foundations.

All existence is movement and dream-like, but words can make the shifting seem solid. God becomes noun, and noun becomes god – separating and keeping apart what is entwined; fixing the fluid into forms that bind or hide the verbs beneath them. This can be wondrous magic or terrible sorcery. Born of one mother, our utterances arrive like Sacred Twins. Divine or demonic, they wield the awe-full power of polarity. Able to undertake heroic journeys beyond the borders of the known to boundless joy, they have an endless capacity for communion or violence, to destroy or renew the world, to make love or war. All it takes is a word.

The dark curtains part. The sun sails forward, shining brightly on a sea of blue.

"In the beginning was the word. And the breath of god moved upon the water..."

But before the word was breath, was water. Ocean, wind, sun, sky, stone... fire, air, animal.... plant, promise, seed, and soil – all were one before they became every-thing.

"And the word was god."

All existence is sound. Life is vibration, music, song, movement. Words are magic. They are screens, filters, lenses for experience. Sifting, selecting, and sorting sensations... they create worlds. Words are maya. Manipulative, playful, liberating, confining; revealing and concealing... They are dangerous, beautiful, seductive... Sirens to the mind.

So let us be mindful.

These ancient echoes and past pronouncements are still resonating in the strings of our hearts. They can destroy or undo us... they can call us to wholeness and harmony, dancing and dreaming. Take a chance; take your turn; speak your truth! Forget your parents, old prohibitions and priests. Pledge allegiance to what is eternal. Find your voice and lift it beyond your shame and sorrow. Give a modern melody to the music that's immemorial, and as the sun rises... sometime or soon... you will sing a new world into existence.

Silent Words, Invisible Worlds

The wind dies down, and the sun falls to earth. Flies swarm in the slanting light, catching the rays like specks of gold dust that sparkle above diamonds dancing on water. They land, turning dark and hungry, ready to sample some flesh for dinner.

Songs of thrush and sparrow echo in the woods lining the lake, melodic and peaceful, and a woodpecker's drumming drifts across the inlet as waves gently lap the shore. The evening is soothing, save for the ravenous flies, but they will depart with the fading light, bedding under leaves and moss in flight from falling temperatures. The moon emerges slowly, a slim crescent that follows the sun westward.

This is a real world, so far from human shores. Heaven, earth, wind, and water are more than mere phrases. They are expressions, energies alive and eternally transforming that can be tender, testing... terrible. They speak to our senses and in feelings flowing together undivided by definitions.

We must leave home and bid farewell to old habits, routines, and language to enter this world beyond words. Water and air are separate in speech, but they mingle in mist and fog. The still surface of the lake is a looking glass filled with liquid visions of mountain and sky. Ocean bottoms rise and ridges erode over eons, above becoming below, the foundation reforming from figure to ground. Granite boulders are softened by lichen and scoured by wind, their distinctness slowly disintegrating to sand in the gristmill of millennia. Eternity echoes like waves that wash through the tide of time, slapping on the shores of a great silence that surrounds and sustains all sound.

Our language rarely changes, but everything else shifts. Life forever moves on. There is nothing solid to speak about or stand on. And we – in some ways substantial – are not all that solid either. We are verbs, fields of energy, capable of taking flight with the imagination, or – Christ-like – walking on water. We can swim, surf, dance or drift; become more fluid; rock with the rhythms, and move with the music. We can float, fly, soar or sail, or we can be serious and sink like a stone.

Does this need to be a problem? There are no lines, rules, rights, or wrongs in the realms of what's authentic. Reality is entirely unreasonable. It's rigid rules that are restricting, confining categories that are criminal. Words can never do justice to the world for beauty will break every law created by logic. Judgments are made and sentences passed, but all our assumptions and abstract assertions have no basis in the playground of primal forces. The will of the gods shall not be bent or broken. We can neither avoid nor overcome the great powers, nor win any argument against Nature for, eventually, she has only to change the subject.

*   *   *

Thunder peals across the landscape, and lightning bathes the gardens and hedges in fire. The tempest is kept outside of the tearoom. Spoons and saucers clink softly as rain beats against the window pane. The curtain is drawn, the discourse discreet, and the conversation civilized, but the castle will eventually fall.

*   *   *

The sun settles south of the horizon. Light fades like an aging rose, the world turning as stars wink and watch overhead. The wind whispers. The earth rocks me in her arms as I lay upon the ground. Pines sway, sigh, and sing me to sleep. Reason and rationality slowly run down. Thinking stops; deduction goes dormant. Descartes dies. The conscious self slides into an abyss.

The night fills as the ego empties; a veil is lifted as the curtain falls. Other sensations awaken while we slumber. Vision goes vacant; sounds swell and saturate the air. A small animal stirs in the bushes. Owls screech in demented delight. Shapes begin shifting, shadows take form. The skin is caressed by soft fingers of black. Venus consorts with the moon.

The song of the earth lilts like a lullaby, and drowsiness draws us to dreaming as the infinite approaches in the invisible night. Sightless and succumbing to sleep, the self drifts to the doorway of the unknowable. Words and individuality are left at the entrance; identity dissolves into liquid radiance. The mind disappears in the ecstatic; the body becomes streaming light.

In the morning we wake up refreshed. Dreams are quickly forgotten as we put on makeup, distance, language.... invest our attention in the ego and eyes. And this little self does not remember where it did not go.

Wordless but True to My Word

Great Mystery, thank you for this day, for this life…

My words start out predictably, but they are heartfelt. I am at a loss – for what can one do with wonder? What can one say in the face of great presence? In these moments, there is only being. Thinking, time, and language stop, and mystical rapture fills the self beyond its container. Eventually thought starts again, and the pen moves over the page. Truth and honesty of description demand I begin with gratitude, and my words become an opening line, but from there, no sentence is adequate, for it is the opening itself that we long for, that moment out of time.

"In the beginning was the word," but the awareness before – so magical, eternal, blessed, creative, and at peace – is what we truly crave. Words begin; thinking starts; sentences are passed. We're squeezed into structure, captured by the clock, our creativity brought into line. Duties and distractions clamor and seize our attention; we succumb to an ordinary life, seduced by saccharin forgetfulness.

But somewhere we remember broader horizons. A hidden compass turns toward something greater. It could be the memory of the Garden, a premonition of paradise, or the pull of destiny that determines the direction or destination we seek. Outside of causality, logic, and sequential time, it draws us forward… or back. Modern life may have come a long way from our origins, but distance is merely a measure of quantity. Our notions of progress are strangely and revealingly silent, dumb about matters of direction. Dominated by rationality, we are unaware of the small parcel of perception rationed out to us – "I think, therefore I am."

There are other openings in the wall. Through the windows of sense and imagination, the landscapes are brilliant and alive, calling with responsiveness and rich in swirling synesthesia. There the foundations are fluid, the shores less solid, and our rock of reason sinks like a stone. The ocean is wide, mysterious, and fathomless. It is the origin, the place we come from, the source to which all rivers return. It is tempting, tantalizing, and terrifying. The currents seem challenging, the depths dangerous. Transformation requires death, disintegration, the dissolution of identity. Separateness must be surrendered in order to swim. The old self cannot see the other side.

Once again I stand at the entrance to the Garden. Snake points the way to the apple, ripe with knowledge and polarity. It's powerful and potentially poison, but it might keep the doctor away! Satan and seduction, evil and exile are just as likely as good. But the irrational has never been welcome where reason rules. The empire of the intellect only sees the threat. It draws a line, pulls the blinds. The thinking mind has no measure for what's infinite or eternal.

Another tree stands in the center of the Garden, and its fruit contains the seeds of everlasting life. The flesh is succulent, full of promise, and beyond polarity. Imagination, sense, and feeling draw us forward. Their windows open to this world in wonder. The air is refreshing, the clouds ever-changing. The view is full.

*   *   *

Great Mystery, you are within and all around me.
Boundless, you swirl in breeze, body, man, and manifest breathing.

You are in sun, fire, light, wave, and particle. You are a flame, formless and burning in the heavens and in my cells. My cells and my selves – a thousand, thousand identities combine into one. I would merge again, join the flow, and become a face, a facet, an eye to look upon itself in wonder. For all is wondrous.

Life is but a dream. The boundary of self and other is permeable. I am a dream and the dreaming, a dreamer awakening in life. Time is a river, its shores ever-changing. I am the long body, the movement, the journey through time, forward and back, beginning beyond.

River, rock, current, canyon, and mountain are moving, merging, and mutually defining. My small dream flows into other streams, my definition and distinctive droplet dissolving into deeper, broader being. I am not invested in banks or bed. Both evolve together. All motion is relative. And we are all relatives here.

Language is limited. "Thanks" is not enough, but it is all I can say. You have given me body, eyes, sense, a heart… such a great dream. It's one worth living.

Eternal Life

A chorus of songbirds sings "Yes!" to the dawning day as the horizon lightens over the rolling mirror of a slate-silver sea. I am touched by beauty, and my thoughts become tender to match the soft reflections of sunrise on the shimmering waves.

How do we appear in the looking glass of life? Are we happy? Do we dare to love this earth enough, to let it in so we truly can see it?

This earth... this world... is neither out there, nor within. It is not solid or static. Its features are not objects. Our universe arises from contact with something other than us. Perception is a dance, and our partner is not standing still. And neither are we. As rhythms change one leads, then the other, and there is nothing predetermined or mechanical about it.

Sea, sky, stone, and stream are movements, music; pattern, puzzle, change; in call and response with the senses that touch them. They too are reaching, longing to be seen, loved, or listened to; crying to be caressed and cared for. Their senses are diverse – strange, foreign, fantastic... and sometimes familiar. But beyond all division, boundaries, and borders, we share a common ground: this living earth that spawned and sustains us. All her children are kinfolk, family, related. Have you spoken to your relatives lately?

The words describing existence – "me, you, river, cloud... " – remain ever the same, but the subjects constantly change. We are not skin-encased selves, nor minds occupying some abstract, ephemeral space. We are process and perception, permeable membranes that move with the living earth around and within us. Sunrises inspire us; autumn makes us reflective and melancholy.

The humidity is oppressive; when it's cold, we shiver. Outlooks are sunny or overcast. Moods are meteorological; the weather unpredictable.

Our inner life reflects the outer. Losing contact with earth or water, I feel hunger or thirst. Can this longing be just *my* feeling? The definition and membrane between "self" and "world" changes. Sometimes it grows impenetrable, and senses atrophy from lack of attention. Months go by, and what was formerly important I barely notice. I listen to conversations in my head, emotions mesmerized, caught by the spell of words. The living earth moves from foreground to back, forgotten; the natural and non-human world grows silent. Some stay in this condition for months, years, or even lifetimes. It gets lonely; our worlds grow static, still, and senseless. And mere things cannot fill the dark hole where once there was a tender heart.

It takes a choice or sometimes a crisis to open again. Pain, loss, disease, or recurring dreams can be warnings, callings, omens. They are messengers, reminders that say "Reach out beyond yourself. There is another You greater than anything you have imagined."

Our concepts, categories, and all we know and are certain of are so small and confining. They constitute an island in the ocean, a rowboat on the sea – high, dry, and destitute. Fear grips us. Our hands cling to the tiller of comfort, convention, or control, but another being – beastly or beautiful – longs to be capsized or swept away in the tide.

We are not the mind. A great ocean of air breathes through

our bodies, chest rising and falling on the waves. We are not alone. The salt blood of the sea is encased in our skin. Sunlight enters the eyes, penetrates the flesh, and lightens the heavy heart. We belong here. We are not sinners. Becoming and going, we are being itself, being itself.

Across this shifting and permeable surface, impermanent sensations pass betwixt and between self and world. Actions and interpretations arise; messages move through our membranes.... conflict or communion; open or close; communication or contraction. We see the world the way we are, and the universe is dancing with our reflections.

Communion is a two-way street. You must do your share. A rock is not a rock, for it too is sentient and shifting in tune with rhythms much slower than ours. Stop your normal life and sit with this rock for an hour. You may become bored or frustrated, but the lens of language will gradually fall away as you enter its world, on its terms, its time. Its seemingly-solid surface will reveal itself to be textured, grainy, smooth, faulted, and fractured. Its seemingly harsh exterior may be home to mites, spiders, lichens, and mosses that flourish in miraculous miniature forests.

Continue sitting. Grays, greens, sages, and saffrons may merge in mottled mixings of overlapping layers richer than any impressionist painting. Images pulse and proliferate. Patterns emerge and are reabsorbed like a restless and relentless Rorschach. Sing to it and forget for how long. Become lost, found; disappear in delirious moments; find yourself rolling and rocking – happy and whole in a soft, sweet, slow center of stone.

When attention finally wanders – responding to another

undetermined invocation – leave in gratitude, your steps joyous and light on this sacred ground. The exile from the Garden is our own doing, and it <u>can</u> be undone. The landscape is living and vibrant, awaiting our notice, love, and attention. Remember, you are not alone. Something is reaching to make contact from the other side.

The song of the earth is sung through our senses and woven in strings that tug at our hearts. It is the original language, the living breath, the beating pulse, the great presence that spoke long before the word was made God. It surrounds us, background and foundation underlying all our thinking and separation. It sustains us and supports the roots of the sacred tree. The fruit of eternal life need not be feared, forbidden, or forgotten. Let your eyes be pulled to it like the red, rising sun.

The path home is before us. There lies our true direction, destiny, everything desirable. Take the first step. Foray past your fears; release the words of authority and find your own voice. Savor the succulent flesh and fortify yourself with gratitude, smiling as you walk through the valley of death. And say one word, one word only:

"Yes!"

Human, Nature

The sun rises over the river, its deep, gurgling tones evoking quiet strength and peace amidst great power. Songbirds flutter within the spring-green foliage – thick and brilliant along the water – their calling chatter bouncing back and forth across the bank like some fast-paced game, while swallows cut through the air like feathered darts flung from the hands of gods. A raven squawks and flees downstream, chased by two small, but protective parents.

There is wisdom here, and my tongue fashions a song of praise, a prayer of gratitude. But these words are just one of many voices along the riverbank. Their form is different – spoken through mouth or pen – and they seem more solid when shaped upon the page, captured and stored in sentences that can spring to life in a far-off and unseen future. But they are of this place and time – here and now – grown from sun, soil, and those seeds planted in the heart and watered by the good will and grace of this great river.

There's profound power and a harmony that's healing in nature – this nature, your nature, mine. The forms around us are infinite: flower, cliff-face, cloud.... bear, beetle, cottonwood.... eagle, stone, wind. All these beings are our relations, each with its special medicine and voice. Yet we all come from the same place, and home to it we shall return.

We are of nature – the earth our mother, the sky our father. The source is with and within us, and we carry it always – this sense of sentience, the stamp of oneness beyond the shapes of inner and outer, self and world. It is our essence as we radiate and reflect on every "other." Lightness and humor fill the canyons, valleys, and sky as *Presence* – a free and formless energy that confronts itself again and again in beautiful and brilliant disguise.

A stinkbug marches across the red-clay ground. A hummingbird hovers, intense and motionlessness, surveying the flowering chamisa. Ants scurry, their multitudes almost invisible, yet everywhere on the earth. My heart sings with joy and satisfaction; the pen moves across the page. And I am just one voice – a bird calling in the morning, the ears of my kind far, far away.

The expressions of all these forms are different, and their lifespans vary. Clouds twist themselves together and tear apart constantly. A fruit fly runs its course in a day; a beetle, amoeba, or cell maybe longer. Mammals can survive a century; trees endure millennia; while the life of a river, canyon, or star stretches out toward the infinite. The songs of these friendly, feathered folk quickly fade, while human words can fall silent or be passed down by people and pages through the long corridors of time.

We are human, nature… part of and present to what is here and now, in love with this moment and reaching out to eternity. Ultimately all forms are momentary; all stances of separation are comical. Assuming an ego in its separate world has its consequences. All our questions of you and me, inner and outer, subject and object are temporary and self-fulfilling.

In planting the seeds of isolation, we remove ourselves from the Garden. We reap what we sow, and the Fall brings a lonely harvest. Having divided spirit from flesh, inner from outer, self and psyche from world, we feel insufficient, alone, and lacking. Ill-at-ease and full of doubt, our questions never cease… "Why do I feel this way?" But disconnection drives the inquiry – the results are incomplete for incompleteness is the result. The answers do not

222

come, and those that do, do not satisfy.

At the heart of all our deep questions is the quest – for another course, a new story, a greater dream, a different song. Our home is in the Garden. The way to our true nature is nature.

The sun sparkles on the moving water. The birds continue to sing. My eyes close, and all space is awash in sound. Is this tumult "out there," in the river or throat of the thrush that moves molecules of air, eardrum, and cochlea? Or is the clamor created "in here," – (wherever here is) – among minerals, bones, and blood; in the heart's pumping, the brain's sensing; thoughts, theories, and images... signals transmitted and transformed by nerves, chemicals, electrons, and... then what? Where is the "I" and the "it" in all this?

All is nature: one sound, one sight or many.... co-arising, interdependent.... here and there, everywhere, everything, and nothing. It is me and you, bug, bird, beast, mind, and matter; all cells, signals, movements in the great body of Gaia.

The river streams onward, but the river is in me. It journeys between mountains and ocean and back again. I too am embarking on a journey. I am seeking the Garden. I am walking to the mountains, the forests, or the deserts; toward nature and myself. I have come here searching for vision, the sacred... for God and my deepest truth. I am sincere, scared, small, serious, lonely, and looking-for-something as I enter the wilderness.

But as I soften my eyes, relax, and surrender my self, I may discover that it has already – now and long ago – entered me.

Living Your Dreams

A thought comes; a thought goes. *"It was here just a moment ago, where did I put it?"* The mind searches, wandering, looking for clues: *"I was standing by that bush. What was I doing?" "I was thinking about women. I imagined talking to Jill. What was I saying?"* It is not far away, that thought; it must still be in the area. If we turn aside it will soon disappear, dissolved in the landscape, blown over the horizon, dispersed by the wind.

It is a shadow, a flicker of movement in the corner of the eye. It is here, there, present but not yet visible. In what direction shall I face? Each bearing diverges from all potential others. *"How shall I shine a light into the darkness? Broad beam or narrow?"* Like fog or a smoky vapor, perhaps what I am seeking is all about me.

I want to write about writing about writing. I want to think about thinking, speak about speaking. I want to balance these inner and outer lives, but there is only one life, though I talk as if they are somehow separate.

Consciousness is a stream, fluid, moving to and from some grand ocean. It is one moment torrential, another tepid and meandering.... rapid, cold, clear, still, stagnant. But it is all water, one river through many forms, shifting and transformative. And who am I, the ocean or the drop?

Can I create a new language to step outside the ways I see and think about things? Am I a man who dreams he is a butterfly or a butterfly dreaming.... dreaming.... dreaming?

Life is but a dream.

I went to the desert with its vast open spaces
seeking god and myself in our infinite faces.
Crystalline stars, hot days and cold nights,
without houses and cars, without wrongs without rights.
Under one sky, born of one mother,
where are the walls between self and the other?

For we are the earth, and we are the skies,
and we are the seeing, as much as the eyes.
Monsters and dragons, fairies and elves,
Just transient facets of changeable selves.
Ideas and cognition, knowledge and knowing,
Are but a tide or a current in perceptual flowing.

We are what we win, sometimes what we lose;
We become what we get and are what we choose.
Afraid of deception, afraid of believing,
And it's all our perception and our way of perceiving.

"I think, therefore I am," but if you are do you move?
Your existence in doubt, what else must you prove?
The problem with language and the way that we think
is that it studies all water in a vase or a sink.
Trying to be stable, your thoughts are erratic,
since the picture is process, and you are just static.
With impermanent self and mutable mind,
love is the answer for you are what you find.

In me's an addict, in me a monk,
in me an eagle, a slug, and a skunk.
In me a saint, in me a killer,
the sleek butterfly and a fat caterpillar.
A dark lump of coal, a rare precious gem;
but are they all in me or am I all in them?
I am a raven; life's just a joke.
Can I find my true calling before I croak?

The meaning of life, the meaning of power,
the meaning of meaning, this moment, this hour.
I dreamed I was dreaming. I dreamed I awoke.
I dreamed I was solid and raised up in smoke.

I dreamed I was lost, here and now, so I found,
the sense I was singing, if my memory's sound.

You are the river, you are the drop,
so come join the dancing for it never stops.
There's fun in the flowing, so heed this advice:
If you're solid you're rigid, and cold as ice.
Inside our stories, our stances, our dreams;
there's ecstatic freedom or nightmares and screams.

Life is both sacred and original sin,
and what we let out is what we let in.
We are a dream, a dreamer, a dreaming,
just droplets and currents in consciousness streaming.
We are the water, the boat, and the bank.
And we are all one, so whom should I thank?

The Dance Hall of Maya

Like sand being shoveled and sifted,
The veil is both lowered and lifted.
Illusion is real and reality illusion.
As beliefs drop like fruit in profoundest profusion.
I hold one in my hand and look at them all.
I don't understand, but I do love the fall.

The lake glistens like a mirror, reflecting a thousand dreams. What's above appears below – clouds appear to float upon it – and beneath its smooth skin another world – raw or in repose – supports the still surface of the glassy waters. There, life goes on unseen. Concealed, but conjectured, we sense a hidden landscape of crags, stumps, mud, and murky bottom. Its fluid fields are filled with fish, frog, and polliwog, while rock, cast-off beer cans, and fishing lines mix with algae and brown slime in the feeding grounds of diving fowl.

All is maya, everything illusion. The lake's liquid veneer is a millimeter thick; the world below, real, but only imagined. All is appearance in this looking glass landscape, as islands and trees seemingly grow downward to a gray sky. Appearance yes, but so beautiful. And this feeling of beauty itself.... is it real, unreal, illusion, or truth? If a response to the illusory, how solid is its foundation? Can the world of illusion lead us to truth? Perhaps it can, for I've heard wise ones say the deepest truths are rooted in a profound recognition of an ever more elusive mystery.

Is there any ultimate meaning to experience? Sensations arise, but from what? A finger touches a stone, and we describe it as rough or smooth, flaky, compact, heavy, striated, and a thousand other "things." Philosophers have questioned the reality of the stone for centuries, but what of the finger? I feel it, sense it or through it, but what of "it" or sense itself? Is sense a complex pattern of electrochemical firings in the brain? If so, are we just chasing our tails, since our knowledge of brain and electrochemical firings themselves are a result of observation and sense?

Interpretations are based on interpretations in infinite and varied meetings of self, words, and world, themselves mere interpretations.... We live in a house of cards – fragile and miraculous! – constructed of categories whose foundation sits upon the shifting sands of capricious and inexhaustible perceptions.

All is maya. Ten-thousand forms and faces appear round the risings and fallings at the moving interface of self and other. Boundaries fluctuate; interpretations change. Existence and "reality" are experienced, but arbitrary. The self can expand or contract, and the world moves inversely. Oneness becomes many, and many become one as Maya dances across the universe like smoke, cloud, or thunderclap. She casts her spell, and our senses "make sense" to us.

But others make sense quite differently. A dragonfly has thousands of eyes; dolphins emit sonar and speak in poetry. Birds and butterflies can journey ten-thousand miles to find a feeding place they have never seen. Rattlesnakes sense heat while shellfish know the position of the moon. Bats hunt in the darkness; salmon return to their spawning grounds; swallows to Capistrano. How many species, and what abundance of senses swirl around us? How countless the possibilities of perception – dimensions so different, yet overlapping ours – among the surfeit of secret corridors and rooms in this dance hall of Maya?

Maya, mysterious goddess… She fascinates or fixes us with bottomless, hypnotic eyes. Spellbound by her tricks, frozen by her sinuous movements, she smiles and draws a veil across her face.

The fog descends. The lake disappears in the mist. Clarity eludes me. Logic is lost in the mystery; the weather too complex to predict. The air is invisible, but the mystery is real, and magic – though illusion – is also illumined truth. Confusion reigns. Will the real lake please stand up? A passing shower ceases, and a soft breeze caresses my cheek and the shore.

Maya…. Onward she goes in flashes of quicksilver, always uncontained. Her images dance on the wall of Plato's cave in concealed and revealed truth. Equally at home in heavens or hell, she draws us ever onward through foreground and back. Faster than quarks or quanta, too cagey to be caught by chaos theory, on and on she spins, twirling through synapse and space.

She's teaser, temptress, and teacher;
lover and leaver; window and wall;
she's nowhere and everywhere,
in nothing and all….

The source of our nightmares, our terror and screams.
The lure and the love that makes us follow our dreams.
She's the shadow of night, the light of the days;
She stands for the truth and lies where she lays.

She's virtue and vixen, goddess and whore.
Impure offers and honor, mixed blesser amor.
Never begrudging, whether lavish or stark;
And gods jealous and judging are gospels missing the mark.
Beyond peace or perfection, a miss as good as a mile,
And in every direction is her kiss and a smile.

*   *   *

Rain lets loose from the silver bowl of the sky, a curtain dropping upon the smooth glass of the lake as sprinkles spatter its surface. A thousand converging voices create chattering conversations as a deluge of droplets strike and stroke layer upon layer of leaves under the woodland's green canopy.

This language seems familiar and friendly. Though I do not know a word or recognize a pattern amidst all the pattering, I will join in and add my voice. I can sing out to the forest, dance in the dialogue, and speak out in witness to the wonder of it all. Soon I will be forced to seek shelter instead of meaning, but for now this moment is beautiful and deeply satisfying.

Everything feels right, and it makes sense. And what is meant by that, who am I to say?

The River

Relatives in Motion

The storm has passed. The Colorado River surges past the waterfront, turbulent, mud-filled, and turned brown like coffee with cream. Lapping waves cough up undigested debris from gully and arroyo, depositing sticks all along the bank. Silt settles upon new shores in its halting, but irreversible journey to the sea. The mud slowly dries out and returns to dust.

Life is not constant. It moves in fits and spurts. Weeks of drought preceded the downpours. Gray clouds thickened, dispersed, then gathered again in billowing darkness, releasing their wet cargo to deliver a deluge that cut a soaking swath across vast mesas and canyons. The river continues onward.

Life is not simple or saccharin sweet. It is neither a series of appointments nor an accumulation of steadily-ascending achievements that lead to high plateaus, pinnacles of success, and retirement. It is a collection of choices taken or not; expanding routines, failures, sudden reversals and accelerations. Each day a single grain of sand moves from one side of the scale to the other. Nothing changes – each mass a molecule larger or smaller. Nothing changes. But one day the balance shifts; equilibrium is lost; and nothing seems the same again.

Children are born, and their arrival alters everything. Relationships wither. Marriages dissolve; new ones form. Thunder rumbles on the horizon. Conflicts, long building, break out in storms, floods of feelings released in the torrent. When the waters recede and currents finally calm, the river has found a new bed. A cripple finds faith and throws away his crutches, while illness or accident fells another. The office door, once so familiar, becomes an entrance to a prison. A young girl drops out of school and wanders. A single stone, motionless for a thousand years, is unloosed from the cliff and falls.

The talus slopes of this canyon are a resting place for thousands of these stones, each one once a part of the "solid" cliff above. The craggy faces – seemingly ageless and impassive – are scrubbed by wind, water, and sun. Sand settles, swirls, and scours the walls to a dark polish. Elements erode and dust is deposited, molecule by molecule. One day a small pebble or a prodigious slab will let go, releasing itself into the wispy embrace of the air. Toppling free and plummeting in a furious and fearsome fall, its tumbling will trace a trail to the river, its momentum exhausted in the embrace of muddy waters or spent on the soft red shoulder above. The moment passes and the cliff shows a new face, while erosion begins anew, piece by piece, till molecule becomes mudslide, and flow turns to flood and back again.

Dear River, thank you for this day, this life, and the bittersweet sadness of change. Yin becomes yang. All that has been built up must tumble down; all that has been put together will be pulled apart. A billion birthings and dyings are becoming and breaking down in my body in the time it takes to write this sentence. Nothing stands still. You are not the same river you were moments ago, and I sense a profound and bottomless wisdom beneath those coffee-colored currents.

All motion is relative, and there is no absolute reality, no still point. This ancient canyon slowly evolves as it moves along with the sun, moon, and stars. The river streams on in relation to the bank, the world in relation to the self, and my identity is moving with them. Shifts can be subtle or cataclysmic – some happen more quickly than others. All motion is relative, yet something remains – a background against which we discern these varying faces and forms.

I call it The River. It is the fluid ground of being within the forming and flowing; it's the polarities and the kinships and unions that hold them all together. It is silence and stillness surging, a presence beyond opposition or judgment where all things pass without fail.

All motion is relative and, dear River, you are mine. I feel you as friend, family, and something more. I am at one with you and completely myself, beginning and endless, nothing, everywhere. I am a tourist in time, invested in this bank, standing on the shifting sands of this shore. And you are the liquid of life, ever-slipping from my grasp as I embrace the water on its eternal journey to the sea.

The River's Dream

Our campsite is a wooded bench jutting south into the river. The Chama flows onward, wrapping itself around our temporary home, this plateau of piñon and oak surrounded on three sides by water. On the west and south, the river meanders, placid and lazy, but toward the east it quickens, tumbling hurriedly as it bends and rushes away toward the rising sun.

On baking desert days, it's a pleasure to enter, lie back, and drift in reverie, passing sandbar and red-rock cliffs as clouds roll past mesa-tops thousands of feet above. In moments like these, we can know majesty. Suspended in the water's magical arms, our bodies and souls released from gravity and held buoyant like an eagle soaring through the air, we slip slowly into sweet surrender. Brisk and bold, the cool liquid restores our vigor, and downstream we emerge refreshed, our wilted flowers in bloom again, our listlessness carried away in the cold currents coursing from snowfield to sea.

The river has a thousand faces and as many lovers. Sandbars, stumps, beavers, and boulders lie in her bed. Raccoon, deer, muskrat, and scorpion press their lips to her heaving body. The dusty, dry desert brightens with her passing. Grasses, greasewood, cottonwood, and oak dress in emerald display, happy just to be near her. Towering mesas show their painted cliffs in her honor, two hundred-million years of history hung on canyon walls cut by her current, the bones of the earth laid bare and beautiful to celebrate her presence.

We are touched and surrounded by her creations. Calmed by her lilting lullaby and grateful for her restorative powers, we sit at the shore like acolytes and apprentices in appreciation of some great healer. She is a master shaman, ceaselessly shape-shifting. Constantly journeying through creek beds and canyons, she can rage or ramble in traversing the countryside from highlands to harbor. Golden in the morning, ghostlike and surreal in darkness, she mirrors the moon in shimmering silver.

Her movements and magnetism tug at my solid self, and I sense something phantom and formless slip from my being to travel downstream past red rock and mud. Continuously changing, her waters snake, twist, and turn, drawing me away into speechless depths. Dancing in a dream-like delight, informed and dissolved in a fluid landscape, mere words are inadequate. Like the self I know, they stop at the shore, reaching out to grasp what cannot be captured in an irresistible frolic with folly. Intent on the intangible, what I seek forever slips through my fingers like liquid, and my hands hold nothing but the memory of a delightful and cleansing coolness.

A greater dream beckons. The tug is compelling, frightening, incessant. I must leave everything I know behind. Beyond the banks, beyond reason and "reality," the river keeps flowing.

And there, with her and the grace of God, go I.

Gently Down the Stream

I sit close by the river, and tranquil waters wander through the cold valley dawning. It sings in stereo – rolling around rocks on my right, dancing till it drops downstream over logs to the left – as it skips and slides onward in its gentle journey toward the sea. It is a soothing presence, but like a shaman's rattle or the siren's call, it tugs at the edge of my awareness. It courts and captivates me, tempts me to enter its flowing, whispering "Come. Come. Release yourself. Let go and return home for a moment."

Ebb tides are moving out under the surface of the ocean; currents undercut the bank of my rational mind. My dreams drift away from the shoreline, swimming seaward with the salmon, while bones, blood, body and brain – seemingly solid and stable – stay here on the sand.

Reason rebels. It stays in the shoals, drawn to but dreading its dissolution. It admires the surface, revels in rippling patterns, clings to empty chatter while shunning a soulful descent. It cherishes comfort, distance, and objective discourse, refusing a more passionate plunge. Numbed by the narcotic of social conversation, it turns toward its own reflections – forgoing what's raw or real – and, like Narcissus, stays on the shore and starves.

But the sounds of streams and splashes of surf send their summons to the fluid-filled flesh. Ancient appetites reappear, the thirst for union washing over me with waves of longing. A caress, a challenge, a call laps against my inner ear.

"Come, come… come back. Return to the land of water. Give yourself to gravity; flow down from the mountain; sing out to the seven seas"

236

Great Mother Ocean is origin and first cause, a womb without words for eons before tongues and the telling of tales clad our amphibious flesh with the dry skin of history. She is still here, mermaid or monster, a heaving bathtub of blood beneath the flat boardwalks of the brain. She is surge and swell, calm, or frothing with foam, eating away at the proud pilings of our abstract identity, ever ready to shatter our saccharin musings with a splash of cold salt.

She is here, now, ever-inviting us to swim, float, fill ourselves with the fathomless, to drink or drown in holy hunger. Untied from the mast, slowly I settle, sink... surrender, submerging in a swirling sweep of strange shapes and unexplored depths. Leaving behind the lackluster moorings of logic and drifting dry-docks of deduction, reason's rope unravels as I slip away from shore. Carried by uncharted currents that spawn new streams of consciousness, fresh dreams are born as slumbering senses awaken in her yawning abyss.

And I can't go back to sleep.

Solutions

Dear River,

Thank you for this day. I sit by your bank, your long body disappearing in the distance. Pulsing and powerful, you are a vein that leads to the heart of the world. My complex identity is a mere story, an island around which you relentlessly run as you build up, then erode my existence. Fluid and fertile, you are far greater than I.

There is so much I want to see, but my vision has been a servant of the mind, and reason and rationality have too long sat at the head of the table. Comparison, judgment, measure, and meaning seem so small when facing the miracle of the world. Other mouths wish to be fed. Sense, emotion, and imagination open different windows, portals and passageways that lead to exotic lands beyond that room called "me." And it's there that I must travel!

The sun rises and radiance showers upon me like warm rain. My pores open like sparkles on the water; a cool breeze massages my flesh. I want to close my eyes and relax under this languid caress. I am skin… sensuous, prickly, ticklish, and alive… and breath, the hair on belly and body swaying like branches in the wind. I am touch, touching, and touched, a million interactions along an interface that forms a foundation whose upper stories are called "I."

Earth, how I want you! There are vast landscapes I want to explore and think about, but thought falls short. I have wandered far away, living in my head while soaring in solitude through a spacious and impersonal sky. But I am skeleton, bone, and muscle, hungry once again to devour your sunlight and swallow your fir-scented air. Touch me! Welcome me into your arms as I embrace your moss-coated hummocks, rivers, and lakes. Reach into me and pluck this loneliness from my heart.

Life is an endless return, and slowly I am coming back. Daylight dances across the river, its particle-wave dazzle splitting liquid – molecule by molecule – into vapors gathered by wind and delivered to a distant atmosphere. Rising invisibly heavenward, their warmth slowly dissipates, condensing with cold into drifting clouds and droplets – separate and individual – that fall to earth to once again begin the long journey back to their source.

All life began in the ocean. The sea birthed the first animal onto some sharp and stony shore, its smooth, tender skin turning hard, supple, and scaly. Eyes became focused, ears stereophonic. Vision, hearing, smell, and taste were housed in the head. But all skin surrounds a wet interior, and water is the ground of being on which we build "I think, therefore I am."

Mother Ocean, born of your body, I am bags of fluid surrounded by flesh. Rock me in your cradle of waves... all gravity released, all wanting forgotten. Drown me in deep currents of delight. I thirst for water, a second baptism, a sacred immersion in the immediacy of your silky sensuousness. Draw me to your whirlpools. Sweep me from my shallow sciences into fathomless, dreaming depth.

Liquid Lover, take me back... forward and back. Toss and tumble me in the rolling rhythm of your thick-textured tongue. Lick me like mother wolf; wash me with lapping waves; cleanse all sin, separation, and cynicism from ego and psyche. Take me in your warm wet mouth and swallow me. Let me slip through your luscious labia to reenter the womb of life.

I will swim in the source, the river of shape-shifting sensation, that fluid flesh that surrounds and supports each individual island. Scrubbed of self and bathed in beauty, rinse me of identity until I am nothing but wind, blood, and water... wave, pulse... perception.

I am a solid still held in solution, sensations without separation, feelings before form. I am snakes spun round the staff, melody uncontained by measure, a verb dancing about each immovable noun. I'm particle, light, pattern and play, energy and movement that does not matter. Relative, I am yours.

Spark of truth, devotion;
void and stillness, always in motion.
Turning tide, source and flame,
I'm every one without a name.

Help me to surrender, to soften, to release my hard-won knowledge and remember a form more sensate and sinuous. Your lapping tongue speaks a wisdom beyond words, and you run on more beautifully than any sentence I could speak. Complacent in the sickness of solitude, dissolve my defenses and all need for definitions. Draw me out of myself; sink me like a stone, for I must enter you to touch the truth of my origins.

Carry me far away and, in so doing, take me home. Drink me in – as I do you – and I will be your voice, crying out with newborn joy. And I will sing your praise where your mouth empties into the primal sea.

Dreaming on the Dark Sea

Spirit of the Canyons,

The moon moves in and out of shadows, mysterious and ghostly; almost full, yet hidden. Night hawks scream and sweep the darkening skies, their sudden dives for bugs booming like freight trains passing by. Swarms of insects converge and cluster in the juniper and piñon pines; a low humming seems to come from everywhere. The clouds slowly thin, and the night holds the possibility of starlight and sleeping under an open sky. The gray blankets gradually lift, and the earth lies wet, receptive, and fruitful; opened to the inscrutable influence of the moon and the fecund and fertile fluid of the Milky Way.

A cricket casts its lonely call to the dark, while the voices of birds grow silent in the twilight. The moon appears again as the clouds briefly part, her black skirts swirling in sharp contrast to a radiant blouse. She's a sorcerer in silver, a shape-shifter, a maiden who hides and reveals her face. She's a mother, full and fruitful; the crone whose crescent hand first holds the newborn; a grandmother who watches over the night. She powers the surging tides, calls forth lovers and the howling of wolves. Her face has moved the pens of poets, guided ships and armies, fixed the time of harvests, and filled police blotters with strange stories and statistics.

There is magic in the night sky, a deep call to dreaming that moves us beyond all logic. Let yourself be moved! The intellect is but one island in a strange and surging ocean. Other worlds are calling us. Just launch your boat upon the water. Enter the sacred river!

This sea is rich, eternal, our first home, a swaying cradle of drifting dreams that sustained us long before we became ourselves. Tugged by the tides, lulled by her lullabies, and spellbound by moonlight, we once rocked in her surge and swell as foam, froth, and gold-a-glittering swirled on the surface. The spray of surf and strange sensings strike against stones on the solid shore of reason, with a threat, and promise, that we might lose ourselves again.

All appears different when adrift in her watery arms. Moved toward a horizon deep with possibility; riding hidden currents with the stars above to guide us; reason's rocks become our enemy, a jagged edge to tear our craft, to shear, shatter, or sink us.

There are secrets and sanctuary in the moonlit waters. Boundaries dissolve with no solid shore to cling to. All becomes fluid, all problems forgotten as we set out upon a sea that shimmers with unknown solutions. Land appears and is swallowed as the waves rise and fall. The fortress of the intellect is neither the tallest pinnacle nor the only vantage point. Even today's highest mountains were once shifting sands on the bottom of the ocean, time and great forces having thrust them heavenward. Other circles of power, purpose, and perception are at play in the world, and each has a window, a bridge, or a doorway… a threshold that can be crossed.

Step through. Climb down from your turreted tower; move out beyond the castle wall! The bridge is down; the mote removed; true sight restored in the blink of an eye as midnight's silver beams strike the optic nerve. Step through the looking glass and entertain some different reflections. Sail out upon the seven seas, howl like a wolf, and walk upon the water!

The moon pours forth a golden path across a liquid

landscape. The die is cast like light upon the oceans. A more rapturous reality streams, swirls, and splashes, its deluge of delight drowning all our prosaic prisons. Floating freely with neither rhyme nor reason, self or story, we shall swim in a radiant river without boundaries or banks, until finally, our passage becomes poetry. Stare at her sparkling face and dare to dream till you are swept through that hole in the sky to a luminous world beyond.

Water Colors

Dear Morning,

Thick fog saturates the air, and the trees appear to stand underwater. But the riverbed is dry – save for a few pools in low-lying hollows whose still surfaces tremble, tickled by the touch of skittish insects. The atmosphere is heavy. Silence hangs like a wet garment; sun and wind are nowhere about. The forest waits in enigmatic and timeless tension.

The eyes and mind want clarity. Logic would separate the world into yes and no, up and down, black and white, but today gray is everywhere. It spreads across the sky and seeps into space; coats log and stone with dew-like dampness. Its wet breath enters the body and pulses in the blood. Clothes feel burdensome, clammy, confining. They cling to the skin. Thinking slows down as sight stares into space with little or nothing to focus on.

Stray thoughts and wishes for "good" weather dissolve in the mist; plans for the future fade away into the thick-textured moment. Reason recoils from the touch of a tactile world, and the caress of cool air makes hair stand on end. A salamander strides up from the streambed and sits on a stone, the wet atmosphere welcoming to its soft and lustrous skin. Life is but a dream, and we find ourselves back in a primeval garden. Immersed in earth and water, embedded in a rich humus of being, we reach out to the world with different senses. Like roots searching for secret springs in clotted and stony soil, we stretch our tendrils toward some hidden sweetness in the damp and dreary daylight.

Sharp lines soften like watercolors; fern, moss, and stone seem to slide into one another. Forms formerly separate bleed together in moist mergings, a movement within a larger symphony. Horizons and boundaries are hazy. Introspection moves outward; the riverbank starts to shift.

Sharp distinctions dwindle as the sense of sight shrinks. The moisture teases us onward, tempting us to open a door and bridge the membrane between inner and outer. Images and impressions swirl within the psyche; borders blur in the mist.

A question or a calling hangs in the air. What longs to come to the surface or cross over? Inside the body, a salt ocean of blood harbors strange and emergent life-forms in its swaying and shifting womb as it pounds a sturdy rhythm like waves upon the shore. The separate self struggles to keep its head above water.

Life is a river, life is a dream.
Let go of anchors to drift down the stream.
A call from the left side, "Be fluid and merge!"
And fear on the right resisting the urge.

Each breath is a living, each breath is a dying;
constantly giving without even trying.
Chest rising and falling like waves on the sea,
as inner meets outer in world making me.

The senses not separate, and new senses are found,
like musical notes of sights that are sound.
Stirred in the cauldron, nothing stays pure,
as the dream mixes potions that can kill or can cure.

Foreground meets back, like stream meeting shore,
god found at the edge of mine being your.
Solid as wood, or fluid as fire,
everything's good in the dream dance of maya.

Twistings and turnings, prance 'cross the screen
in the flirtings and yearnings between seer and seen.
Certainty's guess, appearance is show;
and we must ever say 'yes' to what we don't know.

Music and magic, mystery mined,
the endings so tragic, the birthings divine.
Caterpillar cocoons, and its whole life soon shatters;
but when beauty emerges, the hurt hardly matters.

From Sea to Shining

Light grows along the rim of the ocean. The wind is quiet, and the voice of mystery rushes forth, a river of sound and silence, containing all. It speaks in lilting and lapping waves as dogs bark in the distance. Tropical birds chatter softly in the palms. Somewhere a motor starts up inland as great cranes load their cargo onto barges bound for Cozumel.

The sun lifts off from the horizon and rises slowly out of the mirrored sea. The one flaming disc appears as two, then one again; illumination and illusion reflected in its gradual, imperceptible movement. What is moving and what is still when all motion is relative and we are all related?

Shorebirds cross the beach searching for food, their tiny legs a blur. Crabs emerge from the sand, scuttle away in a tumble of limbs, then bolt back to their burrows. Seagulls pick through curving lines of driftwood and debris left by the retreating tide. A lone heron cautiously stalks the waterfront to the south as pelicans drift by overhead. Dolphins leap, carving graceful and glittering arcs through the air. A ferry slowly emerges out of the horizon, while jet planes leave cloud trails through the sky.

To the south, the coast fades away into the faint distance. A hazy line separates the twin sisters of Mother Earth and Ocean, one our blood, the other our bones. People comb the beach, wandering that borderline betwixt and between. Coated with sand and splashes of salt, their attention explores distant landscapes as shells rattle in their pockets.

Long jetties reach out to the sea, their fingers of stone softening the waves. In the sheltered and quiet places, earth's human children cautiously enter the water; testing the tide with tentative steps, while its tug insistently draws them from shore.

Rocks, slippery with seaweed and sharp with barnacle, call out to us. Drifting lazily on the surface propelled by soft rubber flippers, luminous fish float by our masks. Deep currents wash over our bodies as human concerns are carried far away. One spell lifts while another casts its sensuous net, engaging us in dimensions more dreamlike than distinct. Drawn back and forth, out and in, we waver between fear and fascination.

The moon moves as if within us; our moods responding like the tide to her changing faces. Perception crosses a permeable membrane; perspective becomes fluid and impermanent, the self neither static nor solid. Bodies waver between above and below, separate and one, all borders dissolving. We search for direction, meaning, answers.

Tensions expand and diminish; shapes shift. Born from the sea and buried in the ground, delivered and dying in the embrace of two great mothers, we stretch between matter and spirit, great peace and polarity. Storms and sunshine merge at the end of a rainbow. Lines form themselves into circles, opposite poles are no longer far apart. All forms are fluid. Wood erupts into flame and crumbles into coals. The smoke brings tears to our eyes. Ashes to ashes, dust to dust, death and decay... Daily we're created, consumed; birthed, broken, and scattered over sand, shore, and sea... our vision swimming.

Clouds of fireflies dance with the stars overhead, momentarily merging their brief, but brilliant torches with those that guide us through endless nights in the hourglass of eternity. Time is ever now, a river without banks. Past, present, and future undulate like waves, and we bob on the surface of this great ocean. Dolphins leap and pelicans dive, hunting for crayfish or quanta, hungry for fish and fleeting glimpses of another world.

Showers of sunlight rain down on the sea; fields of energy sparkle in silver. Rocking in her gentle swells, renewed and rebirthed by the rhythm of her heartbeat, we are buoyant in amniotic fluid. Old appetites die as new ones awaken, craving the smell of salt and the taste of infinity.

Dreaming and the Dream

Do Whatever You Quanta

Cold winds sweep down the canyon. High clouds drift in from the west; cirrus curtains that wave in the breeze. A crescent moon, half hidden, winks in and out.

Smoke drifts by from a fire downstream. The river flows steadily onward, sinuous and serpentine, snaking its way to the sea. A few birds rush past in search of a late meal before settling in nests for the night. Across the water, a cliff juts into the river, a horizontal cleft across its face conjuring impressions of a hungry mouth in the head of some great eel.

Sense makes image; image makes sense. Faces of stone, faces in clouds, faces embedded in gnarled bark.... the voices of robin, river, and wind... a taste of sunshine, the fragrance of ponderosa, cedar, and smoke. Textures tease and touch, as ten thousand threads are spun into a tantalizing tapestry of life.

The dragon moves, the sleeper awakes. Call it God, Nature, Great Mystery, Dreamer... Something stirs beneath the visible world. Near at hand, below the surface, over the horizon, just beyond our grasp... it is inaccessible to the rational mind.

Academic prose and scholarly research split hairs while cyclotrons are splitting particles. Fragments of the unknown become known, but the skyline recedes indefinitely. There is no final say. Descartes and Newton grow silent like unwound clocks, their lonely universe ending in entropy, nary a tick for their talk.

The gods are grinning. The mechanical dream – our magnificent and futile folly – is over. The literate mind reaches out and runs around in circles as the thrust of knowledge carries us toward the new territories of tomorrow. There, space has become pregnant and sexual, with curves, black holes, and big bangs. Emptiness is fertile; linear time is sterile. Tomorrow never comes.

The new science now speaks with shamans. Physics whispers to metaphysics, muses about meaning, and, by god, what's a meta for? Chaos chases order across morphic fields. Poetry rhymes without reason and winks with a wave and a smile. Logos and Eros discuss wedding plans; eternity has a blind date with time.

Being melts into nothingness; matter fills with spirit, but all that's immaterial. The universe is a song; everything is relative. Everything coexists, is one, is possible. And the time is now.

We know through the senses, through feeling and thought.
We know what we're knowing, whether we know how or not.
The insight of science, the wisdom of dreams;
the fabric of space-time, unraveling seams.
The eyes of the daytime are not the same as the night.
The unknown is left when what's known is proved right.
Breathe into the present, slow down and just saunter.
For the moment's eternal and you can do what you quanta.

Flights of the Imagination

A boulder juts out of the leaves, its stark silhouette chiseled in charcoal and gray. Lichen spreads over its surface, softening an excess of earthy energy grounded in granite. From this angle, its features look like the head of a hawk, its sharp beak and hollowed eye pointing south over the lake, as if some immense, ancient bird of stone wished to rise up from the land and ascend to the heavens. There it waits, ready to burst from the ground in an upheaval that would snap roots and rip grasses and mosses asunder. Shuddering free of soil, shock-waves would shatter the silence, the woodland trembling in terror as trees were overturned and tossed left and right in twist and tangle. Shaking leaves and clumps of dark loam from its stony wings, the forest would flatten under those first flapping beats, until the beast slowly rose to darken the sky with its monstrous and magnificent form.

But this morning nothing takes flight other than my imagination and the insects and woodland birds darting along the shore. Nevertheless, there is a magic, a wonder, a truth to the imagination that is not found in the long-house of logic or the stark halls of science. The soil we tread on is not a discarded clutter of dull and uninteresting "dirt," but a forgotten storehouse of mystery and memory… So too the water, the wind, and the sun.

This earth is truly home, and it can also be heaven if we only open our hearts. Awakened from unconsciousness with unobstructed eyes, we could walk in worlds of wonder and step on sacred, hallowed ground. Perhaps we would hear music – the melodies of the earth – and remember ourselves in the songlines of our ancient and aboriginal past. Our passage might become a pilgrimage, our strides a dance, the journey a joy in living lives of love suffused with spirit, our strident voices turning to harmony.

If this were so, slumbering giants would awaken and take an interest in us again. This is the Promised Land. The landscape is alive with the footprints of gods and goddesses. Our birthplace and home is the playground of Gaia. Our anger can be assuaged, our sins swept away, for we are not in exile or alone. Terror can be transformed and freedom found – along with ourselves – in the wonder of terra firma. Then we shall find ourselves on solid footing, and granite no longer will be taken for granted.

Imagination is a faculty of the heart as well as the mind, and every bit as important as vision to the life of the spirit. There is nothing noble or romantic in being blind or allowing an attribute to atrophy. Why dismiss it as dreamy and irrelevant when it can move us from the mundane to the miraculous, the pedestrian to the profound?

One day this great stone bird will fly. It is no more foolish or fanciful than the ocean's floor rising heavenward to the tops of the Himalayas – which we accept as geologic fact. Her ascent may be slower than I imagined, but she has the time. Her movements are measured in multitudes of millennia. Her magic emerges in expanses of eons, that billion-yeared backdrop to the short-term sitcom of history.

Can controlled experiments and reductionist rationality come close to grasping all this? Hardly. Having only recently realized that we live in an environment, unable to fathom in what manner we lift a finger, develop cancer, or how to stop killing ourselves, it's time to admit how little we have named or know. It is folly and outright foolishness to close the doorways to dream and lock the gateways to greater and grander worlds.

There is much to gain and so little to lose. Our comfort zones are littered with the wrappers and residue of limited and hollow happiness. Beyond our framed pictures and still lives, there is motion and mystery. Countless cycles, both immense and infinitesimal, move within and upon each other, to be slowed or quickened by imagination. Vibrations, rhythms, pulsing streams of light can be surfed or swum in ecstasy; infinite strands of the web can be plucked and played to create choice music. This morning, while sitting on this shore, a thousand small lives will wink out and die. Robin and raven feed their young, while India slowly smashes into Asia, raising ranges of rock into the towering temples of Tibet.

Prehistoric monsters inhabit black depths of the seas where mountains higher than any we know lie submerged and silent below the surface. A dragonfly sits in the sun and stalks its prey through multifaceted eyes that fracture and focus light in bands beyond our recognition. The seemingly solid earth floats on an ocean of molten metal whose moving magma creates magnetic poles, chaos or calamity, and new islands in the Pacific. Overhead, hawks trace soaring circles below clouds splitting sunlight into rainbows.

The gods are powerful, present, active; and they are alive. It is we who have been slumbering. Neither earth nor deity is dead. They stretch out before and around us like sleeping beauties, awaiting our kiss or song, a signal of our awakening. We must cast off the curse, shake off the stupor, and pass through the doorway of imagination to turn our hell into heaven, our nightmare into dream.

The wind rushes across the lake. A nuclear fire rages on in

the heavens, and sun rains down from the sky. Particles become waves and light dances upon the waters. An afternoon, a season, a century passes. The great stone bird smiles and bides this time betwixt burial and birth. I have slipped into reverie, taken flight with imagination, ridden on her shoulders and savored her soaring. She has gazed into eternity, seen millennia past, and carried me to new dimensions.

We were made in the Creator's image, and we are both dreamer and dream. The path to the imagination is the entrance to the Garden, and it's the gateway to the god within us.

Dream of the Dark

Dear River,

A cool breeze caresses the boughs of a cedar, swaying and moaning from this welcome massage. The sun retreats over the ridgeline, and stars appear like an advancing army, slowly taking up positions across the night sky. Crickets and cicadas call across the distance; night hawks boom in their blurring dives for bugs. A pair of flickers return to their fledglings in a hollowed-out oak, resting from a never-ending search for food. The hands of dusk settle slowly, passing over the drowsy eyelids of a desert drifting off to sleep.

But others awaken during the night. Mice and rodents scratch for seeds and scurry across the soil, safe from the teeth and talons of snake and hawk. Coyote crosses the sage flats, slipping in and out of shadows, stopping to listen and sniff the air, trotting onward in a slow dance with hunger. An owl hoots in the distance, ready for the hunt. For those who seek coolness, or shadow, or stealth, the day begins at dark.

In time, the moon rises over the mesa, a few days past full. The canyon fills with ghostly silver. Heavenly candles flicker and are slowly snuffed out as battalions of stars beat a hasty retreat and slip under cover. The boundaries of known and unknown are blurred in shades of gray, cobalt, and charcoal. Shifting shapes and shadows tempt and trick the eyes. Mystery reveals itself as certainty is stripped away, shrouded gods dancing beyond the borders of the clearing, beckoning us to enter their world. Projecting our demons into the darkness, most will retreat to their houses and huts, tents or tenements, and surrender themselves to soft beds and the comforting oblivion of sleep.

The clouds stream across the sky like primal herds, their trails of dust veiling the face of the moon. An ancient part of us longs to awaken and join the hunt, to leave boundaries, body, and beliefs behind within our withdrawn and wary shelters. A warrior, tracker, and hunter slips quietly away from the slumbering form and merges into the mystery, stalking prey and power in the shape-shifting landscape of sightlessness. Unafraid of who he is and what he might find, another form of seeing emerges, tracking things which cannot be spoken about, seeking a knowledge which cannot be caught.

Something snorts in the shadows, and a great steed – nostrils flaring and black as a raven – stares at him across a clearing. With no desire to break or tame it, he turns, reaching out with his own wildness, forming bonds of unbridled affection. Fierce in his fearless love, he mounts this night mare, flying through the air and embracing the wind in a wild race across the dark sky.

Ahead, clouds separate and mill together like great hordes in the moonlight. The drum of the heart beats a dance of danger and desire. All future is formless, all outcomes unknown and uncertain. Abandoned to the pull of his passion, the rider gallops onward drawn by the magnet of destiny. Shapes swirl and solidity shifts like luminous soot drifting around the black hole of eternity.

The clouds wrap around and dissolve him. The self drifts apart as everything comes together in streaks of streaming silver. Light collides and refracts in kaleidoscopic display, free and unfettered in its reflections and prisms. The heart grows wings and breaks free of the chest, at play in a greater and endless pulsing.

Hurled headlong into the rich void of his vision, the hunter suffers the joy of what he seeks. Armed with only intention, his bow bends, but does not break. Strung with gut and sinew, the twisted cord sings in release. Searching for the invisible and at peace with the infinite folly of his task, he sends his prey a prayer and lets go. In this, his aim is pure.

The hunt is soon over. The arrow flies to the quivering heart. Burst open, it falls in love. Killer and Cupid both, the prey becomes us. We are what we seek. Tears and blood flow like soft rain in the night.

A crimson sun rises in the mourning.

Ascending to Heaven

Dear River,

Today we strap on boots and packs, leave this canyon, and head toward the mountains. Ascending to heaven, we'll labor up steep trails to where sparkling streams have their source, tumbling and laughing like children. There the vegetation thickens, and the sparse grasses, juniper, and piñon of the lowlands give way to ponderosa pines, aspen, spruce, and fir. Meadows, thick and luxuriant, wave in the wind, and wildflowers offer their bright faces to the sun. Onward we'll climb, ever higher, to where the winds gust and trees grow smaller again – stunted, skewed, and thinning out – leaving only mosses and lichens, themselves giving way to rock.

We are called to seek out that zone where earth reaches toward the sky. The mountains have long been seen as a sacred place, a home to spirit, a metaphor for the upward flight. But in gazing heavenward we sometimes miss what is at our feet. We ignore the roots, become blind to gods that dwell in the depths, and do not conceive the spiritual path as a journey to center.

Vast power surges beneath the earth's crust in movements of magma and molten metal. There – melting and molding matter – Vulcan labors, his volcanic forge also home to strange alchemies that test, transform, and temper men's souls. Those surging fires shape continents, shift great floating plates of earth, and erupt into new landforms. Solid steel dissolves, and rocks melt into rivers whose swirling currents fabricate force fields into magnetic poles.

Out in the sea's fathomless depths, strange shapes slither through the darkness, forms so fantastic, alien, and other as to shake our assumptions about life, intelligence, or purpose. They seem mindless, somehow monstrous, and we shudder at where we have come from; or perhaps wonder where we are going.

History is a story spread across a rich, thickly-textured landscape of space-time. We tell our tales, fashion maps of metaphor, and images of evolution or progress direct our attention upward. The sky beckons us in our longing for liberation. Perhaps this is natural for our species of surface-dwellers: The earth seems dark, confining, a place for burial. The sea is fluid, mysterious, ungraspable. There we are out of our league, our thoughts fear drowning when faced with its depths. A choice was made eons ago when we were cast up on the shore, gasping for breath. We resist the tug of those tides and refuse to go back like the whales and dolphins did. Chained to the ground by gravity, we imagine being free like a bird, unaware of any constraining threads that might be woven through the invisible cloth of the air.

We turn our eyes to the heavens. Perhaps it is as simple as this – trained and overdeveloped in our visual sense, there is no other way we can go. Sight is distorted in the water, useless below the ground, and dependent on the sun. If we want to "see" where we're headed, we have only one direction to turn. There are many other doorways that can take one to spirit, but most we pass by, unconscious of even their presence. The orientation of our vision is preordained, and our path follows the sense that makes sense for us.

The mountains call to us with a strong, clear voice. They are ancient, beautiful, a place of power and home to the gods. Vision is grand, palpable; insight comes easy. The earth reaches heavenward; cold winds blow; clouds wrap around the summits. Thunder and lightning crash along the crags and crests. Snow, hail, and sleet are common, even in summertime. The ridges collect rain and are the source of great rivers. Immense vistas reveal themselves through parting mists, and ordinary human concerns become small or irrelevant. As we scurry like fleas through their forested slopes, our self-importance shrinks, an opening where spirit can find a place to enter.

I will offer myself to this grander vision, let spirit enter me and plant its seeds within my field of dreams.

Like many, I am a novice, uninitiated in the art of dreaming, whose treasures and transformative power threaten the realities of the rational mind. We've been well schooled – steered away from its forbidden fruits, offered the bruised apple of Isaac Newton, and told to figure the cost per pound. Dreams are dismissed, their buoyant magic ignored, and gravity pulls us down.

Our waking consciousness steers us down a straight and narrow corridor. Old and oft-repeated prohibitions, punishments, and programming create the walls that shrink our horizons and waste our potential. The possibilities shrivel: "Pay attention to what's in front of you. Come back to reality. Stay in line… keep off the grass!" A doorway closes, and the numinous visions of the night are put to rest.

But in that world of dreams, the surroundings continually shift. When the dreamer steps through that shimmering doorway, he sheds the constant and unified self. Flesh and form become fluid, vaporous, composed of cloud, capable of flight or passing through whatever was thought to be solid.

I shall enter this different body that can be at ease under

water, span interstellar space, or admire the inner architecture of a diamond. I will remain cool and curious within the raging furnace, blaze a trail beyond the horizon of eternity, and be a familiar stranger in landscapes no stranger than myself. I will expand, shrink, dissolve and reform; discover secret passages; and learn other ways to climb a mountain, or how to become one.

In this waking dream, the slope is steep, and I must wear my heavy boots. But reality is growing soft and melting – mingling with reverence and merging with reverie as the mountains grow within me, lifting me upward. It seems fanciful, crazy, or capricious, but when I reach the lofty summit, I will leave my pack on the highest pinnacle and keep on walking. Below me a body will sit, panting for breath, while something unseen takes flight and ascends, to blissfully soar through the spirit and sky.

The Morning After; The Night Before

Sunlight oozes down the hill across the valley. Water tumbles over rocks in the river, sounding like wind in trees. The grass is damp, the morning cold. Fingers are stiff as they reach for coffee and pen under gnarled oaks, ancient and craggy. Stoic, silent, and suffused with wisdom, they watch over the fields as a few jays screech and pierce the morning quiet.

Last night candles burned in the clearing, casting their light over wood and stone around an old fire pit that stood like a navel in the earth. A breeze rolled through the canyon, bending the single flames to the north. Footsteps shuffled around the circle as a host of stars gleaming overhead. A rattle shook, sending its call into the blackness.

Words came hard at first, the voice uncertain. The rattle wavered, almost hesitant, wary of shattering the silence and disturbing the dream of darkness. But the rhythms slowly grew, like trickles turning into streams, and waves of movement spread through the shaman's weathered body like swells upon a vast ocean. The sluggish pace increased and doorways opened – invisible thresholds crossed by legs that bore a dancer growing younger as his feet stood upon the living earth.

His roots reached deep into the wellspring of the sacred. A song of gratitude poured from his lips:

"Hey ya hey, yah hey a hay.... hey ya hey, ya hey ya hay.... Thank you, spirits, for this beautiful place, this wonderful dwelling. We're blessed by one more night to breathe in this living air; to see, hear... to sense your presence above, below, and around us; by one more chance to find you within, and to find ourselves in you."

His songs of supplication rose to the velvet of night's vaulted roof, twinkling with sparkling crystal. His footsteps slid and shuffled in a slow turning around the navel of the earth. Thankfulness flowed like healing water to all those around him: the marvelous trees – ponderosa, oak, juniper, and piñon... the grasses and flowers... the stones and mountains... the wind and space itself... the animals, silent and listening. Their spirits danced alongside, their attention meeting and matching his.

The land came closer, shaking off slumber in tune with the rattle. The ears of eternity listened, attuned to the timeless. A quickening – something invisible, active, and alert – filled the gaps and arced across openings in the evening air. The great presence smiled.

Great Mystery, you are so great, and we are so small. Help our people to awaken to the living wonder around them. The streets in our cities carve a narrow path, leading nowhere. The words on the radio speak of nothing. May we lift our eyes unto the hills that surround our meager creations. May we hear songs in the silence, whispers in the wind. Let our hearts speak, our bodies stir. Though our fumbling words fall to earth like hollow husks, allow our spirits to flourish. May we remember our home, find our indigenous soul. May the animal arise again, natural and free, to roam and prowl outside the small perimeter of our civilized mind.

The rattling increases. Prayers fall like soft rain. The candles flicker as ancient gods arrive like dormant thunder. We are pilgrims standing vigil on the hilltops, attentive and awaiting a miracle. And our watchful eyes open wider as something dawns in the dark.

Love

The spirit of love called to me as I sat on a graveled shore
by the Gila River. Thoughts are easily placed on paper, but how can
I begin to talk about love? It is so sweet, simple, and universal; so
stormy, complex, and complicated. Love is a witch, a sprite, a siren,
a sorcerer. She's a gypsy goddess who dances among streams and
wildflowers far beyond the level lawns on the grounds of reason.
How can I think in some isolated ivory tower and draw conclusions
about that which desires to draw the utmost out of me?

Goddess, I feel you all around me. Why have you come,
capturing my mind and this moment, my letters and sentences all
scrambled up in the spell you cast? Show me where to find you and
how to listen to what you have to say.

Your presence is a seductive smile, a hidden beauty that
surrounds me. Since all things are interrelated, I must assume
aspects of this very instant are imbued with love, that your features
are concealed and might be revealed in the landscape before me if I
only observe it well enough...

Across the sunlit streaming water, dead stalks strung with
spider webs shimmer like instruments played by the wind. If I were
to contemplate them – the old; the decaying, dead, and dying.... the
seasons gone past as seedpods of summer cast themselves toward
unknown and future springs – there would certainly be lessons to be
learned about love.

Frail, separate, and standing like skeletons, they are
wrapped in flimsy, but glittering garments. Slender strands of
webbing weave them together as seemingly disparate things are
joined by craft and artistry. These strings – tied to their moorings or

shredded by storms – trail in the breeze, their threads thin, transparent, tough, and tenacious. Like the ties to all we care about, these connecting cords reflect the light and the need for renewal and repair as our bonds are broken, our creations tattered and torn apart by the ravages of time.

We are hunters, seekers, word-weaving spiders, and those shimmering lines tremble and resonate like sentences. Our stories are spun and cast like nets into the emptiness, our questions a quest to snare meaning or purpose from the infinite flow of existence. For what do we pray as we seek the fly? What food feeds our bodies and souls? Surely there must be a message here, a taste or a tint to flesh out the palette of love.

*   *   *

The landscape is magnificent; it is deep, diverse, and textured. A thousand scenes and episodes play out around me, awaiting my attention, like this bank and its changing relationship to the water. Swirling images of shores and streams with their shifting shapes and boundaries eddy within me, this self both solid and fluid. Male and female, yin and yang dance in the river as mountain, valley, stream and stone, carve, confine, direct, and define each other in an uninterrupted motion and meeting of mutual sculpture.

Grand movements of sky, soil, sun, ridges, rain, roots, and river stream together as the waters change course, creating and choosing their bed. Great forces are at play, a symphony of so many voices speaking about love. They whisper in the wind and blow in our ears as we reach out to one another between those sheets where we lay.

Things are simple only when our gaze is superficial. An hour examining the bark of ponderosa pine reveals layer upon layer. Colors and patterns multiply and proliferate; movements of forming and fadings, surface and depth, dance like a waltzing between dreamer and dream. Doors open into dimensions unheard-of as cracks, flakes, fissures, ants, aphids, and beetles slowly emerge into the sight of eyes that are spellbound. Great gnarly roots twist through the riches of soil upon which we sit. Saps and pitches ooze and crystallize; scents swirl through the air. Needles fall and decay all around in bunches of three, slowly turning to earth as their sharp ends pierce our pants and poke fun at every point of view.

And here lies the lesson: Love is everywhere if you look.

*   *   *

If beauty is in the eye of the beholder, so it is with love. All joined together, we're part dreamer and dreams, and when we enter it lovingly, there's far more than there seems. This world – woven in wonder – is more than enough, and it is a quality of our vision, our reach, and our regard that midwives the dark, creating demons or delights.

We are not alone. We are not separate. The world is not *"out there."* It ignores our self-absorption and plays with us, like it or not. It is dancing in and beyond the looking glass, constantly shifting its shapes and shattering illusions of image, reality, or who "is the fairest of all."

A seed might fall upon pavement or a freshly plowed field,

and something very different arises. Asleep and dreaming, it may lie dormant and waiting upon the earth until moisture and the warm sun stir something within, its shell bursting open with hope and expansion. Or harsh, unrelenting drought may silence it forever.

The seed is not merely a seed; the world not merely a world. They are possibilities, potential. They reach toward us, ask something of us, inquire, *"Who are you? What might we be together? Are you fertile soil?"*

We are not passive observers. We are both creators and the creation, dreamers and the dream. What is your gaze like? What is the capacity and quality of your seeing? Awaken from your sleep and look more deeply in the mirror! If the world seems cold, nightmarish, and lifeless, is it your harsh gaze that is killing the seed, poisoning the waters, and silencing the birds? Do we really believe that it's life or the river which is shallow?

Love is our vision at its fullest capacity. Impressions and ideas of reality and finite forms are secondary. It is the heart that senses the unknown, the mystery, the longing to be; and it opens the door to the image of possibility. The colossal oak is alive in the acorn. Grand forces are at play in a child, a lover, a spider web. They are alive, already here, wishing and aching to be seen by a gaze that is nurturing. And it is love – and a sign of respect – to stop, pause, remember to look again.

Love is our highest potential, but it must be given to the world. We must participate, build a temple, fashion an altar, enter this dance and this river. We can meet the world as a warm sun or a spring rain, and something will emerge, grow, flower, proliferate wildly around and about us.

Love is the greatest of magic. We are catalysts, contributors, creators... lovers, meant to engage and marry the life rushing toward us. There is no objective reality; there is nothing (and everything) "out there." Stop waiting for the world to change, to meet your needs or desires, for it is waiting for you! It is waiting... waiting and wanting.

*   *   *

Thank you, Great Mystery, unnamable unknown. You are warmth made manifest, and you move in all things. You are in my bones, my eyes, in the river of my blood. You have never left me, and I am not alone.

I am being becoming, dreaming within dreaming. And I am who I am, both beyond and beside myself with affection and gratitude. I am in your hands, on your banks, on a rock in the sun. And I am at home, at peace, and in love in the world.

Songs in Stone

Dear River,

    The morning is frosty; ice having formed around the edges of this sorrel-stained lake, tinted with tannin from decaying leaves of oak. An October sun dances among high clouds, promising, but fickle, and it teases my layered and longing flesh. Lily pads float on the surface of the water while underneath, great slabs of granite slumber on the bottom, their massive outlines softened by mud. Unmoved for millennia, these megaliths form grand footings, a foundation for invisible columns of yore that seemed to support the sky.

    Massive boulders are strewn all throughout this New England forest, scattered scraps of stone left by ages of ice that scoured this land. Appearing as islands and congregating in cliffs, they stand like sentinels – solid, stable, silent – a repository of geologic memory holding seasons, centuries, and species come and gone.

    I am the latest, and I sense those tracks of dinosaur, drought, and endless winters from my temporary place on the shore. The pulse and presence of eternity is here, now, outside and within me, prowling around the edges of my awareness, tapping on the door between one possibility and another. The water looks cold, uncomfortable from a customary standpoint, but something hovers in the shadowlands of my perceptions and entices me to enter.

*   *   *

    There are ten thousand depictions or dreams of what we call

life. The possibilities are endless. In one reality we swim in a sea of daily affairs, rapidly moving from here to there like tadpoles in a puddle. Avoiding the matters of the soul as if they were predators, we amass knowledge and power like piles of poker chips, trading them for trinkets to display in the cabinets of our circumscribed social life. Shallowness and superficiality are served up with saccharin smiles. Conversations and clichés come with crumpets and coffee – a banquet of empty calories that can damage the heart. In that dream, perhaps we are already dead.

But there are scores of senses uncharted by the ordinary self, worlds of wonder inaccessible to this everyday coat of flesh. Quanta leap, and fluid fields of energy dance. Universes assemble, rise, and fall; parallel realities converge. Time and space intertwine and merge, spawning new dimensions.

Something expands; a doorway opens. The sentient landscape smiles, my simple friendship mirrored in its infinitely expressive face. It has many secrets to tell me: about God... about love, death, and beauty... about stones who sing through silence... about life which is but a dream.

But what a dream it is!

I won't go back to sleep.

Facing the Shadow

The Coming Storm

The morning is overcast; wind roars through the trees in intimations of winter. The darkness from an approaching storm fills the narrow valley – a deeply cut slot in the furrowed earth. Sharp rocks etch lines into my hands as I climb over boulders in search of a high perch. Raven croaks and soars above a stark and lonely pinnacle. A single tree clings to its rough face, somehow finding soil in stone.

Memories prowl around the edges of my awareness. Gossamer fingers of dreams pry open the cupboards of consciousness, and images tumble out onto the counter of waking life. Strange symbols surface from deep seas to float over landscapes of language and logic, casting nets of mystery and fascination to capture all those who would seek some deity or drown. They are lures of the unknown, the siren's calling, mirages or markers to those who seek truth. The boat rocks in the waters, adrift in the mist, while the solid self clings to its comforting confinement by calling itself dreamer and not dreamed.

The great rocks stand motionless. Silence holds sound in an invisible grip. A falcon patiently waits, watching from atop a granite sentinel. Danger and possibility gather in a foreboding fullness, for life feeds on life, and every dinner brings a banquet of death.

Far away, in the world of humans, babies lie starving in the cradle of civilization, while the armies prepare for war. Life is but a dream, but "reality" cultivates the seeds of nightmare as the "righteous" harvest infected fruits and contaminated crops beneath their bitter and judgmental gods. Bombs are assembled in factories, kitchens, and cellars; poisons are dumped in the waters; heroin enters another vein.

The economy expands; people consume. Houses fill with possessions while the lives within become more desolate and empty. Ever more fearful and isolated, their hearts grow colder as the heat is turned up, millions murdered for the oil.

The learned hide out in their heads, assuming themselves to be special, smart, above it all. Thought is valued at the expense of sense, emotion, imagination; mind is cherished over matter. The ivory tower is blind to the long, ominous shadow it casts in looking down upon the world. The biosphere shudders, the flesh and very foundation of life trembling while the university ignores the universe. Science searches for the ultimate particle, but only the wise discover nothingness.

The storm is coming. Raw winds blow across these massive boulders, quiet and enduring, the stones speaking volumes through their stillness.

Life is a dream, reality a myth. Raven calls loudly and lands on a treetop behind me. Bird of mystery, trickster, creator of the world, he cackles at human folly and laughs with the cosmic joke. For a moment, he too stops, waits, watches, his feathers shining iridescent with the darkness.

Boarding Pass to the New World

Dear River,

I'm tearing through the atmosphere in an aluminum shell thirty thousand feet above the Midwest as the brown earth passes by miles below. Outside our metal cocoon the air is cold and thin. The wind shrieks, but its howling is drowned out by the thunderous roar of jet engines. Their propeller blades whirl like dervishes, driving oxygen into a bellowing furnace where fuel bursts to flame, harnessing the heat of hell to hurtle us through the heavens.

The seats are small; the aisle is narrow. The air is stale and the noise, constant and irritating. My body is cramped, and it complains about this cage it finds itself in. Movement is minimized; muscles are stressed by inactivity. Inside a metallic monster, a prisoner of technology trapped within a tin can; the animal rebels. Something in the psyche paces as if behind bars. The mind mutinies and looks for a way out, but resistance is futile, for energy flows where attention goes, and we are going nowhere very fast.

Progress has its price. I should just pay it and be thankful. I have made this choice – it would be a long walk to Albuquerque – and I could go with gratitude. Outside this high-tech husk I would quickly be frozen or torn to pieces. Every seed needs its shell, something hard and constricting that shelters the fertile, but fragile core.

My seed wants to open. I long to feel the sun on my face and my feet on the ground, to breathe the bracing air of early fall. I dream of lying on the soft earth, listening to the lullabies sung by bird and brook as I say "good night" and sleep under starry heavens.

Restless, my roots reach out for water and soil, but I must wait, for right now nature and nurture are nowhere around. It's cold outside and a long fall to earth. The feast of the senses sends forth its siren's call, and the taste of tomorrow is tantalizing, but I must rein in my longing, remain in my seat, and temporarily settle for plain fare. I sniff the stale air and eat the empty food. I will gestate in the belly of this iron bird, impatiently picking at the shell, and suffer this restriction before release as the cramped contractions of a coming birth.

In a matter of hours, I will be delivered to my destination, drawn along by moving walkways to claim my baggage and liberty, discharged from the airport to fly on my own. With mountains, forests, and the wide world waiting, my wings will be tested. Old songs of freedom echo in my inner ear, and they both question and mock me as they challenge me to throw off my shackles and dance.

"Am I a man? Will I run from the immediacy of the body to the isolation of the mind and wander aimlessly through the alleys of some abstract order, never learning to stand with my two feet on the ground?

Am I a lover? Will I reject the beast and sacrifice beauty in the process?

Am I a warrior? Will I shy away from the wilderness in fear of facing myself and – shamed by should – proceed along well-worn paths that are not my own? Is my spirit strong enough to soar above society's mundane and material concerns, or do I bear too much baggage and – momentarily freed from external chains – will I retreat to the cage I carry within?"

Every day, battles rage between civilization and the natural mind. Skirmishes take place in the halls of Congress and schools, in forests, jungles, and living rooms. Crops are genetically engineered, animals hormonally altered, the natural world improved as the artificial and synthetic storm our very cells. When the body breaks down, its organs are removed or reconstructed in the comforting embrace of managed care.

Timber is cut, homes and highways built; rivers are dammed. The wilderness is tamed and – confined within classrooms – children are taught to choose mind over matter, write between the lines, walk single file, and value books over bodies. Shamanism must surrender to science. Native cultures are smashed, subdued, and swept into the twentieth century to make way for progress. The rainforest burns. Minerals, resources, and powerful economic interests are at stake in questioning our allegiance and asking who we really are.

I must ask the question. The truth, they say, will set you free, but real knowledge does not come from the mind and merely thinking. The body, soul, and senses are only united through acting. Will I find the man I seek?

True freedom is frightening. There's no safety net in the leap to one's destiny. The messiah, the monster, and the harsh hand of reality are extraordinary and immensely endowed with energy. Life and death walk arm in arm – powerful, but not always pretty – and looking in the mirror of the soul may reveal the face of the witch or the one who is fairest of all.

Those mirrors are rife with reflections, but I must choose, "Which side am I on?" It's time to act, move through the looking glass to find out who and what I am. Perhaps on the other side lies freedom and the fulfillment of my dreams... or the sound of shattering panes.

The airplane has arrived at the gate.

Crucifixion

The sun rises slowly over the Sangre de Christos Mountains. It seeps down and pools in the valley. The morning chill holds on tenaciously as curtains of high clouds drape themselves to the east. Taos still sleeps in the shadows, the roar of an occasional truck shattering the day-break peace.

Old stories still reverberate in this strange place called New Mexico, and the land can seem enchanting, enigmatic, magical. Names like Geronimo, Coronado, and Kit Carson echo across the mesas, and plaques are erected telling of battles, treaties, gunfights, and settlements. But what strange god did the Spanish worship as they set their eyes upon these lovely mountains they called the Sangre de Christo, blood of Christ? They came searching for gold, plunder, and easy riches, and the blood that was shed was rarely their own.

Hispanics, Anglos, and Natives in pueblos now rub shoulders in uneasy alliance, but the old mythology still shows its ugly face. The mad rush for gold has moved into real estate and the scramble for the tourist dollar. This magical valley will be surveyed, subdivided, then sold off, lavish houses for the rich ruining the vast uncluttered vistas everyone wants outside their picture windows. New golf courses are built, and the ski areas expand. "Growth" is already wreaking havoc. An ugly sprawl moves north and south from Pueblo and Plaza like a rash, shops and malls spreading like strip mines for the extraction of money. The quality of life degrades to the tune of "more is better," and Beauty is raped like an innocent on the altar of a booming economy. It's a good bang for the buck.

Out here in the sage flats it's still quiet except for the

growling trucks. Sound carries. It is beautiful at a distance, a lovely green undulating its way to black cinder cones and the sharp and spectacular cut of the Rio Grande Gorge.

But this too will soon be gone. Dirt roads and surveyors' strips are carving up the hillsides. Up close it's already ugly. Plastic bottles and broken glass are everywhere; canyons and forests are fly-infested and eroded from the overgrazing of cattle. Paper, Styrofoam, straws, and the universal beer can are scattered throughout the sage, as the conquistador psyche joins the throw-away culture to loot and litter this "Land of Enchantment."

Out on the pueblo the people struggle to maintain their ancient and sacred way of life. The corn dances and fertility rites are still performed, but the casinos bring in a far-better harvest.

The moon will be full tonight, and it will rise, orange-yellow, over the Blood of Christ mountains. Tracking its way across a wide expanse of sky, dark shadows and silver shall rain down upon the landscape and dance through fields of sage. At dawn, she will settle, round and plump, and smile at her golden lover opening his arms to the east.

Most of the populace will miss it, huddled indoors under artificial light, watching television and nodding off to sleep. In the morning they'll wake up with alarm and – still tired and restless – force themselves to head out to work, lusting for silver and gold.

Have we gone insane? Must we stimulate and bludgeon and numb ourselves senseless? Are we unable to see the light?

This magnificent, jeweled earth dances through the depths of space, and turns its face to the sun. The grasses, chamisa, and

281

sage rise up through the litter to feed upon its shimmering radiance. Beauty is around us everywhere, but it seems we've gone blind. The kingdom of heaven is spread all over the earth, while we hope and pray for an afterlife somewhere else.

The Sangre de Christos frame the valley to the east. Are they not part of our mother? Are they just resources, matter, minerals… material to be bought, sold, assaulted and mined, mined, mine-d?

The Blood of Christ mountains are rising up toward the heavens, home to the gods, and godlike themselves. Even the Spanish saw something divine in them and named them after their savior.

But before us lie thirty pieces of silver, so what the hell.... Let them bleed!

Feathers for the Serpent

Springtime arrives. Bear leaves his lair to wander over ridges; serpents emerge from the ground. This is a time of remembrance. Ceremonies, circles of stone, and primeval memories stir in the land of the soul, recollections of prayers and promises made to ageless gods and bonds of blood forged in pulsing dances around ritual fires.

The megaliths and monuments are now overgrown and forgotten. The fierce faces of distant deities fade into the past. Those ancient obligations remain unfulfilled; offerings are seldom given as the new brain ignores the old. The surface of the earth is marked by fences, wires, and roads. We navigate now by satellite. An information net cuts across every border; televisions flicker in jungle huts. The old worlds of emotion and instinct seem obsolete. Why don't we all feel better?

Reason owns the mind, but it cannot capture the heart. The blueprint is well designed; the architecture impeccable; but the foundation – the contact with earth beneath its system of rules – is unstable. Armies of judgment are arrayed against the irrational, but chaos proliferates. Children are beaten at home and gunned down in schools; city streets devolve into combat zones. Wealth is amassed through wars and weaponry. Poverty proliferates; the earth is pillaged; might makes right. Welcome to the new world order.

The soul is hungry. Its landscapes are unmapped by GPS, and its appetites can't be pacified by another useless thing bought at the mall. It aches for deeper knowledge and primal passion; seeks extraordinary encounters with something real, but intangible.

A hawk circles in the clear blue air, attentive to what's

happening below. An eye opens in the reptile brain; archaic images appear in stone and cliff. The wind seems to speak. Neural nets are trailed in deep oceans, the home of monsters and fish that feed multitudes. Somewhere a drum, or a heart, begins to beat.

*   *   *

Steam rises from the ground before the ancient oracle. A priestess speaks in riddles, expressing a truth that's hard to understand, but the body knows. The mind rebels. It waves appointment books like magic objects, but the spirit is drawn to the swirling mists.

Curiosity calls. The flesh wants to experience. What lies below the ground or within it? How does it feel to enter the water or burn with fire? The heart beats in excitement, anticipation, worry. Fear stalks the outskirts around the sphere of action, and reason raises the specter of the worst possible outcomes. It counsels comfort, security, study and planning.

But the new brain is a poor friend and lover. It is allied with fear, committed to observation, enamored of its own creations. It sits and stagnates like Narcissus, regards its reflections as reality. Shackled by the limitations of its vision and "cogito ergo sum," it suffers with thirst, stays on the shore, and starves.

The body wants none of it. It aches for a true companion and – "in a new voice, slowly dawning as its own" – it tells the mind "No!" [1]

The hawk circles. Steam continues to rise. Something is moving beneath the earth, simmering in the depths where remnants of the Hydra – the many-headed serpent slain by Hercules – were buried underground. That central head – golden, immortal, and still breathing fire – awaits resurrection.

Banished from the Garden by the patriarchs and pathology of the Old Testament, it slumbers within our psyche. Buried by millennia of mindless morality from the church and clergy of the chosen people, it sleeps beneath the surface. It shows its face far from civilization, appears in thick woods and canyons suffused with untamed energies, in wild places where twisted spires of volcanic rock evoke dark forces and archaic creations curdled from the cauldron of chaos.

A rumbling resounds in the mountains. It could be thunder, or rocks rolling away from a tomb as the sleeper awakens. But this is no gentle shepherd serving us manners and mutton. The landscape shudders. This resurrected god opens its cold, unblinking eye, the animal arising, attuned to sense and a more sinuous sacred. Everything is as it is, monstrous and miraculous. The body of the old brain moves instinctively. Civilized sight sheds its skin.

Old rites are remembered and wrongs are forgotten as ancient knowledge flows through a newly-reopened doorway. Theology crumbles, for judgment day has no meaning without shame or sin, though the flesh of this god has scales a plenty.

"Skree, skree, skree...." a voice calls from on high. Hawk, fiercely alive with its own glowing gaze, releases a cry of joy, burns with fire, and dives as the great serpent rises to meet it in a dance of death, desire, and dinner. The god above returns to earth. The snake grows wings and ascends to the sky.

The sleeper is stirring, burning with desire to awaken. Fierce, forceful, our first God, his forked tongue tells of forgotten truths long before language, logic, or form… the union of opposites, our dance with death, the light and the shadow. He speaks in appetites, smolders in senses, breathes in the body. He beats in our hearts, flares in our bellies, flowers in the flesh. This is an old story and a good one, but silent too long. We can listen and learn, but we must live it to be wise.

All is as it should be. Kundalini is rising up the spine. The feathered serpent appears in the east; the great healer arrives with the caduceus; Venus sparkles in the morning light. Life is but a dream, and this _is_ a dream worth living. Awaken to it! We must open our eyes, our hearts, our senses. We must open our mouths. We must roar, howl, shriek, rattle, and laugh. We must shatter the silence and speak out for the serpent who long ago swallowed his tale.

(1) From Mary Oliver, "The Journey."

Eating the Apple

Poison and passion… passion and poison. Adam and Eve approach the fruit of knowledge; Pandora opens the box. Sleeping Beauty licks her lips. She's tempted, can't resist the taste. Prometheus rushes for the shimmering flame; Snow White swallows and topples to the ground. The goddess, Strife, enters the banquet hall, hurling the golden apples across the floor to be claimed by the "one who is fairest of all."

Craving and desire. *"I want! … I need!"* This moment, this life, this job…. this day, this relationship… This self is never enough.

Dissatisfaction won't stay away. Hope and hunger undulate like waves on the sea; optimism rises, then falls along with blood sugar. Light arrives with darkness and shadow. The young body grows old and tired. Sex is no longer what it used to be, though what it used to be might be better forgotten. Everything leads to its opposite. The future holds death along with promises of a better tomorrow.

The river drifts by the bank, constant and endlessly changing. Gravel and dried stalks dominate the shore, the grand seasonal cycles arriving and departing as rocks, seeds, and silt tumble in the sweeping stream of time.

We see the world the way we are. Our eyes gather light, blend it into patterns of neural pulsing, send it to the brain. They – along with ears, nose, and mouth – are all placed upon and within the swiveling skull. Perception and identity becomes housed in the head, and it dominates our attention and conversation, but the greater part of our vital organs are lodged elsewhere.

We are far more than our thoughts. A serpent sleeps at the base of the spine and dreams of awakening. There's an animal who lives in our belly, and there the child curls up with the wolf. Our feelings are visceral; antipathies appear as things we can't stomach. We can be full, satisfied, unsettled, sick. Primal perceptions take a different form, and feelings have no distance or abstract language. We are hungry for love or experience. We are what we eat.

Our eyes look out and race across distance, an elm tree or galaxy a mere blink away. Clarity, focus, vision – these metaphors of controlled attention and the values of an organized mind – depend upon light and unclouded properties of the atmosphere.

But the eye was birthed long ago in the ocean, and its soft, bulbous surface is constantly rinsed with water and salt. Of aquatic origin, like heaving viscera and pulsing waves of blood, it's a sibling of the sea, kin to ancient jellyfish organs and most at home when crying.

So cry, cry, cry! Cry out for this craving called life, stretched out on a rack of desire and disappointment. Cry for your wounds or the tightness of the dressings you wear. Cry for your expectations, and the blindness they've caused you; for promises past and dear blessings left behind. Cry for the eyes that looked into your own, softened with trust, love, or innocence, now clouded with hurt and the pain of betrayal.

Cry for your shame, cry out your sorrow, for treasures ignored at your feet as you plan for tomorrow. Cry for love, the heart breaking, and the limitations of every path no matter how sweet. Cry for wonder, the divine, blessed union; and the sure, slow falling from grace. Cry for the land, the buffalo, the Indian nations bulldozed and broken, the grand dreams crushed under the wheels of greed, glory and god.

Cry for the pain – yours and the world's – the part given to you as the price of admission. All things must pass; all we love will be taken away. Cry for your family and those bonds made to be broken, as the sure shadow of death falls upon every one of them. Cry for this love – or worse, for its lack. The promise of spring becomes broken stalks in the fall, and the price of desire's required suffering for all.

Spirit, thank you for this painful passion play of life. I have eaten the apple, tasted desire, sweetness, and suffering; and tears will join the river on its way to the ocean. I know not what seeds await them, but may they water new growth and nourish something somewhere round the bend. My cheeks are wet with weeping, yet my vision has cleared, and I feel serenity and relief beneath the residue of this bittersweet sadness. I was blind, but now I see.

The Prodigal Child

Sweet Spirits of this place,

Thank you for this day. The evening sunlight breaks through clouds, dark and dramatic. Cicadas buzz madly in the cottonwood above the rustle of the river. A raven calls. Silence fills with echoes of thunder and the hushed voices of an unwritten past.

Long ago, the Mogollon people built settlements of rock in the caves and cliffs above the Gila River. The stories of their short stay etched in stone, from whence they came and why and to where they went remains a mystery for us to ponder and puzzle upon. The land whispers of their presence. These spirits of another time move behind an invisible wall encasing our world, waiting for us to return.

*   *   *

Much has changed and – just as true – nothing has changed. The spirits remain. The earth lies fertile and enchanting, and it is we who do not see or hear her. Let's be real! We are not victims! We were not thrown out of the Garden. We turned our backs and walked away. Life in the past, a life close to nature, was not "savage, brutal, and short." Daily we tell ourselves stories that twist the truth and ignore our roots. Like prodigal children, we squander our inheritance and distance ourselves from our own darkness.

There is a fork in the road, an unavoidable choice. Shall we take part in life or not? To participate with integrity and authenticity requires us to engage in the struggle with self and change the only part of existence we really control, to become wiser, more tolerant and compassionate. Are we capable of opening ourselves to the world, accepting it all, and loving it the way it is in all its imperfections? Can we attune ourselves to hear the song being sung and – finding our voice and our deepest chord – blend it with the grander and more universal rhythm?

Many have chosen "no," and they shrink from the darkness and difficulty. Aggressively asserting their childish wants, they seek to fashion the earth for their own comfort and convenience. They defend and dominate, attempting to remake the world – the domain they have least control over – so their self-centered desires can remain unchanged and unchallenged.

It seems to have worked with a vengeance. Forests are cut down, rivers are damned, fields fenced in barbed wire. The great bison, the grizzly, and the wolf have been hunted to near extinction. Mountains are gutted; minerals are mined and extracted in a never-ending rush for more and more. The Promised Land is looted; the Garden – where man walked in peace and spoke with the plants and animals – plundered.

The earth that created us is daily raped and ransacked for resources. Our relatives and kin – those forms of life who share this planetary home with us – are auctioned for our pleasure, convenience, or use. What's real has been replaced by real estate, what's right by property rights. After selling our mother and treating her like a slave, we have no remedy or answer for our discomfort and loneliness but to consume more.

We take and take and take. We take a break, a vacation, a shot, a swing, a pill, a piss, a path, or a photograph.... all with dogged determination: whatever it "takes." But what does it take to turn this thing around, to stop, step outside the box, and see the stupidity and stark horror of the colonial mind? Do we have what it takes to change, to love and give ourselves to the earth?

There are so many choices to make between giving and taking.... between love and fear, acceptance or aggression, addiction or recovery, gratitude or grievance... between a more fluid freedom and fight or flight. We must wisely choose our gods – (for we make ourselves in their image) – asking what it will take to bring Spirit back into daily life?

What will we give; what do we have to offer? The sacred tree can never be sold for timber; the holy realm cannot be mined for profit. The prodigal child can close the gate to the Garden, but the Other World will not go away. It does not disappear merely because we've shut our eyes and bolted the doorway to its numinous and dreamlike dimensions.

*   *   *

The spirits still roam these hollows and hills. I sense them in the clouds, the wind, and moonlight. They will not show themselves to those who have turned aside. They congregate in all the blind spots created by our lack of vision. They abide and endure, hovering at the edges of our awareness, ready to emerge from space and stillness, from the source behind the ten-thousand sights and sounds.

Shape-shifting, fluid, and free, they cavort and frolic behind the veil. Perhaps they are lonely or long for human contact, waiting for that prodigal child who has gone far away. One day, when this child has taken and squandered all he can, he may wake up in the pig sty and see what he has created.

Perhaps then he will find the humility to become human and set his sights and heart on home. Throwing himself down on the doorstep, begging forgiveness and asking only the chance to serve, tears may wash his gaze and restore a vision of the wonder of what he left behind.

That moment may be a long time coming, but I can hardly wait. The earth and all our relations shall dance in celebration. I pledge allegiance to the day when we return to the Garden, to our senses, to our Natural Mind. To it and the spirit world, I give my commitment; I give my words, my hands, my heart. I offer it my hopes, my desires, my dreams, grateful for all it has given me – everything I've got.

Oh Say Can You See?

Oh say, can you see, by the dawn's early light? What so
proudly we hail....

The national anthem plays on, and I wonder, "Oh say, can
you see the ignorance, the fear, and the blood shed over this land?
Twenty million Native Americans annihilated..."

The wind is troubled, the earth uneasy, the rivers run
crimson with blood. Two hundred nations destroyed; broken, and
battered into submission; their vision smashed like potsherds and
tossed in the rubble of history. *"This land is your land. This land is*
my land... " Eighty million buffalo reduced to a handful; the gray
wolf, the carrier pigeon slaughtered to extinction. Twenty million
people – massacred, deceived, decimated – dwindled to a few
hundred thousand.... Disease, deception, and death – this the dirty
shadow of Manifest Destiny run rampant in the land of the free.

This heartbreaking tale remains unspoken by the lying
tongue of history. Falsehoods, fables, and fantasies obscure the
obvious. Bones and bodies are bulldozed into unmarked graves and
covered over with soiled speeches about "settling an uninhabited
wilderness." Our consciences are conned with the proper words, our
advances advertised, but the truth is lost, and a great dream lies
forgotten beneath our beautiful and spacious skies.

We are still in denial of the demon inside us. For those who
once lived in harmony and loved this land, our amber waves of
grain spread out like the yellow tape of a crime scene. The wheels of
wagon trains rolled westward on a tide of genocide, their ship of
destruction driven by a deadly gale from the east. Songbirds were
silenced; wolves eradicated; the buffalo butchered... all the relatives

of the Red Man rubbed out in bringing "brotherhood, from sea to shining sea."

How can we be at home here? How can we lift our eyes to the horizon and not feel shame?

Spirit in all things, I ask forgiveness for myself and my people. It may be too much to ask, for amends need to be made, penances performed. The past is still living alongside and within us. Unspoken and unacknowledged, the epidemic continues to spread. Sick, greedy for gold, and lusting for things, we hide behind sanitized slogans of gain. "Resources" are "extracted;" rainforests destroyed for "development," and ancient ways are sacrificed on the altar of abundance. Each new pathology gets promoted as progress, and our destiny, our dream, even our decency dies to keep the economy growing.

Spirit, help us to take on the work of becoming worthy. Sadness, shame, and sorrow slink through the shadows around our surface optimism. We are not free and may never be. This will never be the home of the brave until we have the courage to stand up and face what we have done.

But we are silent, censored, civilized. What will it take to change? Who will choke on those force-fed falsehoods and fracture the phony facade of happy hour? Who will shatter the silence to challenge these counterfeit chronicles and manufactured memories of Manifest Destiny?

The Sacred Tree appears barren. It survives, enduring through this drought by withholding its fruit and flowers. Its withered vines await the water of life, while within us, a deluge of desolation and despair grows like a river that's been damned. Who will cry in the wilderness and shed the first teardrop?

Spirit, please help us. All are tainted, and the stain of blood is on our souls. You have saved me and given me a dream of life. I would return something to you, bring this one small portion of your creation into balance, but I cannot do it alone. Remove this disease from my heart and make yourself at home there. Give me courage to suffer my sorrow and lament the lives and the life that has been lost.

Our roots are soaked in slaughter. Give us the will to cleanse the carnage and heal our heritage. May we truly be brave and bewail our bloody birth, and in so doing, bring our darkness to light.

Crying in the Wilderness

Great Mystery, Mother and Father Gods,

How can I sing my song for you? How can I express my love and gratitude, my wonder and reverence? How will I open this heart when it is filled with shame? Will you touch my reaching hands, crimson and drenched with blood?

The wind blows cold from the north, carrying the birds southward. The sky is a deep blue. The morning sun sparkles on the water as the leaves turn golden, scarlet, and russet. A fish breaks the surface; ducks thunder by on beating wings. Granite boulders and ledges of shale line the shore like footprints of eternity, the remnants of glacial epochs leaving magnificent tracks as ancient time crisscrosses the fields of the present. The beauty is unspeakable.

The earth cries out in pain, and I do nothing. Aboriginal people are pushed into history, millennial forests burned and bulldozed, biological diversity sacrificed for another billion burgers. Oceans are fished out and coated with oil. Chemical spills, pesticide spraying; garbage, greenhouse gasses, and genetic engineering; Middle East wars, pipelines, and plutonium... A thousand species are slaughtered for profit and progress, the sacred earth treated as sewer... and our voices are silent.

"And the rockets' red glare, the bombs bursting in air," gave proof of our fright and our struggle to care. Now the dawn's early light is clouded and green with smog. Clear vision is difficult. It will take many tears before we can see again. Why can't we cry out when there is so much to cry about?

Anger, grief, frustration, despair; shame, isolation,

powerlessness, and guilt... There are as many poisons in the mind as in the biosphere. And why not? We're merely cells in a larger body. It is so painful to remember, so enticing to forget. Can we really hope or expect to shit in our nest and come out smelling pretty?

Deodorants, breath mints, perfumes, toothpaste, air fresheners – can we buy a solution for everything? Our assumptions and outlook are symptomatic of the sickness, our perspectives afflicted with pathology. Barcaloungers, television, shopping malls; antidepressants, cocktails, crack, and cynicism. Nationalism, alienation, and apathy; self-absorption and victimhood. Shell-shocked, the soul atrophies and starves, but the shelves stay full.

Industries spring up to fill the hole, medicate the pain, or distract us; make us numb-out, forget, splinter. Purchase a little peace of mind, while ignoring all the other pieces. Become a single sell in a great buy-a-sphere! The highway to disconnection is wide, well-paved, and promoted, but it exacts a silent toll.

Death and disease press upon us everywhere, not only in the fallen forests and rotting fish, but in the refusal to live, feel, and suffer the pain and wounding of our world. They fill the bottles that stock the pharmacy shelves and laugh at the signs that read "*Heath and Beauty*." They spread like viruses in computers, cyberspace, and commercials; live in air conditioning, chlorinated water, and urban ugliness. Their hollow sockets gleam like the shiny headlights on our sport utility vehicles.

The malady mushrooms in our way of thinking, and it thrives in the denial of its presence. It haunts the heartless hallways of reason, objectivity, and science; poisons us with patriotism, progress, and self-interest. It proliferates in punishing gods and child abuse, Manifest Destiny and the separate self. It breeds at the core of control, capitalism, and cancer, like a parasite destroying the host.

Death is here and everywhere, in my-side-versus-your-side, in ecocide or suicide. It flourishes in fantasies of great wealth, lottery numbers, and get-away vacations. But the dice have been cast, and snake eyes stare back behind all our visions of paradise.

Spirits of the sacred earth, here on this shore, surrounded by beauty, I would thank you. My life is yours and soon will be returned. I would sing for you and for all you have given. But my words are scratched on paper from the ground-up forests of the Northwest; my coffee produced at the price of a peasant's poverty. My metal cup echoes with the cries of a miner's bleeding lungs; my daypack and sandals assembled in the slave shops of Malaysia.

Great Mystery, how can I bear the guilt I carry? How can I come to you without shame? Your flesh shrieks out in pain. The poison is in me, my people, and in the living, dying earth. Tears fill my eyes as I turn and face you. I want to cry, howl, rage, and froth like an animal, for I am. I do not want to be polite, optimistic, or rational. The body of the beast speaks in bawdiness. My body aches, and my heart cries out, "Stop! Stop this insanity!"

Your beauty and embrace fill me with gratitude and grief for all we are losing. Rivers must be cried before we are cleansed. May we start now, releasing all that we have dammed. The tender shoots of a new life are calling to us. The seeds you've planted in our souls will only take root with the water from our tears.

My song is a voice crying in the wilderness, but I would cry in living rooms, in city streets and public parks. I would cry until there is no need for sitcoms, until the stain is washed from our souls and the blood from our hands. I will cry until we reach out to one another and hold the living earth as precious. I will cry, cry, cry... and cry again.

I will cry until the tears stop running, and, finally, so do we.

Spirit and Soul: As Above, So Below

Waltzing with a Wild God

Children climb over iron railings on the gazebo while busses circle the square. Adults drift from store to store and shop. The park is small, but grass, trees, and flowers cool the air and soften the noise of the highway, slowing the speed of the city. Rock music spills out the window of a passing pickup. The beat goes on.

Yesterday, clouds let loose as we hiked out of the canyon. Step by step, our breath rapid and in rhythm with muddy boots gripping and slipping, we climbed a thousand feet through thunder, lightning, rain, and hail, sweating up a trail turned to a trough of silt streaming to the canyon below. The thunder was ominous, the downpour steady. Fear mounted with each booming flash. Our footsteps marked time as we counted the seconds between sight and sound, blaze and blast, gauging the distance and danger.

The wind picked up, and water hurtled down in sheets, stinging our bare legs like needles. It funneled into our boots and filled them, already heavy from their cargo of thickly-caked clay. Brown sludge surged down the hillside and plummeted over rock.

Each glance toward the ridge brought another bolt of lightning.

The seconds seemed to shrink with the crackle of fiery bursts, their concussions growing sharper and more searing. A ponderosa blew apart above us, flames billowing, seemingly unaffected by the deluge. Smoke rose from what little remained of the trunk. Reaching the trailhead, we raced for the car, throwing our packs and ourselves – shivering and soaked – into the shelter and safety of its metallic arms.

Zeus stamped like a madman; the fury of the wind increased. Windshield wipers were useless against the deluge spilling down from the sky. Explosions rocked the car with shock waves, the detonations concurrent with their blinding brilliance.

*　　*　　*

It's easy to speak of God when he's far away. We converse about enlightenment around the coffee table and give lip service to this longing, while investing most our energy in other places. We imagine encounters with spirit like the rapture before a radiant sunrise and picture its presence making a dull life more fulfilling. And sometimes it comes that way – a slowly-growing gratitude suffusing a life, the feeling comforting and constant.

But illumination is often not so domestic. The deity arrives like a demon: snarling, wanton, and wild. The divine appears, not in silent stillness as we sit on a meditation pillow, but in a searing fire that destroys whatever it touches. And when suddenly the distance closes like a charging bear, do we really want what is offered? Like the foolish Semele who demanded to see the naked Zeus and was

302

burned to death, we are often unaware of what we are asking for.

Fire fascinates us. Lightning flickers, and we scan the horizon in search of the electric charge. We are drawn to it like a moth to flame, thrilled at its approach and the deep rumbling of this voice from heaven. We approach the edge and grow excited, moved beyond ourselves in the face of its majesty and power.

But suddenly it is too close, and – overwhelmed by its force and fury – an abyss yawns before us like an open mouth. God comes on too strong. He arrives ready to rumble, and we take flight in fear, trembling at the prospect of this sudden transcendence. Talons of terror pierce our hearts. Beauty becomes the beast. Angelic harps are drowned out by the raw power of rock and roll, as the deity-turned-demon desires to dance. Are you available?

Yesterday I was human and humbled, my self-image shrunk to size by the power of God's great gale. One day perhaps, I'll run toward and not away. I'll stand in the rain and join in the howling – my throat raspy and hoarse with thunder – giving voice to a turbulent tempest that swirls in my heart. I'll stamp my feet on the muddy ground, hurling my small fire from the earth back to the skies. Committing myself to chaos and the utter folly of this task, I will meet this wildness on its terms and become the storm.

These thoughts seem fanciful, flaky, and foolish. But everyone's time is coming, and if I'm to be taken, may it not be by timidity. Perhaps the gods will smile and look fondly on this spirit – soaked and silly – as he spits back at the eye of a hurricane. May they find me worthy and be merciful as I roar and wrestle to a decisive defeat. I may lose this battle and perhaps my mind, but sometimes something wondrous can be found in losing so grandly.

Perhaps I will. I have no certainty; no assurances of safety, satisfaction, or survival; no sure solution to this wonder and wondering. But my spirit smiles and whispers, "Yes."

Soul Retrieval

The arrow points down; the elevator descends to the
basement; the bottom drops out. Shadows expand and grow into
darkness. Vision is clouded; Innana and Persephone enter the
horizonless house of death. The soul is unsettled, and it shivers,
shakes, suffers… but there is nowhere to run.

We're alone in a dangerous labyrinth, with no light at the
end of the tunnel. The cave is close and confining, the air too stuffy
to breathe. Nightmares slip through doorways of dreams; demons
dance around the edges of awareness. The armies of order are routed
by chaos; the tower of reason crumbles; libraries burn. Landmarks
are useless. The world sinks into primordial soup.

Strange images surface, belly up in the dark waters, one
replacing another. Drunken sailors stumble into boats and drift
rudderless toward some vague and distant horizon. A crippled man
totters on one leg, refusing help, his flesh falling off the bone.

We sit and wait for explanation, direction, an answer.
Nothing comes, and the silence mocks us. We are floating in the
stomach of the snake, the belly of the monster. We search for a
destination, but the darkness doubles. Eternity eats at us;
determination perishes in peristaltic waves of despair. Emptiness
weighs upon us; the ground gives. Night expands; nothing is
everywhere. We pray for peace or patience; hope for vision,
passion, and power; but we languish in limbo, passive and
preoccupied, pausing in all the wrong places.

Persephone pines away in loneliness, and flowers fade and
fall without her shining face. But the grasses and glades will not join

her for a holiday in the house of gloom. The sun beams outside the entrance to the cavern, but it will not set foot in those dark chasms of carbon. It calls us to rise up and walk. The goddess must find her way back any way she can. Is there no one who can help her?

*   *   *

Meanwhile, sage is smoldering in the smudge bowl, and a ladder leads out through the roof of the kiva. The shaman raises his rattle; stones sing out from inside the gourd. A plane taxis down the runway; Spirit ascends to the sky. Hawks circle their way to the sun, their feathers on fire in luminous gold.

A Fire in the Desert

It's a new beginning, a new day. A barrel cactus blooms, an eruption of vermilion splashed on the sage-green palette of this desert... gentle, subtle, and quiet in its beauty. Sunlight dances on spider webs, and a prickly pear raises its spiny head from the soil. Morning doves coo ever-so softly, but other birds send out sharper notes. Yellow flowers, thin and wispy, sway in the breeze.

The faint smell of smoke drifts past from a fire on the mesa above, touched off by the crackling thunder of yesterday. The creative spark – alive, electric, and destructive.... We watch and check the wind, cautious lest it come our way.

Christ, Moses, Mohammed... they all came to the desert. Wandering in its incessant harshness and impossible beauty, it was here they spoke to Spirit, listened to the voice of God, suffered the temptation of the world and its treasures. Moses – heeding this call – stood and conversed with the burning bush. We have a thousand of them on the mesa above us, but our minds run in more predictable routes, concerned with safety, security, and loss of possessions.

The gods have spoken, and the hillside has burst into flame! Our attention wanders. Our mind flutters like a moth, but is persistently brought back. Something whispers, "Go there! Speak! Listen!"

This god has expressed himself in fire. What do you have to say, Emissary of lightning, smoke, and thunder? What is your message? Do you tell us of heat, burnout, or an approaching time of purification?

Old growth is being swept away to make a home for the

new to abide, and this clearing is hot, raging, and destructive. Letting go of the old is never easy. Umbilical cords must be tied off and severed. Letting go is rarely gracious. The boy screams for his mother as he is carried off to join the circle of men in the woods. A release is required, and often this entails smashing, burning, burying... cutting off, bloodletting... peeling, ripping, tearing, cleaving.

Separation, discrimination, severance... The symbol of the sword is sacred, and its blade cuts both ways. Fire – the center of home and hearth, stolen from the gods, and divinity itself – blisters, maims, and turns to ashes. The primal spark, bringer of life, the male principle – dynamic and penetrating – pulses onto and into the receptive earth, and it lays waste in drought, famine, and desert. It is holy, this heavenly power. It is energy, the motivating force. Breathing, eating, consuming oxygen and fuel, it is the flame which ignites in our very cells. It is desire, vitality, Father Sun, creator, prime mover, first cause. It is God – warm, nurturing, and demonic – drawing and driving us, and it rages unchecked on the hillside. Shall we worship or flee?

The power of fire can comfort or burn. The waters of life cool, quench, or drown. The breeze wraps around and brings us breath; calms, refreshes, and revives us; then blows us away. The earth bestows body and belonging. It feeds, befriends, succors, and supports us, until it slides or swallows us, and we are buried and taken back.

The One Glorious God has different faces: darkness and light, night and day, male and female. He is Brahma, Vishnu, and Shiva, a deity of death and resurrection, bearer of salvation and

Armageddon, the desirer of human sacrifice. He dances in a ring of fire above us – lord of initiation or injury, source of the sacred wound. He's the god of radiance, his thunderbolts – fiery and threatening – full of light as the earth erupts and cracks open. He comes in the cutting, the crucifixion, the scarring, the sun dance.... the shaman torn apart and dismembered.

The goddess can be wet, watery, womb-like... slick, slimy, and blood-soaked. Smiling in submersion and suffocation, delighted to be drowning in deluge; in her arms we swim, surrender, and are swallowed by the whale. Fluid, and close friend of Fate, she's the sacred source of all life and sweeps us away in the flood.

Spirit is like air, the foundation of existence. It's inspiring, omnipresent, invisible, and it roars, uproots, and flattens as it twists itself into a dark funnel to suck out your breath at last.

Set your eyes upon the god and the demon, the Buddha with the sword. He has come to cut away illusion; break open the shell; to level, bury, and burn as he makes way for new growth. The lamb of god must meet the butcher; the path to heaven begins with nails and a cross. We conjure up angelic images of transformation... envision honeyed meadows with butterflies, lighthearted and free, but dark Kali dances to different music. With dripping fangs and a necklace of skulls, the goddess of change coaxes the caterpillar to constrict itself, break all boundaries, dissolve, and perish.

To know eternal life we must die; to find the greater self, the smaller must be torn asunder. We want the ecstatic, but not the transforming knife. We would know our animal nature, but not be devoured; rise to the heavens, but run from the fire. But death is our sacrifice, the sacred wound, the necessary offering at the doorway to another world. Blood comes with birth, and it colors the good red road on the path to the heart.

Our ancestors, champions of the great ball court, climbed those stone steps to the altar, content and proud. As warriors they went willingly to their dying, welcoming the blade, giving themselves to the gods and presenting their hearts to the sky.

Welcome this breaking of boundaries, the transformative tearing, those sacred surrenders to life! The shields must soften. The container must crack, crumble, or be crushed. Every shell must split apart for the seed to grow. If it does not open – by fire or water, to warmth or wetness – the living core will perish.

Above us on the hillside, God is speaking as the bushes burn. We might hear him if we didn't talk so much. The illumination is captivating and alluring, but we define it as danger, or a distraction to our more important conversations. We could come closer, but our tendency is to move away.

But something is summoning us. It tempts us to draw near, to walk on this bed of coals, to step into a wheel of fire and follow the light in the desert. It is mesmerizing… shimmering, pulsing, and alive. Perhaps here, in this ring of blackened acres, glows the center of our purpose, inviting us to walk in wonder, approach in awe. We are called to enter that circle as a moth drawn to flame, spiraling closer and faster until – in the final moments of ecstasy and dissolution – everything is forgotten and we know ourselves completely.

GPS

God is....

Running, walking, dancing, drumming;
laughing, shouting, be becoming,
Elders, babies, saints and sages,
sands of time and rock of ages;
Fog and darkness, turns and twists,
plans, agendas, goals all mist,
Shifting shapes, diffuse and dense,
skin and synapse making sense...
Judge and jury, good and evil,
fork and cup, bowl and weevil,
Manna, mother, milk and honey,
starving souls and lotsa money,

The earthy body births a two,
creating meaning, me and you;
The seamless whole divides and fractures,
Sensing, feeling, thinking, actors....
One world inner, one world out
One a sinner, one devout.
Self and other, loss and wins;
One great mother, sacred twins.
Matter, pain, and pleasure paired,
As bodies, teeth, and souls are bared.
Primal passions, restless drives,
Creation's garden, chaos thrives.
Rights and wrongs, no one prevails,
For snakes and justice both have scales.

Swirling winds, breath in and out,
connecting webs are torn by doubt.
They call it progress; claim it's fated,
you must be trained, domesticated;
Establish borders, tame the wild,
follow orders, kill the child;
Love her, leave her, hurt and hate her;
destroy the now and wait till later;
The prairies paved, the lands defiled,
the peoples broken, meek and mild;

311

Cities roar in rage and violence,
the voice of sense reduced to silence.
Vocation shrunk to work and wages,
to buy more stuff to fill the cages;
Polluted rivers, soot-filled air;
wonder withers, hearts despair.
The cosmic joke, the tragic funny
In falling darkness, watch it sunny.

Within these dark nights of the soul,
Light can find us, make us whole.
Cast out shame, release all doubt,
for life makes sense as words run out.
Dismissing hell, rejecting sin,
embrace the heaven we're always in.
The land, the air, the fire and water,
our mother, father, son, and daughter.
The breath of god and love of living,
gifts and grace and all forgiving.
It softly whispers, no commands,
With the gentle touch of healing hands.

A journey starts of endless miles,
convention frowns, but spirit smiles.
You'll risk rejection, feel alone,
but find protection and a home.
Misled by maps and trails of tears,
just take a step, the path appears.
Tested often, no one fails,
who perseveres to find the Grail.
Finding courage and will undaunted,
you'll find god if god is wanted.

Forgetting fear, ignoring how;
god is here, and god is now.
God is movement, god is word;
god is meaning that's absurd.
God's a phrase which we have coined,
which can't be captured, but can be joined.
God can be entered, like a stream,
For god is real and god is dream.
God's a river without banks;

god is giver, give god your thanks.
God's receiving, god is sending,
both limitless and never ending.
God is infinite as grains of sand,
god is friend, give god a hand.
God is earth, and god is sun,
and god is you when you're the One.

The Brutal Banquet of Life

The sun rises above the mountains as the stars hide their
faces behind a brightening veil of blue. Great Mystery, Creator,
thank you for this day. Thank you for this beautiful world, for water,
wind, earth, and fire. Thank you for life, the miracles above, below,
and around me.

I want to sing to the morning, shout "Yes!" to this glorious
place I call home. Creation, destruction, order and chaos play out
their extraordinary dramas on an immense and magnificent stage.
Joy, sorrow, fascination, and fear compose compelling and
counterpoint movements in a grand symphony of pleasure and pain.
Delight and distress are entrees in our elaborate dinner; compassion
and cruelty are served with a smile. Hope and despair join hands to
dance in a circle of magic; weeping and wonder gather twigs and
fashion a nest – these mixtures of darkness and light moving us to
tears of affection or anguish.

Spiders, birds, and lizards scavenge the ground. Feeding on
insects, cast-off seeds, and each other, they dine on the fallen scraps
of yesterday, fattening and flourishing from this rich banquet of
death.

Life, sweet life, so mysterious… It arises in shadow and
sun, in calm seas or storm. One moment mother, then monster; it's
friendly or frightening, stable, then shifting. The waves are
relentless. They rise up and then fall, rocking us to sleep or eroding
the shore.

And the shore is never really solid. The stones break down
into sand, are abraded and shaped over time. Water and land, sea
and shore, self and other... Always the mystery without meets the

mystery within, each one cause and effect, altered, changing, evolving, emerging.

Clouds amass, disperse, and reform; squalls pass through. Trees topple, decay, and dissolve into humus. Shells split and soften; seeds germinate, take root, and flourish in the rot. Stems shoot skyward. Thick forests take hold and soon cover up old definitions.

*   *   *

Bright flowers of crimson and pink unfurl, smiling in the shadows cast by adobe walls. Automobiles, old and new, rumble down the highway, gleaming chrome and rusted fenders rubbing shoulders along the way. A limousine with the newly married passes a hearse heading in the other direction.

Tears of joy and tears of sorrow... each have their seasons. It is how it is. Love is lost and love is found. The celebrations are sweet, high-spirited, and often far too short. The wheel turns; the ceremonies and receptions are over. Love found must begin to build a foundation. The journey to the unknown starts with intention, desire, direction. Plans are drawn up, ground is broken, a floor is laid. Walls are built, and dreams become concrete... sometimes for better and sometimes for worse.

For foundations can be untrue or crumble. Walls become prisons, and the sills start to rot. Decay sets in, termites and beetles boring holes in what once was solid. The roof sags, the door sticks, the windows become opaque with dust and grime. Soon we can no longer see through the pains. Beds become battlegrounds. Wedding

315

dresses are exchanged for butcher's aprons, the carcass is cut up.
Tears are shed or hidden away in closed containers. Life moves on;
the garden goes untended; everything collapses.

Wildflowers sometimes blossom amidst the rubble.

Save the Last Dance for Me

Bullets of fire bounce off the water as the sun shoots westward. The spirits of darkness approach. Sparrows and thrushes trill in counterpoint, their duet played against a background of spring peepers. A loon sends a lonely call from somewhere down the lake.

The weekend is cloudless and unseasonably warm, bringing swarms of motorboats and black flies buzzing over the water. The bugs are troublesome, but tolerable; the boats less so. They whine with anger and aggression, taking pleasure in power, sending waves slapping against the shore in the wake of the shattered stillness.

I look forward to the night. The black flies will abandon the air, driven away by dropping temperatures, as the motorboats and their occupants head home toward beer and dinner. Light fades, and the horizon comes closer. Vision flickers, soon snuffed out by the inky hand of dusk. Sight – swallowed by shadow – is replaced by a rising tide of sound as fluted songs float over the forest. Frogs and peepers up their urgent calling, and loons wail with longing, while owls screech back and forth, their deranged hooting conjuring up images of hideous creatures in the darkness.

The leaves rustle. A coyote howls in the distance. Small sounds magnify in the blackness without the moderating influence of the eyes. We keep flashlights by our side and scrounge for kindling to ignite a reassuring fire. Flames dance around the circle of rocks as we move close to the friendly glow, seeking security in sight, though tear-stained and squinting from the smoke. The crackling wood is comforting, but beyond the clearing sounds of the night hold sway, and the call of the wild beckons to the beating heart of the beast we keep at bay.

Life feeds on life. It is the way of the world. Bats and swallows dart through the air, intent on their banquet of bugs. The nuthatch kicks up leaves in lust for beetles. The fish takes the fly, while eagle, osprey, or kingfisher eyes him for lunch.

This beast is a savage, but he's our savior as well. Christ is crucified; the incarnate are crushed, chewed, and metabolized into muscle. Life is an eternal dying and return, a sacred dance of a divine and devouring deity. The great wheel turns. The serpent swallows its tail, eating itself. Empires rise and crumble while grasses are plowed under to fertilize the soil.

Winter turns to spring, seeds take root, and the fallen rise again, delivered from the dead into new coats of flesh. There is no world of peace and perfection, placid and pure, where good exists without evil. We enter this temple of transformation to be sacrificed on the altar. The forms are fluid; our time is temporary; all things pass without fail. Any wise man knows he's wicked; any priest a pawn or predator.

So let us all prey.

The temperatures fall with the sun; a chill creeps into the air. Cirrus clouds swirl around the circumference of the sky; the moon is newborn and not yet visible. Crystalline stars will blaze in the cold, clear heavens. The body shivers as night draws steadily closer, stalking the retreating day.

Tonight I will arrive at the doorway to the Dreamtime and kneel upon the threshold. Before me I see death, dissolution, ecstatic bliss, my breath upon the mirror. I see a long black tunnel, an entrance to heaven or hell, the gateway to the Garden, the gaping mouth of mystery.

And something waits there, smiling.

Spirit, I give thanks for this life, for one more day to behold your beauty. Each dusk and dawning brings a banquet of delight and difficulties. One day your lips will part and take me, but I will neither fear nor flee. With eyes, heart, and arms wide open, I'll run to them as a lover, intent on one passionate and final kiss... wanting to be swallowed whole.

Dying Suns, Guiding Lights

The wind sweeps across the water, carrying with it the first chill of early autumn. A hurricane spins like a turbine somewhere over the Atlantic, and high clouds spread across the morning sky like a film of oil.

Last night the heavens were radiant. A throng of stars blinked like crystal in the cold clean air. The northern lights appeared and pulsed with eerie life, enchanted ribbons of radiance snaking across an ebony sky. Loons and owls cast their haunting calls into the hollow blackness.

The seasons are turning. The days grow shorter; and the sun sinks lower in the sky. The carefree ease of summer shrivels with the anxious arrival of autumn. The solar powers slow; the endless expansion is arrested. As the forest approaches the intersection of the equinox, the trees turn, – their sap responding to signals of an ancient stoplight – leaves changing from green through yellow and red. Heat and cold, dark and light battle or hang in a tenuous balance, as waves of warmth and winter move back and forth over the landscape like advancing armies, the final outcome never in doubt.

Butterflies and birds are heading south. Roses wither on the vine, the innocence of youth lost as its full-fleshed face confronts the hollow sockets of death. Crickets still buzz in the yellowing grasses, but their songs will soon be silenced. A few hardy flowers turn to the sun, savoring the last moments of a slow and sad goodbye, their green turning golden, then gone. Stalks stand brown and wooden, as life contracts and moves inward and down to the soil. Summer's spirit vanishes; soul takes root.

It is a melancholy time. Apollo turns his bright gaze away. Persephone is raped and abducted into the underworld. Demeter, grief-stricken and suddenly old, looks upon life with disinterest. The ascending arc has passed the pinnacle; promise and pride shattering in the fall. Warm rains and crashing thunderstorms are infrequent. Fruits are picked; the reaper cuts down fields with his scythe; Saturn returns to eat his children. Seeds are stored away for a far-off spring.

Spirit, be with us as winter extends its icy hands. We drift into darkness, enter a long black tunnel – destination unknown-- succumbing to death or dreamlike dormancy to await an elusive resurrection. Either way the contractions are painful. As the sun in the sky grows dim, we tend our fires and lanterns, determined to live on what's been stored away.

Wisdom is the harvest of experience. It is the seed that endures when all our chaff is screened and sifted. It is the grain, the germ of new growth; food and fuel for the future; the staff of life ground into bread that feeds the people. We have all eaten the fruit on the tree of knowledge. Good and evil weave through the web of life; terror and wonder walk arm and arm through the world. It is wisdom – or a warrior's choice – to track this wonder, to attune one's eyes to awe, and in so doing, end the exile and enter the Garden again.

Great Spirit, help us open our eyes and feast on the light you've placed within us. We are not the center of the universe, and we will not solve the mystery. May we adjust to your cycles and seasons, humbly gathering in gratitude for all you have given. Help us fan the flames burning in the hearths of our hearts, and cast forth a circle of warmth to weather the cold gusts of winter.

Evening comes, and the breeze grows chilly. I shall celebrate the fall and the rich harvest of summer. May all the chaff and dead stalks of my life be blown away. I accept the losses in life, but I will give my heart to thanksgiving. Thank you for everything.

The pearls of wisdom shine brilliantly. Their beauty is magnified against dark backgrounds, like a necklace of stars in the cold night sky, like a light in the long dark tunnel. They call out, give comfort, and lift my spirits. May they guide all those who are lost toward home.

The Challenging Quest for Vision

We enter the wilderness to seek a vision and return. The faint tracks of Christ, Buddha, or Black Elk stretch before us. We encounter the unknown, its presence and power awesome and palpable. Sunshine, cloudless days, storms with sleet are all possibilities. Fear and loneliness are constant companions; culture, consensus, society, and small talk fall by the wayside. We walk to the mountains, dark forest, or desert. We descend to the underworld.

The fog of unknowing blocks our vision. Rain and raw winds feed our worries. Rattlesnakes, mountain lions, or bears prowl 'round the edges of our awareness. Accident, injury, hunger and thirst chatter in the corners of consciousness. Swamps of despair wait on either side. What we have run from lies in ambush – hiding everywhere – as we step forward, trembling.

Empty days extend into the distance. Watches, schedules, and appointment books have all been left behind. Aimlessness invades our attention, and our boat is rudderless… the sails slack as we are spun this way and that by changing winds on a sea of boredom. Plans dissolve; intention scatters in every direction. Statements of purpose, images of achievement, and stories of success mock us. Resignation enters our body and eats away toward our hearts, like a cutworm chewing a tunnel at the core of our being. It will not stop. Anger flares up and lashes out. We shake our fists at God or Gaia; call them stupid, ugly, or foolish. They are dead, delusions, abstract and empty categories. *"Why did I ever come here?"* We feel lonely and lost; abandoned.

The old self is obstinate, and its unraveling is difficult. As the well-maintained walls of the known crack and begin to crumble, they brace themselves against the assault, but the enemy lies everywhere. The unknown stalks us inside the shadows of night. It's camped out and camouflaged in forest and field, roams in the surrounding hills, moves through mazes of underground passageways. We reinforce our battlements, but it burrows beneath us, undermining our foundations. We steel ourselves to stand our ground, but the ground is no longer solid.

Humility comes hard, but it is like manna from heaven. The miasma melts away, and the self's importance shrinks. The cauldron bubbles; the soup thickening as movement gathers steam. Fog condenses into rain, and tears fall from the eyes to water the parched and barren earth. Waves of grief hurl themselves against the shore.

The castle walls are battered and soon begin to break. The shell softens or shatters; the cocoon splits asunder; the egg hatches. A small crack slowly expands into an opening – an entry or exit, a window where two worlds can meet. A portal appears in the psyche, an aperture in the air... Inner becomes outer, outer meets inner. Emergence and entry, essence and existence are merged within magical moments as new life struggles to be born, reaching for food, form, and freedom. Light and a gust of wind rush forward into the vacuum, filling the lungs and eyes with sweet and searing beauty. The trail of tears or the road less traveled becomes the path with heart.

*   *   *

In the light of a new day, the tracks of saints become visible. They too crossed the river Styx and journeyed through the

Valley of Death. Their drumbeats echo in canyon and hillside. Their songs can be heard on currents of wind. Their presence yet remains, their footfalls felt in the shifting sands of eternity, their imprints barely perceptible along the shore.

I will ascend to the mountaintop, and lift mine eyes to the hills in spirit flight. I have fasted, foregone food for this feast of vision, this banquet of the soul. Transformed by tears, washed of wanting and willfulness, my gaze is clear.

The beauty of the earth extends out below me. The valley stretches out vibrant and voluptuous, the river radiant in the sun. Diamonds dance in a luminous landscape of liquid, its surface ashimmer with glistening gemstones. It calls me to enter its currents, to wrap myself in its ribbon of gold, to drown in devotion. Before me lies the source of life, the fountain of youth, the entrance to the temple.

A voice cries in the wilderness: *"This is the Promised Land! Wash away your sins, release your regrets, shed the old skin! Step through the doorway. Enter the water! Be baptized, blessed, cleansed, and reborn."*

The ego has come undone, the stench of death and decay swept away by the breeze. The shaman is dismembered, then remembers. Flowers take root in the rot as the dark night of the soul surrenders to the new dawning of the spirit.

All is as it should be. This moment and I are enough.

*   *   *

The sun vaults over the hillside and runs across a cloudless sky. The river wraps itself around a gravel spit and bounces off

325

boulders across the way. A stiff breeze from the south ruffles the surface of the water. Swirls and eddies form and disappear, scouring a deep bowl at the foot of a rocky face and dropping sand in steppes and terraces along the shore. The temperature climbs along with the sun. Soon I will enter those waters to float and frolic through the lazy afternoon, delighted and adrift in the welcoming embrace of its clear, cold currents.

Vision, rebirth, transformation… a new dream. Euphoria cannot be held onto. Time and the river move on, though eternity is always. Eventually I will descend into darkness again. Spirit shall become flesh; the raw, tender skin will develop new armor. My fluid movement may be frozen into rigid form when touched by the cold hand of fear. Definition will become defense and concreteness constraint once again.

I may build another house to inhabit – a structure of the self more simple or solid – to temporarily shelter a secret interior. I may feel pride in my workmanship as new walls divide within from without; deadbolts blocking the doors; protection becoming prison again. The sashes will be lowered and locked, the openings closed, and the air grow stale as I look upon the world through the pains of my windows.

*   *   *

Will I once more disregard what I know and grow deaf to the song of the soul? Shall I ignore the tapping on the glass, forgetting the wind and breath of god until the foundation trembles again in some great storm, and lightning hurls a flash of illumination through my tightly-closed eyes?

Today the world is filled with enchantment, and I cry with gratitude rather than regret. Tomorrow is a new landscape, but the same choice awaits. The tides and sun rise and fall; the river seems glistening or gloomy as tragedy and terror, comedy and wonder, dance around the circle. The seasons pass. Ten thousand forms burst forth and fade as the cycles turn like a whirling dervish. They spin in ecstatic dance, but sometimes it makes us nauseous and dizzy. It depends on where we focus our vision.

There's an invisible point, a stillness, a center in all the spinning. Spirit, I will struggle to see you everywhere. You are wind and water, sun and soil. You are the trees and the tides, in all I know and in the knowing. You are in eternity and now, in nothing and everything.

The passage to another world is rarely easy. Something ends in each beginning. A vulture passes overhead, its silver underwings like those of an angel. Life and death go hand in hand… and there are many forms of praying.

Spirit, you shine in the sun and run in the river. You are above, below, behind, before, beside, and within me. In the "I" and eye that sees you, you are the seeing. Welcome into my life, for it is your life. I know not where you lead me, but I will follow. I will enter the Valley of Death for "Thou" art with me.

And I will fear no evil.

Dreaming with the Deer

Early this morning I awoke to a clattering of rocks as a doe picked her way down the stony hillside, bounded into the river, and crossed. She did not see me sit up in the tall grasses where I had been sleeping, and came closer – gazing upstream and down, head alert, great ears turning left and right. Finally, suspecting something, she swerved and strode steadily away.

I went back to sleep and sank into hazy dreams. Awakened by a cough, I quickly stood up, searching for the source of the sound to find five more deer facing me across a short stretch of sand. Three bounded away, but two remained, eyes upon me. On a whim I spoke to them, and they set to flight.

I do not know the reasons for things, but I am in love with the mysteries of the world. Roused from sleep in a bed of sand beneath the white oak, I feel as if I've been awakened by angels. Something delicate and beautiful came close and flitted away, an awareness so bright and precious I'd hesitate to touch it. Every morning I pray to live in balance and harmony, and I earnestly speak to the hills, sky, and river, but I am still too coarse, too human, too civilized to fully enter this temple. But each day I try again.

The deer speak to my heart of walking through life with grace, taking soft steps upon a solid footing. I am gradually learning to walk like them, stepping tenderly on the earth, adjusting my path to not crush the grasses and shrubs along the riverbank. I learn slowly. Like most, I've had no teachers in this art, but I do my best and persevere. Many of my fellows do less, approaching the land with gun or bulldozer, determined to take something from it, leaving cigarettes or beer cans in their wake. Others just ignore it, fascinated only with human creations, able to name more brands of soda than species of trees.

Nature is the visible face of the spirit, the source and sustenance of our lives. In her, creation is constant and right now, not some mytho-historic event. The kingdom of heaven is of the earth, and here, amidst box elder, coyote willow, and the ten thousand forms of life, we face something equal to and greater than us. It speaks in a language we recognize, but did not create. It is a humbling experience to truly encounter what we can't comprehend, and what is in many ways superior to us. To be human is to come from humus, to be of the earth. Soul and soil grow from the same root.

The deer survive on grasses, oak leaves, and instinct. They do not question if they are, or have enough. Sitting by the river with my back against the juniper, I see a profound wisdom in these clear brown eyes. I do not want the piles of things crowding the shelves of stores. There is no deep emptiness needing to be filled by money or matter, no vacant hollow that craves approval or adulation.

The deer have arrived. Soft and strong, they've come to open the heart. In loving this world – its mountains, valleys, and streams – I have found heaven on earth. In the sacred moments of utter connectedness, I partake of and participate in creation. I am, and have, it all. There is nothing to buy that could bring me more happiness.

The deer have touched me, and I want nothing more. I am richer than any king, and the trappings and treasures of the world neither tempt nor trouble me. This earth is my place of power; this bank holds my interest. Fidelity and trust will not be found in institutions, and they cannot tender an offer to match this simple offer of tenderness.

The deer have eaten, drunk their fill, and once again they ascend to the mountain. They walk a path with heart. And my spirit leaps to follow them.

Fearing the Fall

The Mimbres River, bone-dry a week ago, now chatters happily in its streambed. The sun reaches out toward the ridgeline to the west in radiant glory, its waves of ethereal fire slowly descending into this frosty valley. The moon, half-faded, hovers in the morning sky; the cottonwoods are turning yellow. I rest beneath a ponderosa on a soft carpet of needles, my back against its sweet-scented trunk, listening to the song of birds, brook, and breath, my heart and the world in balance.

Soon I must leave these mountains, bidding farewell to the rocks, rivers, cottonwoods, and campfire, turning my back on swallows, stellar jays, and silence. For weeks I have slept under oak, piñon, and juniper with the stars blazing overhead. I've weathered storms and sunshine, rain and rattlesnakes, while hawks soared through the sky circling to heaven. I've been blessed, bathed in love and loneliness, and a bittersweet joy nests in my heart as I await the light and warmth, breath visible in the cold morning.

In two days my plane will be ready to gather and lift me skyward to descend in a different dream. There lies a good life – small town, friends, and a lovely little house. But when I open its door another closes behind me. The seamless landscape shall become broken. The phone will ring, lights go on, and these star-studded nights will disappear and be forgotten. The pace will pick up, and I'll stumble through landscapes of lists and errands, my friendly forest pathway replaced by a succession of hurdles.

Dear Spirit, be with me. The earth turns, colors change, and winter will soon be here. Loneliness and loss are beside me already, and I dread to be leaving. I would hold fast to your fire in the swift-fading light. Walk with me through the coming days. Grant me courage and the strength to tend your flame in the approaching times of cold and darkness.

Thank you for this life in the body of earth, for reminding me I am not alone. Though often distracted or adrift in thought, I am always somewhere – today among the grasses and scrub oaks, tomorrow...

I am afraid. Many dark nights of the soul are waiting amidst the well-lit avenues of human association. The cords of connection are routinely cut by comfort, convenience, and other civilized concerns. The heart easily becomes confused by language; purpose and direction are lost in labyrinths of peoples' self-reflecting creations.

Help me, Great Spirit, for I am yours. I know that now, but I stand before the entrance to darkness, and demons flit about in the shadows. Inside is a dragon which I must slay, seduce, or befriend. Routines, habits, avarice, addictions.... Multitudes of distractions and diversions pull me from the circle of life. Money, fame, power – the threats and temptations of society draw me away from my center.

But who I am remains the sum of my relations, and I am tied to you by breath, thirst, and hunger. My days are determined by your cycles. May I find sun, soil, and rainfall in the food I eat; feel the wind, grassland, and forest in your life-giving air. Guide me to remember and to mend those threads that fray. May I discover you in the landscape that lives within me and tend this garden with a life-giving gratitude.

The birds head south, the branches grow bare; the early morning chatter is quiet. The light fades, the sun settles lower in the sky. Bleak times are approaching, and we all must live on what's been stored away. I will gather your harvest in the cupboards of memory, these storms and sunsets stacked like cordwood in my heart. I shall learn faith, live frugally, and feed the fire of my passion while lighting a candle in honor of all the departed. I will sink deep into dreams, descend to the roots, and sing with your voice till the coming of spring.

Bless me on this journey. Ancestors, my Maker, my Love and Destiny… do not fail me now. Be with me as I battle to be with you. I long for an ally and search for a star to guide me home.

In Another World

A warbler calls from a barren branch of the piñon. She whistles, chirps, and clucks – my words seem so inadequate. As I describe these sweet and succulent sounds, I am placing her in my world, and I wonder about her motives, meanings, and to whom she sings.

But she is not in my world. Her instincts, memories, and images are her own. Her senses are unknown to me, attuned to subtle and mysterious whisperings in the ecology of wind and feather. I am blind to her reality, oblivious to the shapes and structures in the make-up of her eye. Unperceived pulses and particles add depth and texture to her surroundings. Unknown wavelengths whisper in her ear. With my awareness and vision, she would quickly die, her vibrant and numinous world turned flat, dull, and uninteresting.

She inhabits a mysterious world far beyond mine, and the universe is revealed to her in forms I cannot fathom. Creation pours forth, endless and evolving, and she – sister, friend, relative.... a "small bird," we say – drinks in knowledge as vast and deep as ours. We all catch just a glimmer, and great Gaia shows to her a face that I will never see.

As I lean against the rough bark of an oak, cicadas are clicking all around me, but they quickly hush as high clouds cloak the beaming circle of the sun. Science would make their speaking dumb, mere stimulus-response, a mindless reflex to temperature or chemicals. But it may be we who are stupid, unable to feel the love and longing, the brilliance in these bonds between their bodies and the sky. They're aware of my presence, also growing silent as I draw near. It could be something simple that makes them speechless – my sounds, smell, or light – but perhaps they sense darker shadows and refuse to cast their pearls before swine.

The branches all about me are alive with movement as ants, aphids, flies, and honeybees scour their bark. Spider webs and golden strands of sap shimmer with sunlight, sparkling droplets falling to the ground from undetected sources. The trees may also be observing us as they capture sunlight with chlorophyll hardly different from the retinal matter in our eyes.

This is holy ground. Heaven is not somewhere else. The world is not simply "out there." It is here – above, below, before, behind, beside, and within – asking to be participated in, engaged with, met.

I am drawn to this living earth by desire as well as gravity. Vision is not merely a matter of the eyes. The complex, layered, and thickening textures of existence draw me onward, and this rich synthesis and stew of the senses is somehow as much of heart as mind. Given time enough to follow this fascination, the growing realization of "what-is-all-around-me" results in ever-deepening revelations of the sacredness and miracle of life.

Beyond the old house of reason lies another landscape, and there I'm offered communion and challenged to treat the living earth with love and respect. It's not a simple task. Old habits of self-centeredness, separateness, and arrogance die hard. Before me is the Promised Land, the Garden, my true home; but the return comes with the humbling realization that they are all watching me.

I am in other worlds – their worlds – so far different than

mine to be unimaginable. The hawk's clear and brilliant eye and the dragonfly's thirty-thousand mirrored lenses perceive me moving through surroundings I will never see. I am small, stupid, blind, deaf, and dumb in dimensions I can only dream of.

The possibilities are overwhelming. But the path is simple – it's one of the heart.

Spirit Who Moves in all Things, I must learn to love you, challenge myself to willingly open the doors of perception, and cherish this earth if I'm to find communion with life. I am a human, born with my own unique brilliance, fashioned by fire in creation's cauldron, woven by webs of infinite power and possibility and poured forth into now. I will sing in this symphony, filled with wonder by this wonder-filled life.

My cup runneth over. Around me is mystery and I will be grateful for my small glance at its grandeur. Beside me are friends, family, elders, teachers… relatives all. I am small, but not helpless, for I am not alone. We are in this together, dreaming the universe into being.

The Dreamtime gods, ancestors, and great powers are all about us, calling us to awaken from our slumber, enter this Dream, and celebrate the dawning of a new day. We are on a quest, a sacred journey, as we have been since the moment of creation. That journey is endless, but the moment is now.

Sleeping Beauty

The earth spins like a dervish, and the sun rises over a calm Atlantic. All is peaceful, as Gaia, the great Mother-goddess, rests in a hammock. Harlequin birds flit like streamers through vines of the rainforest, vibrant and colorful like orchids in her hair.

The waves lap gently against the shore, the skin of the earth softly licked by the sensuous tongue of the sea. Gaia's dreambody stretches and rocks to the rhythm of the tide; her beauty sparkles like a radiant jewel in dark eyes of the beholder.

This Sleeping Beauty awaits a kiss, but she will not present her face to any fool who passes by. Most miss her completely, their attention seduced by pleasures more petty, profane, and practical. She is subtle, camouflaged, invisible... woven into the web of existence, undetected by those without the sense or senses to see her.

Her spells are cast like nets to capture the intuitive senses. The strings of her hammock are tuned to deep chords that resonate in the octaves of other worlds. Her harmonies can be heard by the inner ear. Her frequencies are felt by those attentive to uplifting vibrations, and mystics and sages dance to her music. Her songs have been sung through eons of time, haunting melodies that move an open heart to realms of mystery and magic.

Only the prince, seeker, or disciple will find her. The path to her is narrow, though entrances are everywhere. The trail passes through the eye of the needle – lost long ago in a haystack – and one will not find it grasping at straws. We must follow our heart's longing, commit ourselves to be guided by something greater than us. Nobility, gratitude, devotion, and childlike wonder are among the keys that unlock the doors to heaven, open the gateways to other dimensions.

She is the goddess, the grail, the cup and water of life. She's the fountain of youth, womb of the world, the cauldron of creation. She's ambrosia, the nectar of the gods, the deep, bubbling spring that feeds the roots of the world tree. The spark of the infinite must enter her ovum to fertilize the egg of existence. All forms flower in her vastness. Life pours forth from her vulva. Spirit becomes matter, stillness meets movement, and silence makes music as the sacred songs of the universe burst from her lips.

Long ago we were guileless and pure of heart. As children, we nestled at her breast and fed from what was freely given: milk, honey, manna from heaven. We walked in the Garden, played in innocence, and grew from her generous offerings... were fruitful and multiplied.

But innocence was lost, calling us to search to find it once again. The journey may be long, frightening, or chaotic. One must enter the darkness; overcome obstacles; negotiate twisted tunnels through a labyrinth led only by longing. Dragons must be fought; ephemera, fantasies, and false friends seen through. Dangers abound. Lonely, lost... the surroundings are strange, the path perilous.

Nightmares fill the troubled heavens. Sleep is restless. Battles rage, buildings burn; civil war scorches the soul. The sky grows dark with destruction, stained with soot – it seems a threat to earth. We join in the struggle, search for something, anything – a solution, cure, miracle... winds of compassion that will cleanse the carnage... a breath of fresh air... a pipe of peace to bring to the smoking cities. We suffocate under the pressure.

We tie ourselves to the mast; wean ourselves from addiction and appearances, what's seductive or superficial. We escape from prison, cast aside our chains; forge new links with what cannot be captured. We break out of the hall of mirrors, pass through to the other side, fashioning new lenses out of the shattered glass, accepting bad luck with the good. We strain and struggle to lift the enchantment, cast off the curse, to rise to the surface and open our eyes, to awaken into light. Our efforts seem endless.

Sleeping Beauty lies before and within us, waiting. Gaia, the Goddess sleeps on, dreaming a greater dream, her true riches hidden from those who would try to take her. From her we come forth and to her we must return, but how shall we come to her now?

Selfish and short-term pleasures must be forgotten. The exile has been long and of our own making. We must acknowledge our losses, accept our grieving. Tears must wash our gaze of willfulness before true sight shall return. The eyes of a child move straight to her breasts, but a greater vision travels inward to the soul. That chest and its treasures can only be opened by a faithful love. Can we truly see what is before and awaits us? Are we worthy of a gift so great, a union so grand?

What she offers is mysterious and magical. What she requires is not complicated. She asks for kindness, caring, a sincere and simple gesture with your heart in your hands. Kiss the ground and offer it now! In embracing everything and demanding nothing her radiance will once again be revealed.

Heaven Upon the Earth

Dear River,

Mammoth pines tower above me, joining with piñons to frame a circle of sky with black-branched borders, a great column open to heaven. Their charcoal silhouettes reach up toward the stars, whose twinkling eyes shimmer in inky space; their faces friendly in the moonless night. Orion rises over the ridgeline, his belt and bow gleaming in the darkness, trailed by ever-faithful Sirius. Meteors shoot like magic across ebony fields. Celestial bodies beam as galaxies gaze upon earth with sparkling eyes.

An owl hoots in the shadows. Rocks clatter as deer make their way down the slope to the streambed, filling their bellies with green grass and drinking black water studded with diamonds. Their muzzles drip, thirst sated by the brimming cup of creation, its contents cold and clear. Exquisite, slight, hard of hoof and soft of eyes, they stare into the velvet void, alert and poised to shatter the stillness with crashing flight.

But no danger approaches. Only my cup and the river runneth over as their inky shapes dissolve into shadows and pass from sight. Gratitude fills me, thoughts about goodness and mercy following their unseen journey as my attention lingers like a lover for one last caress. The night is dark, but the spirit is not hampered by its blackness, and my blessings bound behind them along paths of space-time momentarily crossed.

I lie at the foot of a magnificent ponderosa who protects, guides, and draws my vision upward through the night. Seeking the sustenance of secret springs, he stretches deep below me into the sandy earth, his life a living offering between soil, sun, and sky. His seeds and needles surround me as I surrender to slumber in his arms. I am small, weak, and a visitor to the wilderness, but, enveloped in his rugged embrace, my breathing slows. He sighs with the breeze and whispers in my ear:

"Simply be like me. Make the space sacred about you. Create a circle and sing your song; make holy that four-chambered house within your chest. Purify yourself. Pour out all planning and pretense; clear out the clutter of foregone conclusions. Welcome the world with dance and drumbeat, and give praise to the powers around you. Life is good. Open your heart to the unknown and make room for an honored guest; and thy container will be filled from the bountiful well of being."

Sleep steals upon me and stocks the cupboards of consciousness with a larder full of dreams. A few linger into morning, and I awaken with a sense of feasting well. Aurora – rosy-cheeked and shy – approaches, blushing beyond the eastern horizon. Venus appears, and the gods of gloom descend with the dawning, slipping beneath the surface of a shining sea that washes ashore in waves of light.

The tide slowly turns. The harsh hand of the sun sends its flaming fingers through the sky. They touch and trail across the skin, lingering until clothes peel off the body like shedding bark and hats are donned to shield vision from a god too glorious to gaze upon. The river glitters with gemstones, its waters transformed by day from darkness to delight; its cold currents – inhospitable in evening – now inviting. Insects swarm through the air like gold dust. Red-tailed hawks carve circles in the heavens. Heat increases in a midday haze that sweeps over the hillsides, bleaching color and contrast from cliffs and canyon. Stones shimmer and start to simmer on the baking earth. They can burn the feet, but this too is holy ground.

Life pours out in profusion from a central and sacred source. That center is here and now through black and white, heat and cold, yin and yang. The one, simmering light shatters into bands of brilliant color that catch the eye, as the Gods put on countless different faces, their excess of appearances ever-surprising to a soul being tested and tempered by dark nights, fire, ice, sunshine, and storm.

Beauty is in the eye of the beholder, and, Great Mystery, I am open to be held. I am humble, mentored, made in your image, and molded by the multitude of masks you wear. I will honor and celebrate those endless guises and guests, and offer them a home and hospitality in the chambers of this heart. A thousand textures trail across my fingertips as we reach our hands toward each other. I listen for your voice; my gaze searches out your face; my heart beats its rhythm for you. My soul is singing, and my spirit dances to the bloody pulse of the passionate life that plays in the power of the world.

Reflections in the Mirror

The stars burn through the charcoal velvet above a black silhouette of cottonwood as I lie awake through the night. The moon rises, half past full, her face slowly twisting as she makes her way across the sky. The river plays sweet lullabies, and I rest, cradled upon the earth, but the beauty of the turning heavens draws me wakeful toward the dawn. Coyotes howl in the early light, their sharp cries cutting through soft shades of gray. Joyous, mocking, tempting, garrulous, or haunting – the call of the wild is heard differently by every listening ear.

The inner landscape needs the outer. Our souls are not fed by flat white walls, offices, and apartments. Our calling is not heard on the radio, and the authentic self will not appear on computer screens no matter how long or hard we look.

We need this Other. There is no depth in sameness. We live among life forms unlike ours, a richly woven web of relations, and we are within the web, not outside it. It speaks without words; it is the ground we stand on, the air we breathe, and the light by which we see. It surfaces in cell, synapse, muscle, and molecule... in strange and ancient urgings our reasoning mind will never understand. It is the great presence, the invisible world. It is a great, primal ocean, and on its surface our cherished consensus reality rises and falls like evanescent froth, small flecks of foam floating among far-grander forces above and below.

We must honor and know this Other to know ourselves. It is not to be ruled, used, or eliminated. It has made us who we are in responding to its challenges and callings through the eons; fashioning bone, blood, brain, ears, eyes, skin, and senses to merge with and meet its patterns and pulsing presence. Flesh to feel, organs to probe, protect, or procreate; we are an on-going evolutionary improvisation attuning to the rhythms and chords strummed on the shimmering strings of its intricate net.

Our response vibrates through the strands of existence, for we are of note, though a very small part of the symphony. We cannot go it alone; our set-apart presence is vain, sterile, and out of tune. Our true potential lies in response-ability: in listening, feeling, and finding greater harmonies that can resonate and carry us beyond ourselves.

The Other has made us, our bone, blood, brain, and body formed in this dialogue and dance. So how shall we approach our Creator?

The people wander in exile from the Garden, while the kingdom of heaven surrounds us unnoticed. The caw of the crow reverberates within our inner landscape. The hooting of owls asks "Who" we are. What will we be when they are gone? How much metal must be mined and highways built so our autos can carry us to the country whose sky is empty of birds? How many board feet of lumber will replace the forest that is no more? How many dollars for the price of our soul? We too shall become barren and banal – our people turned hollow, lonely, and lifeless – for in our drive to extinction we are killing ourselves. Each species has played its part and fashioned part of our psyche. Each death is a suicide.

Separateness is our original sin. Our loss of innocence haunts us, and when we look only in the mirror, it is we who are truly lost. Is God really dead, or is he just made in our image? Shall this prodigal child ever return home, or will he stubbornly choose

345

his pig sty over the Promised Land?

*   *   *

The spirit world lives all about us. The invisible is dancing just beyond the shrunken horizon of our sight. Healing may be many different things, but wholeness always draws us to deeper and broader experience. Our sickness is a form of stagnation, a staying in the shallows. The stance of self-importance is a solitary and static affair, a withdrawal from the great dance of life. Living is movement, impermanence, an always-dynamic balance, communication, response, exchange… a breathing in and out. It is fluid – like water, like fire. It is present, pulsing, hypnotic…. engaging, but ungraspable. It is a flame or a river, terrifying or transforming, something that must be opened to and entered.

Union with the Creator is the pathway to eternal life. The Promised Land is everywhere. Can we turn toward the Other and let life find us again?

The world will go on, with or without us. The web is intact, shimmering, seamless, and self-regulating. And it will endure, should our strand and our promise be broken.

Vision

Clear sky, blazing sun; the desert baking. Brown sand searing, shimmers. The plants are parched, the branches brittle, and roots burrow deep below the skillet stone surface of a bleached and barren soil. The skin sweats, spits, sizzles, and blisters, as moisture is sucked away moment-by-moment into a furnace-like heaven. The once-soft flesh is burned, browned, and cracked like the mudflats; etched, eroded, and carved like canyons. Character is being tested by fire, and our faces become formed in testament to beauty, power, and the harsh hand of the living earth.

Snow-capped peaks smile in the distance, pregnant and seemingly pure against the azure horizon. Their promise of richness – refreshing and cool – is a beckoning image across forty miles of bare, burning ground. It's tempting, tantalizing, and almost unreal... a far-off fantasy of wonder, wealth, goodness and mercy. It must be a mirage, a flimsy facade spun by demons or devils... a miasma, a hypnotic hope, a hallucination, delirious and mesmerizing. It's an illusion, a trick of perception, a deceptive dream made up of smoke and mirrors. It's today's promise of power, comfort, and cold-quenched thirst, the riches of the world cast before Christ in his hot and lonely vigil in a waterless wasteland.

Jesus, Moses, Mohammed, and many a prophet were drawn to the desert, seeking fertile soil for their souls amidst the bare rocks, bleached bones, and burning bushes. Pulled by some invisible, common, and holy thread, what brought them beyond the borders of human habitation to this harsh home where landscape and experience lie unbroken by roads, time, or any constraints of civilization or common sense? The answer comes gradually in fire and air... air and fire.

Time slows and soon stops altogether. Silence and empty space whisper to the inner ear. What was once separate dissolves in the vast distances, and a flowering vase of new sensibilities sprout in the dry deluge.

The earth turns and the sun travels westward, the heat slightly abating. Dust devils dance their evening celebrations. A soft breeze washes the parched and dirty skin.

Life is hard. Life is filled with work, disappointment, and sorrow. But we are not alone. The earth holds out its hands in friendship. Beauty, joy, and wonder are also woven into the fabric of existence, and healing – feeling whole and at home here – is an ever-present possibility.

What is vision? Is it a promise, a path, a potential? Is it a goal or a guiding light? Is it an event, a revelation; a meeting on a road or in a market that can change our lives forever? Perhaps that is how it goes sometimes, a singular occurrence altering our trajectory and spinning us off toward a new star.

But in this silence I sense something different – a living presence, an active power, subtle and quietly relentless. The doorway to the Dreamtime stands slightly ajar, and ancient gods cavort just beyond the gates of my imagination. Something circles around me and its palpable presence flows over the empty landscape. I am not alone. I am prey to larger forces, and spirit, an entity, a hawk or a raven wraps its wings about me and suffuses my awareness. I stare into the world same as before. Nothing has changed. There is food to be made, pots to be washed, coffee to brew.

But something is rising to the heavens as I pick up the dishes. The horizons are limitless. As the distances grow, my small life plays out before me. The wind tells me secrets. Outside the ego, I am beside myself with wonder as cravings, dissatisfactions, and discomforts slip away, my hunger satisfied as I am swallowed by the sky.

Coming to Our Senses

Wind moves in the branches. This morning brings rain and fog, the call of a lonely sparrow, the tapping of dripping leaves. Water is everywhere, above and below. It surrounds and permeates everything, gray upon gray like an endless slate ocean. The grasses are bent. Their wispy heads fill with liquid like cotton-candy spun with dew-drop strands; soft, spongy clouds that shed their cold cargo upon sodden shoes and passing pants.

Waves beat upon the shore in unremitting splashes of salt, and rocks rattle as they tumble across the round stone beach. The spray is gathered up by warm breezes and spread over the landscape like hot, humid breath, spit hanging in the air. All is wet and womb-like. The atmosphere is pregnant with silence and waiting, its motion measured in trickling cadences.

The sun is invisible; the clock slows down. Light, sky, and shadow are all absorbed in dark, spongy tissue; contrast and change are impossible to determine. One might feel close to eternity, but the mind doesn't like it. Space and time seem constant and endless, everything all at once. The air feels clammy, uncomfortable, and confining; smothering, sickening, ill-at-ease. There is nothing to do. Mist continues to fall.

Meanwhile a different and joyful mood is manifesting at our feet. Roots drink in moisture like manna from heaven. The soil softens, its arteries opening to expanding rivulets as elements mix and melt, what's formerly separate dissolved or held in suspension. Newts and salamanders emerge from musty leaves, their skin – tender as newborns – caressed by the damp and dew. Earthworms dance below the ground. Molds, mushrooms, and fungi declare a holiday. Snakes slither in sensuous delight.

But our eyes are looking up. We set them toward the sky, for it's there we've placed all goodness – heaven, exalted planes, the infinite stars. We seek progress, growth, and achievement defined as "higher" education or income brackets. Children are "raised," adults grown "up." Jesus *ascends* to heaven; athletes *elevate* their game; generals *rise* through the ranks. We *over*come our problems; seek a peace or perspective that's *above it all.* Everyone wants to climb up the ladder of success, get the big raise, become part of the upper class, and have that office or penthouse on the top floor.

Our minds go against gravity and its sense. A bad day is a downer, shame a "fall" from grace. Reason is drawn to clear horizons, clarity, and light. It is wedded to the eyes, distant and visual. It longs for sky, wants off the planet. It desires objectivity, an abstract existence, space, grand vistas, generalizations, a bird's eye view, vision…

But the rain is falling. Birds stay in their nests, their damp feathers too heavy for flight. Mud, mist, and wet leaves whisper ancient secrets to the naked skin. The scent of the air is rich with moist earth as other, older senses hold sway. A voice asks us to remember, to remember...

Come down. Come down from the sky, from your head. Come down to your feet, the feeling of toes grasping the solid or slippery earth. Come back to the animal body, scents sent and received, the nose and its knowings.

Come down to the darkness and enter the shadows where

exalted gods, once honored, reigned: Poseidon and dim Pluto, god of underworld riches.... Snake, Salmon, thundering herds led by great bulls... carriers of hoof, horn, fin, and tentacle, beings before becoming. Return to earth, to rest, to your roots. Return to the Garden, to knowledge born before the awareness of time marched onward, separating mind from body, nouns from verbs, and beast from beauty. Come home.

Come home to image and magic, to a golden age when people were out of their minds. Come back before language became human and written into stone, parchment, or key strokes. Come back to a time before words, when living was given and god awe-filled, when mysteries were felt and not solved, before sensing had to "make sense."

Honor your dark roots, the rain, and what's irrational. Each one of our choices has been a way not chosen; every new freedom is also a form of forgetting. The world is pregnant with possibility. The sparrow calls again. "Come down. Go deeper."

Treasures are hidden in caves or rest at the bottom of the sea. Riches are awaiting us in the underworld, our bodies, and on the earth. Feel your feet upon the ground. Live within this world. There you must find your power, your purpose, and your humanity.

The air is musty. Rain continues to fall. Animals walk softly in the Garden. Spiders are spinning nets that catch dewdrops like necklaces of silver. New seeds reach out amidst death and decay.

Find your gift or a god given craft – like great Daedalus – and build a bridge to the sky. But do not try to live there. Gravity is a force of attraction, and we must all come to earth, one way or another.... like Snake... like Bear.... like Christ in his manger.... or like Icarus, who never grew down.

Living in a Larger Story

Footprints in Time

Dusky sages and brilliant greens frame barren rocks towering above the mud and talus slope leading down to the river. Flecks of foam float lazily past like lily pads. A breeze ruffles the water's surface to cool the sweaty skin.

All things come from you, Great Mystery, and to you all will return. Thank you for this time, this moment in eternity. My tracks are etched in clay along the riverbank, but soon they will disappear. They may be here tomorrow, the next day, and the next. A week is not unlikely; a month a slight possibility. My body could last a hundred years, my words even more... or less. But all this shall pass while something greater continues on.

Arrow points and potsherds of the Anasazi are scattered over these cliffs and mesas, fading footprints on the path of a perished people. This trail of a thousand years slowly disappears into dust, yet something still remains. I can hear voices in the silence of these hills; feel the presence of invisible spirits carried in whispers on the wind. A stone plunges into the water, and concentric rings stride out to distant shores, their force decreasing as the radius grows. Do they ever stop, or do the ripples go on forever, passing through the edges of those ponds into some dimension we have forgotten?

Banks of billowing cumulus sweep in from the west, pushed by the relentless broom of an afternoon breeze. A few sprinkles tumble from the sky, spotting the dusky soil in darker brown. Tonight the clouds will disperse to grow themselves afresh tomorrow as the unrelenting sun sends moisture streaming skyward. Cooling and condensing into new clouds, the rain shall fall to earth once more. In the grand cycle nothing lasts, yet nothing is lost. Everything dies, but nothing is destroyed.

Those aboriginal peoples still live in the rocks, the rivers, and in me. They are gone and yet they remain. The canyons hold their secrets. Their blood colors the red clay and rose-complexioned cliffs. Their music reverberates in the mountains and mesas, drumbeats echoing in far-off thunder; ancient songs circling to soar in the winds. Their spirits stream across time, spanning seasons and centuries, an alluring wave that laps at the shores of reason and current reality.

The sands are tumbling in the hourglass of eternity, and our time is short. The footprints on this shore will soon be erased, and today's towering thunderheads will be gone by evening. We live within forces beyond our understanding or control, and we are asked to love something far larger than us. A greater life awaits if only we can surrender to it. We are each a cell, a single note, a stone, but the ripples from our lives can spread beyond all our known horizons. But first we must give ourselves to the water.

The sun settles into its house of dusk. Swallows rocket over the river in search of bugs. My stomach grumbles, and my mind wanders in the direction of dinner. I will soon arise, follow this longing, and join my friends, leaving new sets of tracks in the sandy soil along the shore.

Spirit, thank you once again for this day. I am yours, and it cannot be otherwise. I am clay that's been formed by your fingers, molded by countless powers and pressures like these mud hills and mesas carved by wind and water. Though each moment, minute, and millennia these colored cliffs are being etched and eaten away. The arroyos run off into the river, and silt sweeps onward to the sea to become new earth built on the ocean bottom. Nothing lasts. And nothing is lost.

The landscape shines in the slanting sunlight, magnificent in its exposed and eroded beauty. I accept this life with all its faults and fissures. My fragile footprints will now head toward dinner and away from the river, for I must feed this earthly body as best I can. And its time seems so short in its longing for you.

Witnessing the Miracle

The water breaks; pregnant clouds let loose and shower the desert with cold and drenching rebirth. The river swells and bursts with life, the current rising as brown mud and silt slide over sandbar and gravel. Proud in its power and strong in its course, it swallows the banks and envelopes the grasses and shrubs.

A harsh summer of drought is soothed in the watery fall, the fever of burning forests broken. The skies drip, the scales tip; the earth turns on a path toward wholeness, its blistered skin salved, its blackened wounds washed with cool liquid.

I search the sky for signs of blue, the view limited by the outline of my tarp. My feet are cold, pack and clothes wet, my perceptions framed against the background of my discomfort.

"Great Mystery, living and loving Earth, help me to move beyond myself and the confines of ease and convenience. May gratitude open my heart and expand my perception. Let me have the eyes of the hawk, the heart of a mountain, and the courage to dream a great dream."

Clouds race across the sky from a far-away sea, shape-shifting forms laden with liquid, life-giving blood. Rains fall and the rivers replenish as grand cycles of soaking and drying sound a slow-beating pulse through the body of Gaia.

Thirsty oaks drink from the sodden sand, their great, furrowed trunks turned dark from the drenching. Shaggy cedars twist 'n delight, releasing sweet-scented fragrance into the air that – scattering – mixes with mint, ponderosa, and piñon in a magic potion, a heady brew. I savor the smell, grateful as I breathe in the aroma of good medicine.

"Spirit of this Earth, from thee I receive, to thee I give. Together we share, and from this we live. You are so great, and we are so small. A picture is worth a thousand words, I know, yet may these words create a small snapshot, a simple gesture of gratitude for this grand gift of existence."

Christ, Buddha, Moses, and Mohammed entered the wilderness. They fasted, prayed, had visions, performed miracles, showed us a doorway between the ordinary and an extraordinary life. Vision is grand. Vision is glorious. But vision is not supernatural. Vision is a way of seeing, an offering of attention, an open hand to the unknown, an availability to eternity.

Today, at this moment, miracles are happening all around and before me. Landscape and leaves turn color in the changing face of seasons, sunlight, and shadow, and millennia of geologic memory are etched into textures of stone. Porous and pock-marked from molten explosions... ochre-red, rusty iron, igneous, and iridescent, crushed conglomerate... smooth, polished, and rounded by riverbeds – sediment scatters a million-piece mosaic on this small stretch of riverbank.

Mountains are raked by landslides and rock becomes pebble. Gravel is ground into sand and soon to be soil. The earth feeds and supports the seed as it sprouts and lifts itself up in shoot, stalk, blade, branch, and leaf. Leaves become food, are swallowed and fashioned into flesh, metabolized in muscles whose movements slide pencils of lead across paper milled from memories of tree-trunks. Thought becomes motion and markings that symbolize sound are entwined in webs of words woven from the wonder of it all.

The blood in my body contains salt of ancient oceans. A billion years of DNA is looking through these eyes of love to see itself, the maker and mother, the matrix of miracles. Galaxies, black holes, quarks and quanta... the stone, the river, the velvet tongue of mullein... the song of cicada, spines of cactus, silk of spider... as clouds collide and a red-tailed hawk traces circles in the sky.

The infinite and eternal are here, right now, present in each moment. The oak lives in the acorn, and the acorn lives in the oak. God is in heaven, and heaven is here in the earth.

Beauty is in the eye of the beholder, and Spirit, you have made these eyes. Above, below, before, behind, beside – you are without bounds. I am within you, and you are in me. I am God, man, and miracle. I look out and you are in the looking. I see you everywhere. I am in heaven, for I am on earth and in love.

Circle of Stones

A circle of stones stands before me, marking the wheel of time and eternity. Today's rotations of sun, moon, and turning earth bring bright morning's brilliance to flame upon the red-rocked cliff. The cycles of the seasons converse in hot days and cool nights; in fullness and falling leaves; in dried, golden seed stalks that shine in the slanting light.

Successions of birth and death roll onward all around us. Beetles bore holes in the trunks of dead cottonwoods bleached white in the sun; woodpeckers feed in a stark silhouette of juniper. Stalks of mullein rise from gravel where river banks have been ripped out or resurrected by floods. The child becomes a woman or man, then ages to become childlike again.

Circles turn among circles. Venus sparkles in the twilight. The Milky Way spreads through the velvet black; Orion, Big Dipper, and Cassiopeia pivot in a protracted spin round the northern star. Rivers of air sweep across the continent, while great spirals of clouds dance before the face of the slowly-growing moon. The tides rise and fall like breath. Red corpuscles circle from lung to limbs and back again. The stirrings within a cell move through organs within a body within the biosphere, within a larger framework still. We turn the lens inward and smaller to find molecules, atoms, protons and quarks weaving and whirling like light, while particles wave like grasses in golden fields of probability.

Say "Yes!" quickly! Nothing holds still, and stillness holds everything. Membranes, borders, and boundaries are shifting and impermanent, temporary distinctions in a dance 'twixt this and that. Foreground needs back, change needs constancy, and everything becomes nothing. All motion is relative, and we are surely all related. Can the jellyfish know itself apart from the sea, or the sea the land? Inner and outer are born of one mother, sacred twins always dancing together. All "I's" are ways of seeing, arbitrary apertures in a shape-shifting dwelling of dreams. Go gently and merrily down the stream.

The river sings its way through the valley, from mountain to ocean and back again. Liquid, vaporous, or solid by season, it's a moving mystery set in great cycles of weather and water. Destructive, tranquil, torrential… it can be fertile, frothing, friendly, or frightening, "River" but one name for a multitude of moods, faces, and beings. Separate to streaming, droplet to drink, black at night and brilliant in day, its sounds of lullaby or laughter call and respond to downpours and drying; its deposits of life-giving-death balanced between the ever-changing banks.

There are circles of friendship, circles of truth. Laughter and tears – like sunshine and rain – cry out for one another, each impossible alone. Heaven must know the depths, the branches the roots, the future the past, the ancestors the newborn. Anger and fear, grief and emptiness all undulate like waves, a dance of deep currents that swirl below the surface in an ocean of belonging.

The eternal and infinite shimmer around our field of time, just outside this bubble of awareness. They beckon beyond the border and delight in undefinition. They sound a siren's call: both seductive and alarming. Invisible and there, present and past, potential and process… it's a flicker, a flame, a river, the wind. It's the promise of a butterfly and death to a caterpillar.

It is the opening of eyes long closed and the threat of

blinding realization. It is the body, the taste and the touch, the irrational making sense. It is a cry in the wilderness, the thundering heard, the one calling your name. It is the tender soul, hardened for years, dissolving its defenses; the seed reaching out. It is Christ on the cross, the human sacrifice, suffering made sacred. It is the altar atop the pyramid; the chest cut open and the heart offered.

God will enter the waiting cavity. New life floods in the opening, for birth, blood, and death are all mixed together. The Mystery cannot be solved, and it often arrives in our dissolution. All tension is released as our bubble bursts into nothing. The sun shines on the river; solids shatter into light; infinite reflections stream out into an ocean of awareness. And each is a dream and a doorway to another world.

The Sacred Twins keep turning to see their other face. The Garden of Eden beckons us to come back, to live, die, and know ourselves fully in all that's not us. The tree of eternal life blooms, its flowers of possibility beyond good and evil. The earth, stars, and great wheel slowly revolve, all mirrored in this circle of stones before me. My life, all life, is marked in movement and stillness, center and rim. And all revolutions and progress are spinning round an axis as they march forward and ever return.

Once Upon a Time

Naked we come into this world – vulnerable, soft-skinned and furless – yet we are not alone. Raised in different cultures and continents; rocking in cradles, sleeping in cities, caves, or canyons; we walk beneath the same blue sky – cloud, water, wind, and sun our companions wherever we reside or wander.

The earth both creates and changes us – dark skin in tropics, blue-eyed blondes in the north... lean, wiry desert dwellers, squat stout tribes of the tundra. Eyes, ears, weight... height, skin, lungs, and musculature were all molded, sculpted, teased, and tugged forth from the same gene pool as climate, cataclysm, and changing circumstances – different facets of existence – flowed and were forced upon us. We are Nature.

And in turn we create the world. A thousand decisions – to hunt, farm, wander or stay.... to build cities, temples, roads, nuclear bombs or nothing – mean that life and the landscape are no longer the same. Forests become fields; topsoil runs off into deltas. The air smells different; stars dim; and strange chemicals fill the streams, making a new kind of earth to press upon those who are to come. Nature is us.

So who are we? In the great tree of life, are we roots or branches? Are we defined by above or below, by where we have come from, or where we are going? Are we seed, fruit, trunk, leaf, water, soil, or stone?

Mystery weaves around and through us at every moment as we bob along in the long stream of time. Stars exploded, and Earth's story began. Particle clouds in space condensed to form a planet, a molten cauldron over whose swirling currents the flimsiest skin cooled into crust. Continents and ocean floors floated and sank, molecules were bound into compounds and built into stone.

Chlorophyll evolved to catch photons and eat the sun. It flourished in plankton, proliferating wildly as plants flowered and flung themselves over liquid and land. Ponds and streams flowed; the fecund soil – gestating, greening, and growing – threw up fern, forests, and meadows.

Animals followed from bacteria to beast – soaring, striding, and speaking back and forth in insect, dinosaur, and mammal. Onward they came through darkness and light, heat and cold, ice age and mammoth… spreading, splitting into species, developing and dying in a great back and forth dance, as muscle, brain, bone, ears, and eyes were shaped in call and response with the living earth.

The world lives in us. Mind, thinking, and the awareness of past, present, and future have been drawn out of the rich primal egg to take root in humanity. Blessed with the ability to see stories within the streaming tide of space-time, we emerged out of the great, pulsing fireball at the beginning, carrying this piece of the light.

The drama is not over. It does not – cannot – end in us. Creation continues. The grand dance of differentiation from hydrogen, dust clouds, and elements, to beetles, octopuses, and Einstein takes place in communion, a magnificent and sacred interaction between parts and the whole. We – and all the many faces and forces of the universe we live in – have evolved together to reach this point.

What is our special gift? It is not our eyes – hawk, squid, and dragonfly far surpass us in this kind of vision. Bats, dogs, and deer put our hearing to shame. Smell is undeveloped; our teeth are not sharp; and our skin suffers from lack of fur, feather, or scales.

But we can make these comparisons. We "see" beyond the horizons of space, time, and the immediacy of the senses to weave together these seemingly separate strands into the shared fabric of story.

We are dreamers and myth-makers; bards and the spinners of yarns. That is our genius and glory, this enchanting possibility placed in the primal egg, this grand potential pulled out from the cauldron of chaos and creation. Out of nothingness, gasses, and galaxies, Mystery has shaped itself into us, created a chance to seek and speak of its origins and to chronicle the chapters of the universe.

This wondrous ability was fashioned through relationship – our bodies, brains, and senses shaped by cataclysm, climate, genetics, and geology – as elements were bound into molecule, mammal, and mystery. This mighty power and magnificent purpose placed in our laps, how stupid to waste it, to say it is over, that evolution has ended in us.

The forms of life are infinite, and we have arrived here together. We are storytellers in the story, co-creators in the creation, dreamers and the dreamed. Our history is the universe's history; the strands of our stories are woven together. What can we give back in return for this great gift?

We must narrate a tale worth telling, articulate a dream worth living. We are bound to contribute our best, to create a chronicle that can continue, and use our abilities to the fullest. This

366

story must look into galaxies, subatomic spaces, and the mirror. It will use parable, poetry, and particle accelerators, pledge allegiance to the imagination, and evoke the magic and miraculous embedded in every moment.

It will affirm our uniqueness within a circle of sacred communion, recognize the specialness and rights of all our relations, and call on our creativity to support and celebrate creation in our challenges, choices, and the emerging dream of life.

In the beginning was the word. We must use it well and not let it be the end.

Flight and the Flesh

Dear Hawk, Winged Brother, Friend to the Wind,

You are a teacher, guide, and ally; a feathered dream of lightness, focus, and vision as you carve slow sweeping circles through the heavens. Speak to me! Soar in my heart, mind, and voice! Lift off from the earth in strong flapping beats, and I will do my best to follow.

I have been far away, stranded on the surface, lost in my lists. I have forgotten, but today your piercing gaze shatters the shell of my sleepwalk sight. The time is now.

The stark mountains create billowing breezes that carry you up a staircase to the sky. Great valleys and deserts stretch out beneath you. Your horizons are grand, your motions graceful as you glide across space, alert to movements far below.

My steps are trudging, my feet heavy. My gaze travels barely beyond the appointment book. The miracle of flight has been reduced to something predictable, routine, and rational – airplanes, departure times, and credit cards.

Your call is sharp and challenging, your shrill "skree" a sword that cuts through the clouds and confusion as you separate small from great, grain from chaff, and stop me in my unwilling march to nowhere. It is a slap across the senses, a reminder to remember, a crack in the facade of the ordinary. "Pay attention or pay the price!"

Unexpected images tumble wildly like boulders in an avalanche. But the resistance of routines is strong, and plans and protestations come hand in hand. Shamanic journeys, meditation, religious trance.... "They all sound good, and maybe later, after I finish the chores, phone calls, and e-mail.... Yes, perhaps I can carve out some time, but first things first..."

Dear Friend, fold your wings, dive down, and strike me! Cut open my chest, tear out my heart and lift it on high. Release me from what's reasonable, unoriginal, and repetitious. Fill this earthenware pot with manna from heaven, food for my soul, a gift from the sky.

The world spins on its axis as you circle upward. The sun rises and falls across the heavenly vault. Day, night, spring, fall, moon and Milky Way.... All these circles, round and round they go, mocking my rows and columns, my outlines, goals, and graphs. Career tracks, investments, school plans, promotions – my pedestrian illusions and projections aim ever upward. But they are abstract achievements and mountains of the mundane. These hollow heights are little more than a scramble in a squirrel cage, a frantic and determined dash away from the dreary now to some fantasy future.

Above and below, heaven and earth, great and small – ever higher you watch, witness, and prey. A small speck against a great blue bowl, you turn and twist, your tail flashing red-orange amidst dappled white underwings. You are outside and above, simply there, a concrete fact in some objective world. But a more sacred view stirs among my other senses as new forms of seeing take shape and seep into inner sight.

Ancestral memories flood through my feelings, rivers of remembrance without shore or bank. Cool breezes touch my cheek. A heart of fire leaps in longing for the wind. My arms stretch out to the air, breast exposed, fingers fluttering in a formless fluid caress. Sharp-beaked and searching, a fine-honed gaze cuts through distance like a knife, as cold and abstract fury flexes taloned feet tuned to a beating drum of blood.

Far below, a flicker of movement speaks of warm, wet life. Life gives to life, and I must join the dance. Horizons shrink, funneling into a sudden and frightening fall as I dive downward with death toward that grand feast of the flesh, hoping to rise once again.

Great Winged One, wrap your feathered form around me! Capture my attention and carry me to a grander view. The life of the soul must be fed. Expand my borders and teach me to seek a game worthy of my vision. One day the flesh will fail, the bones break, and this body will return to earth. But today my spirit longs to fly free of form, to dance in dream as I sail upon sunlight and soar through the sky.

I lift up mine eyes. You are protector and promise, guardian and guide, my saving grace. Thy will be done. For this, and with you, I pray.

Sculptures of God

Here in southeastern Utah, the scale is immense. Canyons stretch out in layer upon layer beneath this mesa. Cliffs fall to wide tables and drop away again and again to the river, invisible in the abyss below. Stark towers rise like totem poles; sheer rock faces coil, curve, and wind through mazes of monoliths like plates on the back of some prehistoric stegosaurus. Ten thousand Stonehenges lay scattered about like ancient stele, standing or fallen; spires sprout to the sky like primeval pincushions.

The unseen river moves on through time, its handiwork everywhere apparent. Arroyos become gullies then gorges, plummeting deeper and ending in chasms deeper still. Seen from above, the crevasses extend their dark fingers toward the mesa and, though temporarily safe on this slick-rock rim, we know these rocks too will give way, inevitably tumbling into that deepening hole dredged by great arteries on their way to the sea.

The Green River meets the Colorado. Downstream the Escalante and San Juan join in. Canyons converge in great gorges mile after mile further than the eye can see. The terrain is gigantic, jumbled, twisted and tormented, scarred like an open sore.... a panorama of indescribable beauty. It is a furnace of heat, windswept and barren. Exposed rock and rubble dominate the eyes, the very bones of the earth laid bare, and their raw stumps seem to bleed and color the rust-red soil.

An awesome peace abides in these great expanses; the presence of power is palpable. Strange paradoxes are everywhere about, as fire and air hold sway in a landscape carved and created by water. Colors fade and sharpen with distance, cloud, and sunlight.

Contrasts change constantly, and shadows won't stand still in a land where nothing moves.

Fire, water, earth, and air dance across space and time. Millennia and masses of rock converse leisurely through the centuries, their ears attuned to the slow pulse of eons. Great powers have claimed this land for their own; plants and animals are sparse. It is an inhospitable place, and they learn to survive on sharpened instincts and scraps dropped from the table of gods. Lizards, snakes, and vultures are common. Birds sometimes gather in the cottonwoods lining the river, and a scraggly coyote shows his face, but they are few, and it is the footprints of far bigger players that are visible here.

A thousand years ago, it looked much the same, as it will a thousand years hence. We easily sense its grandeur and majesty, but it is a hard place to enter. Most stand on the rim a few minutes, snap pictures, and move on. It is a sight to see, but its rich and relentless emptiness is somehow foreign to our more fleeting sensibilities. The hours elapse, and little changes but the light. Cumulus clouds come, go, and collide; the sun slowly slips across the sky. The heavens darken, and thunderstorms threaten, but most pass harmlessly by.

The gods are great, but ten minutes in their presence is enough, and twenty can turn into tension. They are so large, and we are so small. We mostly move on, too harried and hurried to grant them an audience. A hundred-million years in the making, and we confront its depths with shallow self-centeredness, dreams cast in decades, and a desire for snapshots before being driven back to the car.

But God is rarely encountered in the comfort zone. Here, in

the intense heat I suffer and sense the harsh hand of creation. I hear a voice and songs weave through all the stark silences. It will not be changed by me or captured in five-minute photo sessions. It is we who are the soft clay, and before us lies a chance, and a choice, to be molded by something greater.

Resting on the rim of this magnificent mesa, I am aware of meeting my maker. I have snapped a few pictures, and I wonder if I have been made in its image or it in mine?

I will put my camera away now, and lift up my eyes unto the hills. I will turn to the sun, the water and wind, and not turn away. I will give them their chance at my salvation, open myself to this harsh and holy land that shifts shapes inside me and carves itself in my features. I will become the son of mountains, brother of rock, a friend to the river. I will surrender my history before its much more magnificent story, and celebrate the grand forces – fire, laughter, and storms – that form the landscapes of my soul.

The canyons stretch out like an endless maze. What's before me is so vast! I may lose myself in the great mystery, but I will work to find it in me.

Make of me what you would! I turn over my will, my life, a new leaf. I'll no longer be apart, and I'll be at peace in the puzzle.

Battered in Thunder,
Birthed in Thankfulness

Cool winds dance in from the north. Streams run in the arroyos, still wet from last evening's rain. Thick clouds, dark and dramatic, swept down the canyon as thunder – at first far-off – grew closer and louder, crashing in its passing by. The first sprinkles and spatters spread and blossomed into hail, battering the tarp and turning the ground ghostly white in the approaching darkness. Fire bolts flared across a smoky sky; tree trunks stood out, black silhouettes against the illumined air.

Ancient gods awakened, filling the landscape with pulsing and fearsome forces. Giant Thunder Birds swept low over the earth like enormous dark-winged ravens – their feathers skimming the mesas above – alive with an awesome and primeval power. We cowered under nylon shelters as they boomed and bellowed past, grateful to escape their notice. The sky cleared. Venus appeared briefly in the west, but was soon blotted out as the great birds circled again.

The tempest moves on; clouds disappear. The heavens open, and stars twinkle above. Mud dries out, reverting to dirt, then dust. We return to our routines and reflections, attend to things that now seem important, and quickly forget how we huddled and hid.

But there is an excitement, an exhilaration in the approach of a great storm. The air becomes alive and electric; self-importance shrivels; and personal dramas are dwarfed and dominated by more awesome dimensions. Zeus, Thor, and Thunder Birds bellow, roar, and rumble like rockslides. The earth trembles; fire bolts flash and strike like hammers hurled from the heavens. There is no escape. It will not go away, and one can only surrender to its divine or demonic supremacy.

Like some great beast shrieking in childbirth, it cannot be stopped. Everything must yield to the power of its harsh progression. Grasses bend, branches thrash. The winds gust and howl like banshees; rain wracks the earth in pummeling pellets. Blackness descends, and the dark sockets of death are illumined by the electric arrows of Eros. Dragons breathe fire and dance like fiends, mad midwives to this labor of love. The air crackles and crashes, the contractions reach climax. All are swept down some tunnel of transformation, uncertain if they face destruction or deliverance.

There is blood in every birth. Something is lost when we are born to a greater life. The snake sheds its skin; the caterpillar dissolves in the cocoon. The tadpole loses its tail and who knows what else? The fledglings forsake the familiar and feathered nest to embrace the expansive but invisible air.

*   *   *

Calm returns as the storm passes. Flowers unfold. The pale desert palette pulses with brighter hues; strange scents are released into the atmosphere. Shells soften and split open; seeds send their shoots toward the dampened soil. Green arms open to the sun, new growth appearing before our eyes amidst all that lies battered and broken.

Great Spirit, I give thanks for this life. I've been spared by the storm and live to see another day. But my time will come. Long ago, I was thrust into a dark corridor and – helpless against irresistible contractions and crushing forces – delivered into this bright and luminous world. And one day I will enter another, filled with faith or fear for the approaching passage.

Grand currents of life sweep us along, and I may never see what lies around the next bend. But I will look upon this day with wonder, eyes newborn and open, the veils of my vision washed away by the storm. I do not know what the future holds, but I will hold this moment dearly, aware of its great and generous gift. For this I express my thanks.

Time rolls on like a river as the banks disappear into the past. I may drift along for decades or quickly lose myself in a headlong rush over some fearsome and falling cataract. The Thunder Birds may return with the darkness and seize me in their talons – snatched, skewered, and plucked from this life – to soar in an unknown and boundless sky. I may be crushed, bones broken and buried in the earth, my shape and identity dissolving as I descend into some final dusk. There, perhaps, lies a doorway to the next dimension – the shell of my body bursting as seeds of the soul stretch toward unknown depths, its roots seeking the sustenance of secret springs to propel themselves upward and shatter the surface of a new world.

I am small and my knowledge limited. I am dwarfed, humbled by the immense storm, but greater for allowing it to touch me. The tempest has come and gone, but part of me has gone with it, and much of it remains within me. Its winds swirl in my psyche, making sense and awakening senses. Its electricity arcs across synapses and produces strange illuminations.

Cloudy curtains descend, and the earth is blanketed in darkness. Rain is feeding the river that surges and carries us onward. It is wise to be humble, but foolish to hide. We cannot go backward or turn away from our destiny. Open yourself to its fearsome and frightening radiance, and let the pull of the dark sea draw you like a moth toward the flame.

Wishing Upon Stars

Morning dawns and camp awakens. Refreshed by the cool winds, people move quietly about, stretching. Last night, clouds blotted out the starlit sky, and the promised meteor shower went on without an audience. Somewhere, asteroids plummeted to earth in sizzling fire, blazing trails of smoking metal through the burning air. Their solid masses evaporating in mere moments, they metamorphosed into light that continues onward throughout the dark eternity.

We too float through the firmament, seemingly secure in some orbit we construe as "reality" or "ourselves." We pretend to be solid and stable, our perspectives and position the reference point to describe and define the universe. We're grounded by gravity and circumscribed by circumstance and other bodies moving around us. But things change. Something happens; we cross course with greater forces. Our trajectory gets altered; the simple life picks up speed; we hurtle onward down a slope too steep for braking. Sweat bursts forth from our brows; time and distance shrink; the cold clarity of space begins to smolder and sear. We cling tightly to our insular and uncertain individuality in the face of an oncoming tidal wave.

Gravity is relentless; our lives begin to unravel and burn. Jaws clench in resistance to change and loss, but the turning of sun, moon, circumstance, and stars is greater than our small will. The tides laugh as we struggle to steer our little boats. Heat increases in a sulphurous smell as we hurtle through the accelerating air like a moth to flame. Everything becomes focused upon that one blinding blaze, intense and seemingly everywhere, as plans, hopes, and dreams are reduced to rubble in the consuming fire. We taste ash in our mouths. When all we know is turned to light, we fear nothing will remain.

*   *   *

But light is eternal, neither created nor destroyed. It is the currency of the cosmos, the medium of exchange. It is in all we experience, our destiny and perceived death. The snake curls in and eats itself. The small self dies that the greater might be released. The man is ripped apart by the monster that he might become god.

Transformation does not happen at the bidding of the relinquished form. It will not be controlled by what is cast aside, and all we treasure must one day be taken from us. Friends grow old, lovers drift away, passion becomes platonic. The family dog – comrade, companion, embodiment of unconditional love – begins to limp and sleep all day. In compassion, we put him out of his misery and enter our own. All who do not abandon us we will eventually leave behind.

What are our choices? Do we hold back the love that we won't feel hurt? Shall we fuss and fume that the universe was not created for our comfort, that eternity will not stop at our personal peaks so we might be stagnant happily ever after? Those are foolish fantasies, yet we wish them anyway. Yin and yang, yes and no, sweetness and sorrow – these sacred twins always appear together in the play of life. It's a great tragedy, yet at the end we must stand up and applaud, and if we do, laughter may arrive along with the tears.

The outcome of our acts is not in our hands. We are a creation of nature and nurture, spirit and flesh, earth and sun. We have a part in this grand drama. We are ill-equipped to run the show, but the show goes on, and we must act. There is no rehearsal, so be here now! Commit to opening your mouth and your heart! Your lines will come to you – look on in wonder as they tumble from your lips.

We are mere filaments of god, and the bulb burns out, but the light goes on. We live in a vacuum and wonder about meaning and purpose, but what does it matter? We did not make this house or string the wires. We are meant to be used for greater things. Something turns us on, throws the switch, and we are there in the socket. It's folly to complain about creation. If God screwed you, at least he screwed you in. Don't be cross-threaded – places of darkness are where we were meant to shine! Give it your all, your very best, and give thanks. In the end, we are exhausted, our bodies ravaged, our flame extinguished. Yet the radiance from our lives can still remain.

Feel the burning as you hurtle toward your destiny. You have illumination to give. The clouds may part, and someone may see your trail. You might bring a smile to their face, make their world brighter, or remind them to wish on a star. Plunge into the water and who knows what shores the ripples will reach?

Thank you Great Mystery, for this day, for the wonder of existence. The clouds still cast shadows on the mountaintop; shafts of sunlight spotlight the hazy blue hills. Each moment is a miracle. And while we sit here in silence, heavenly music is created as worlds collide and are burning to death.

We take in life along with the fragrances of summer, as the breath of god arrives within the shifting breezes. Someday we'll take flight to soar on these winds or be blown away by a storm. We are small specks, motes of dust, flies on the wall. We witness, we worship, we wait. We cannot control what is greater than us.

And for all this we give thanks.

Footnotes:

Introduction: The Call to Adventure

(1) Rainer Maria Rilke, "Untitled." in Selected Poems of Rainer Maria Rilke. Harper and Row Press, 1981. Translated by Robert Bly

Searching for a New Mythology:

(1) James Hollis, The Archetypal Imagination. Texas A&M University Press, 2000, Page 11
(2) Meister Eckhart, "It Is A Lie." translated by Daniel Ladinsky. In Love Poems from God: Twelve Sacred Voices from the East and West. Penguin Books, 2002, page 118.
(3) St. Thomas Aquinas, "God's Nature." translated by Daniel Ladinsky. In Love Poems from God: Twelve Sacred Voices from the East and West. Penguin Books, 2002, page 148.

The Known and the Unknown:

(1) As elaborated in The Teachings of Don Juan, a Yaqui Way of Knowledge (Ballantine Books, 1968) and his series of books that followed.
(2) D.H. Lawrence, "Escape." In Complete Poems of D.H. Lawrence, Wordsworth Editions, 1994, page 397

The Role of Language:

(1) Rumi, translated by Coleman Barks in The Essential Rumi. Harper Collins, 1995, page 36.
(2) Robert A. Johnson, Inner Gold: Understanding Psychological Projection. Koa Books, 2008, page 76.
(3) Kukai (774-835), translation by Jane Hirshfield. Quoted in The Enlightened Heart: An Anthology of Sacred Poetry, edited by Stephen Mitchell. Harper Perennial, 1993, page 36.

The Realm of Primal Forces:

(1) From Rainer Maria Rilke, "The Man Watching," translated by Robert Bly in Selected Poems of Rainer Maria   Rilke. Harper Perennial, 1981.
(2) John A Shedd. Salt from My Attic, 1928.

(3) David Whyte, "The Well of Grief," in <u>Where Many Rivers Meet</u>. ©
David Whyte 2001. Used by permission of Many Rivers Press, Langley,
Washington, USA, <u>www.davidwhyte.com</u>
(4) Thomas Griffin. "As If This Were Your Last." Unpublished.
<u>www.thomasgriffinarts.com</u>.

The River:

(1) Lauren Chamblis, "Dripping." Unpublished poem.
(2) "New Religion" by Bill Holm, from <u>The Chain Letter of the Soul:
New and Selected Poems</u>, (Minneapolis: Milkweed Editions, 2009).
Copyright © 2009 by Bill Holm. Reprinted with permission from
Milkweed Editions. (<u>www.milkweed.org</u>)

Dreaming and the Dream:

(1) David Whyte, "*Sweet Darkness.*" from <u>The House of Belonging</u>. ©
David Whyte 2002. Used by permission of Many Rivers Press, Langley,
Washington, USA, <u>www.davidwhyte.com</u>.
(2) "Imagine" by John Lennon, recorded on <u>Imagine</u>, EMI Records Ltd.
2000.
(3) From Rainer Maria Rilke's <u>The Book of Hours</u>. Translated by Robert
Bly in <u>Selected Poems of Rainer Maria Rilke</u>. Harper and Row Press,
1981.

The Shadow:

(1) Old Hassidic saying.
(2) William Blake, <u>The Marriage of Heaven and Hell</u>, edited by Michael
Philips, page xvi. Oxford University Press, 2011, used by permission.
(3) Joseph Campbell, <u>An Open Life</u>. Harper Perennial, 1990, pages 28-29.
(4) C. Jung, "Commentary on the Secret of the Golden Flower." (<u>Collected
Works</u>; Volume 13).
(5) C. Jung, <u>Psyche and Symbol</u>. Princeton University Press, 1991.
(6) Excerpts from D.H. Lawrence. "Healing" in <u>The Complete Poems of
D.H. Lawrence</u>. Wordsworth Editions, 1994, page 513.
(7) C. Jung, "The Philosophical Tree" in <u>Alchemical Studies</u>. (<u>Collected
Works</u>, Volume 13).
(8) From Kahil Gibran, <u>The Prophet</u>. Alfred A. Knopf, 1973.

The Return:

(1) Jean Houston. <u>The Hero and the Goddess</u>. Ballantine Books, 1992; page 55.
(2) T.S. Eliot, from <u>The Four Quartets</u>. #4, "Little Gidding."

Spirit and Soul: As Above, So Below:

(1) Excerpted from "The Holy Longing," by Johann Wolfgang von Goethe. Translated by Robert Bly in <u>News of the Universe: Poems of Twofold Consciousness</u>, Sierra Club Books 1995, page 70.
(2) William Blake; <u>The Marriage of Heaven and Hell</u>, edited by Michael Philips, page xviii. Oxford University Press, 2011, used by permission.
(3) Sun Bear, personal conversation.
(4) This quote has been variously attributed to, among others, Black Elk, the Oglala Sioux holy man, and an inscription on a church in Sussex England.

Nature:

(1) From D.H. Lawrence, "A Propos of 'Lady Chatterly's Lover,' in <u>Lady Chatterly's Lover</u>. Bantam Books, 1983, page 334.
(2) These ideas owe a debt of gratitude to Jerry Mander, especially his book <u>In the Absence of the Sacred</u>. Sierra Club Books, 1992.
(3) Carlos Castaneda, <u>The Active Side of Infinity</u>. Harper Collins, 1998.
(4) Jerry Mander, ibid.
(5) From <u>The Biology of Belief</u>, by Bruce Lipton, 2006. Audio CD set, Sounds True Inc. Used by permission.
(6) The Gospel of Thomas, #113. The Gospel of Thomas is part of a collection of early Christian writings discovered near Nag Hammadi, Egypt in 1945. Written in the Coptic language, the Thomas Gospel consists of 114 sayings attributed to Jesus.
(7) Meister Eckhart, "When I Was the Forest." translated by Daniel Ladinsky. In <u>Love Poems from God: Twelve Sacred Voices from the East and West</u>. Penguin Books, 2002, page 91.

Living in a Larger Story:

(1) C. G. Jung in <u>Memories, Dreams, Reflections</u>. Princeton University Press, 1973.

(2) Joseph Campbell in <u>Joseph Campbell: A Fire in the Mind</u> by Stephen and Robin Larsen. Inner Traditions Press, 2002.

(3) These ideas were first inspired by Brian Swimme in <u>Canticle to the Cosmos</u>. Sounds True Audio, 1995.

(4) Joseph Campbell, <u>The Hero with a Thousand Faces</u> (Bollingen Series XVII), Princeton University Press, 1973.

(5) Jean Houston, <u>The Hero and the Goddess</u>. Ballantine Books, 1992, page 59.

(6) James Hollis, <u>Tracking the Gods: The Place of Myth in Modern Life</u>. Inner City Books, 1995, Page 115.

(7) Thomas Griffin, "The Praises of this Place." Unpublished. www.thomasgriffinarts.com.

About the Author:

Sparrow Hart has apprenticed himself to nature and the wild for over forty years, exploring inner and outer landscapes beyond the unexamined limits of consensual reality. Seeking something deep and extraordinary, that "dream worth living," his adventures have included a five-month solo in the wilderness, travels to the Amazon, over 30 personal vision quests, and treks to the mountains, forests, canyons, and deserts of Mexico and the United States, as well as apprenticeships with a wide variety of native and non-native "medicine teachers." Through all this, Sparrow considers his greatest mentor to be the Earth itself.

Following his first vision quest in 1980, Sparrow founded Circles of Air and Stone, which has guided small groups of men and women through 11-day vision quest programs for over three decades. He's the creator of Adventures of the Spirit, a series of workshops for men and women that offer a deep encounter with inner and outer nature, and the founder and guide of two programs for men—the annual Men's Wisdom Council at the Rowe Conference Center and The Mythic Warrior Men's Training—that have thrived for over twenty years.

Regarded as an authority on the vision quest process, well-versed in myth and storytelling, he's known for his ability to translate the world's enduring spiritual principles into the concrete challenges and choices of today. He has one daughter, Prairie, and lives with his partner, Willie, in Putney, Vermont.

Sparrow can be contacted through his website at www.questforvision.com.

Now Close the Book

"All that you have read should help close every book.
Any page you have ever turned should have aided in
Dusting off – rending – the veil over your glorious eye.

All talk and words are foreplay.
*I have other things in mind for us now." ***

** Rumi, "Now Close the Book," in The Purity of Desire: 100 Poems of Rumi translated by Daniel Ladinsky. Penguin Books, 2012, page107.

26961098R00232

Made in the USA
Lexington, KY
28 October 2013